The Presidency
and Political Science

INTERPRETING AMERICAN POLITICS

Michael Nelson
Series Editor

The Presidency
and Political Science

Two Hundred Years
of Constitutional
Debate

RAYMOND TATALOVICH
THOMAS S. ENGEMAN

The Johns Hopkins University Press

Baltimore and London

This book has been brought to publication with the generous assistance
of Loyola University Chicago.

The Johns Hopkins University Press
2715 North Charles Street
Baltimore, Maryland 21218-4363
www.press.jhu.edu

Library of Congress Cataloging-in-Publication Data
Tatalovich, Raymond.
The presidency and political science : two hundred years of constitutional debate /
Raymond Tatalovich and Thomas S. Engeman.
    p.   cm. — (Interpreting American politics)
Includes bibliographical references and index.
ISBN 0-8018-7321-5 (alk. paper)
ISBN 0-8018-7322-3 (pbk. : alk. paper)
1. Presidents—United States—History. 2. Political science—United States—History.
I. Engeman, Thomas S. II. Title. III. Series.
JK511 .T38 2003
320.973—dc21
2002013626

A catalog record for this book is available from the British Library.

Dedicated to four thinkers who guided our way

Alexander Hamilton, for his precepts
Edward Corwin, for his scholarship
Richard E. Neustadt, for his legacy
Theodore J. Lowi, for his insights

and

To Anne, my reason for being
R.T.

To Susan and Morgan, with love
T.S.E.

Contents

Contents

Designing the executive was one of the most vexing problems faced by the Constitutional Convention of 1787, and solving this problem was the convention's most creative act. Other issues were more controversial, but they typically lent themselves to compromise solutions, as when the small states split the difference with the large states and provided for the population-based House of Representatives and the state-based Senate. When it came to the structure and powers of the executive, however, the delegates labored in a realm of considerable political and intellectual uncertainty. No one knew what sort of executive would serve the narrow interests of, say, a small state or a slave state. And although experience offered them several models of what they did not want in an executive, it offered few models of what they did want. The British monarch and the royal governors had been, in their eyes, tramplers of liberty. The state constitutions that were written after independence provided for unthreatening governors but also rendered the governors weak to the point of impotence. The national government of the Articles of Confederation, such as it was, had no chief executive at all.

Because the politics of compromise was of little use in designing the executive, the convention became a summer-long seminar on how to achieve the goal of an executive that was strong enough to be effective but not so strong as to be oppressive. The result, according to the historian Jack Rakove, was that "the presidency emerged not from the clash of wills to gain a long-contested point, but from a series of ingenious efforts to design a new institution that would be suitably energetic but safely republican."

"Energy" in the executive was the theme of Alexander Hamilton's series of essays on the presidency in the *Federalist*. Hamilton argued that energetic presidential leadership was secured by several qualities of the presidency that emerged from the Constitutional Convention. One of these was "unity," which Hamilton thought would foster "decision, activity, secrecy, and dispatch" as well as "vigor and expedition." Another was "duration," which was secured by the fixed four-year term. The third was eligibility for reelection, with its shrewd acknowledgment that "the desire of reward is one of the strongest incentives of human conduct." The fourth was "adequate provision for its support" in the form of a presidential salary that could not be altered by Congress either to reward a compliant president or to punish an independent-minded one. The final buttress for presidential energy that Hamilton identified was the long list of enumerated powers granted to the president, including the veto and the treaty and appointment powers.

Just as the convention's design of the presidency and Hamilton's defense of it were grounded more in ideas than in interests, so were the criticisms of the Anti-Federalists who opposed ratification. Cato, for example, based his objection to the president's term on Montesquieu's prescription for one-year terms. Cato also argued that the absence of an executive council from the Constitution meant that the president would be "unsupported by proper information and advice, and . . . generally . . . directed by minions and favorites."

In this book, Raymond Tatalovich, a scholar of the presidency, and Thomas S. Engeman, a political theorist, pick up the torch of the founding generation and carry it through the two centuries that have followed. Like the framers and their Anti-Federalist critics, Tatalovich and Engeman take seriously the ongoing clash of ideas about the presidency. Indeed, they argue, one cannot understand the American executive without understanding what presidents and scholars have thought and said about the office, as well as how they have contested each other's varying conclusions.

Michael Nelson

Preface

This collaboration is, in one respect, the culmination of our collective experiences from a quarter-century of classroom teaching. Along different intellectual paths we nonetheless encountered too many undergraduates who failed to appreciate the significance of the Constitution for the development of popular and energetic government. Students are so quick to personalize the presidency that they can hardly contemplate the notion that the Founders paved the way for presidential activism. Even graduate students, because they are immersed in modern empiricism and the behavioral assumptions of political science, seem disinclined to take constitutionalism seriously.

How does one grasp the ebb and flow of the presidency? No one methodological perspective can capture the essence of this office. The presidency is too complex, too protean, and very much subjected to historical and political developments. Only by looking comprehensively across American political history can we separate the fundamental truths about presidential power from the many transient beliefs that have been, and are today, fueled by ideology or partisanship. This study differs from scientific analyses or triumphal histories because, in our view, the presidency manifests too many problems still seeking remedy to be a model or an end. This intellectual history affords an opportunity for genuine reflection about the different constitutional, political, and personal strategies necessary for the successful conduct of the office.

In searching for the constitutional and political underpinnings of the highest office, we came to identify three presidential paradigms. The Founders sought a strong but limited government with a strong executive; the Jeffersonians of the nineteenth century sought to guarantee local liberties by weakening national and executive power; the Progressives and Liberals of the twentieth century sought a fully national and scientific society, arguing that the president was the natural leader of the modernizing administrative state. Each of these paradigms is comprehensive in its view of the office and is radically different from the others. We will reveal their nature and interrelationships in terms of six analytical questions that are readily found in the presidency literature. Since no paradigm is pristine, these six questions delineate the historical nuances that shape the range of choices in the real world of presidential action.

The Presidency and Political Science is a unique study, the first comprehensive examination of scholarship on the presidency. Although presidential histories are not difficult to find—works that chronicle the activities of incumbents over time—no solitary work could be identified by either of us that represents the vagaries of informed opinion about the world's most powerful office. The insights by Woodrow Wilson, of course, are exceptional, but there are many other perceptive intellectuals who have been all but forgotten, not voices just from the late nineteenth century but also the later twentieth century. We need to carry forward this legacy of learning to those students who enter college and who pursue graduate education in the twenty-first century.

The authors have benefited from the help of many individuals and institutions. This study would not have been possible without many scholars and friends who have instructed, guided, and inspired us over the years. Raymond Tatalovich owes an intellectual debt to Byron W. Daynes, his friend of three decades, since first meeting in graduate school at the University of Chicago. Bill and Raymond have collaborated so often that they are virtually a tag-team in political science. One of their more prophetic observations occurred in 1979 when they authored "Towards a Paradigm to Explain Presidential Power," in the *Presidential Studies Quarterly.* They argued the unfashionable—that prerogative powers and political resources complement each other in the presidential arsenal and it is not necessary for scholars to choose between legalism and behavioralism. The wisdom of that observation, today more readily accepted, is seen in the discussion that follows. Thomas Engeman would like to acknowledge the help and inspiration of Harry V. Jaffa, Martin Diamond, Harry Neumann, Thomas West, George Anastaplo, Frances and Calvin Goldscheider, and William Engeman.

We both especially wish to thank the librarians at Loyola University Chicago who assisted our intellectual journey, and our most capable research assistants, Catherine Thie and Timothy Yetzina. We are especially indebted to Mr. Yetzina, a Ph.D. candidate in political theory, who stimulated our thinking about the nineteenth-century presidential scholarship and whose close reading of the entire manuscript validated our footnoting and identified essential themes for inclusion in the index. At the Johns Hopkins University Press we would like to thank Henry Tom, series editor Michael Nelson, and John P. Burke, who reviewed the manuscript for the publisher, for their collective guidance. This book is much improved thanks to them. Finally, a version of chapter 10 was published as "The Emerging Scholarly Consensus on Presidential Leadership: A New Realism, an Old Idealism" in *White House Studies* 2, no. 2 (2002): 123–37, and we thank Robert P. Watson, Editor, for allowing us to include that material in this volume.

The Presidency
and Political Science

Scope of Study

This volume yields the first comprehensive intellectual history of the American presidency. Although there are solid histories of the presidency, those volumes chronicle historical events as affected by specific presidents rather than studying the interrelationship between the Original Intent of the Founding and the practice over time as assessed by scholarly opinion.[1] Our approach is textual analysis of the leading authorities on the presidency from the Founding until the end of the twentieth century. This interplay will reveal how the leading thinkers of the presidency were influenced in their understandings of this constitutional office by their place in history and, therefore, why they offered different answers to the six fundamental questions that guide this study. Six questions are used as intellectual foils to analyze each thinker and to unearth the developments that have undergirded the transformation of the presidency. To illustrate that these six questions encompass the vital dimensions of presidential leadership, we begin by framing each in terms of the events preceding and following the terrorist attack on the World Trade Center on September 11, 2001.

9/11/01: Transforming a Presidency

George W. Bush, forty-third president of the United States, assumed office after the U.S. Supreme Court ruling in *Bush v. Gore* (2000) that halted the recounting of ballots as ordered by the Florida Supreme Court. That edict delivered to Bush Florida's twenty-five electoral votes, and therefore the majority needed for victory, although Vice-President Gore had amassed a half-million popular-vote plurality nationwide. The legitimacy of Bush's election was called into question, and a newspaper consortium proceeded to commission a systematic recount of the Florida ballots under dispute. Several recent presidents have been elected without a popular-vote majority—Kennedy in 1960, Nixon in 1968, Clinton in 1992 and 1996—but in each case the size of their electoral college majority affirmed the legitimacy of their election. This time, only a few hundred votes tipped the electoral college to Bush, with a four-electoral-vote margin (271 of 538). With some media elites, disgruntled Democrats, and civil rights leaders adding to the chorus that the Supreme Court stole the election, no president in this century entered office with a more fragile political base than George W. Bush. Thus, our first question:

Does presidential power derive from the prerogatives of office or from the incumbent?
We believe this question is most important, cutting to the heart of the nature of presidential leadership. This question was personified in the divergent viewpoints of Edward Corwin, who argued that legal authority undergirded presidential power, and Richard Neustadt's retort that presidential power is influence. Because Neustadt welcomed the behavioral revolution to presidency studies, his interpretation is more fashionable in today's profession of hypothesis-testing empiricists. Students of the Founding hold to the belief that prerogative power is more important to presidential leadership than the use of political resources, an argument usually associated with Richard Pious. Prerogative, according to Pious, is "constitutional authority that the president asserts unilaterally through various rules of constitutional construction and interpretation, in order to resolve crises or important issues facing the nation."[2] With respect to Bush, Pious would argue that cries of illegitimacy, failed mandates, and election by an electoral minority have no bearing on the ability of a president to lead the nation with energy. That is how Abraham Lincoln governed; that is why September 11, 2001, transformed the presidency of George W. Bush. Lincoln acted unilaterally during the eleven-week "constitutional" dictatorship at the outset of the Civil War (before Congress reconvened). Bush exploited presidential prerogative in numerous ways, some not experienced in a generation: orchestrating the multinational coalition, defining the war objectives in the Bush Doctrine, detaining foreign nationals under investigation, and subjecting terrorist suspects to trial by military tribunal, to mention but a few.

Does presidential influence depend upon the force of personality, rhetorical leadership, or partisanship?
During the closely contested election campaign of 2000, intellectual qualities were attributed to Albert Gore, especially his great debating skills, whereas George Bush was the Texan, handsome but hardly charismatic, not especially articulate, and as conservative as Gore was liberal. In popu-

lar votes cast, there have been closer elections—the one hundred thousand votes that separated Kennedy and Nixon—but the closeness of that 1960 election reflected the fact that both candidates were relatively centrist in their views. In 2000 exit polls show that voters cleaved mainly on cultural—less so on economic—grounds: urban versus rural, black versus white, pro-choice versus pro-life. The consequence is that President Bush hardly enjoyed a "honeymoon" period. Since his share of the vote was just below 50 percent, his popularity hovered just above that level during the eight months before September 11 (Gallup's average was 56%). In other words, President Bush began his term untested in national affairs, unworldly in his outlook, and partisan, and the nation did not rally behind his inauguration. However, immediately after the collapse of the World Trade Center, Bush's approval rating soared to 86 percent (Gallup—even higher in other surveys). His high point was higher and lasted longer than that of any other modern president. Bush's image quickly turned, as Americans judged him decisive and ready, and he responded in a bipartisan manner, governing for all America.

If incumbency trumps prerogative, what political resources do presidents exploit apart from their own personal skills? Do they exude charisma or a cult of personality, depend upon party government, or mobilize public opinion behind their cause? Quite a few thinkers view the president as a solitary figure who must develop fine-tuned political instincts because he, alone, must make momentous decisions with awesome consequences for himself and the nation. For that reason this perspective, which was popularized by Richard Neustadt, has been characterized as "statecraft"—literally a Machiavellian who offers pragmatic counsel to our modern-day prince.[3] A president can augment his political skills by mobilizing a supportive public opinion, using his rhetorical abilities, but a more reliable and permanent grounding for presidential leadership is partisanship. There are observers who point to political party as the essential pillar of presidential leadership of both other political leaders and the electorate.

Does presidential leadership depend upon historical context, or is regime-building manifested through political, institutional, and constitutional developments?
Is President George W. Bush a captive of history? He reportedly told his advisers that the War against Terrorism is the raison d'être for his presidency. Or will there be a more lasting political, institutional, and constitutional legacy that flows from Bush precedents to his successors in the White

3

House? Despite being the greatest of our greats, Lincoln was no trendsetter: he faced a domestic crisis so acute that no informed commentator believes that his presidency was a precursor for the rest of the nineteenth century. The crisis of the Great Depression was so pivotal in the twentieth century, however, that it commenced the era of big government and the "modern" presidency. As Theodore J. Lowi put it, the Roosevelt Revolution orchestrated a fundamental change in the political system from what the Framers designed. And at the Founding, George Washington intimately knew that his every action might well create a precedent to guide his successors in the White House. This is regime-building. Regime-building, the degree to which the Constitution of 1787 has given way to new constitutional forms of presidential leadership, cannot blind us from recognizing the pivotal impact of dramatic historical events, such as the realigning elections of 1860 and 1932, which catapulted into power a different majority party and president with radically new policies.

Bush proclaimed the War against Terrorism to be the first war of the twenty-first century, and arguably this crisis may have a long-lasting impact. For now, it remains an open question whether President Bush will join the company of Lincoln and FDR—not necessarily as a great president but as a president who governed under conditions so unusual that meaningful comparisons cannot be made with his immediate predecessors or successors. Whereas "institutionalization" forecasts a trend line based on precedents and the legacy of history, historical context focuses on the impact of singularly important events on one president.

Does presidential leadership vary between domestic and foreign affairs?
Four months after September 11, the crisis presidency of George W. Bush continued, making this war unlike the Persian Gulf War, which his father waged a decade earlier. Nor did the recession of 2001 displace international hostilities as the most important problem facing the United States, as did the economic downturn of 1991. Why was the War against Terrorism different? Because America was attacked on its own soil, something that had not happened since the British burned the White House in the War of 1812 (Hawaii was not a state when Pearl Harbor was attacked). There is a domestic side to this foreign engagement, as Americans were constantly being reminded by National Guard troops at airports, bomb-sniffing dogs going through luggage, and extra-tight security with longer lines at airline ticket counters.

The use of roles to study presidential leadership was popular at one time:

4

both Clinton Rossiter and Edward Corwin used that approach. Even presidency watchers who did not focus explicitly on roles, such as Harold Laski and Herman Finer, made explicit their understanding that domestic policy is unlike foreign affairs. One who did not was Richard Neustadt, says Erwin Hargrove, because "Neustadt reached beyond the conception of the presidency as a collection of separate 'hats,' or roles, such as chief legislator and commander in chief, to the idea that all actions influence the possibility of future actions."[4] In that sense, Neustadt may be alone, because six years after *Presidential Power* was published, Aaron Wildavsky authored his "two presidencies" thesis during the height of the Vietnam War. Vietnam, as we shall see, made more than a few Liberal intellectuals aware that the separated powers operated differently under wartime conditions as compared to the enactment of domestic law.

That was Wildavsky's simple story—Congress is more likely to enact the foreign and military politics that the White House recommends than the president's domestic agenda. Of course the implications of Wildavsky's thesis are much grander than that. To the degree that presidential leadership via Lockean prerogative exists, it surely must exist in foreign affairs. Without debating today's view that the modern presidency began with Franklin D. Roosevelt,[5] we may consider George Washington the first modern president because he established virtually all the essential prerogatives in diplomacy.[6] When the United States was engulfed in "total war"— World War I and World War II—the foreign and domestic sides merged, but more usually presidents are capable of making undeclared war against bandits, pirates, communists, and terrorist states precisely because those unilateral acts of warfare have few domestic repercussions. Americans supported Truman in Korea and Johnson in Vietnam until the body bags arrived home in increasing numbers.

Does the president actively or passively engage the legislative process and promote a policy agenda?

After George W. Bush assumed the presidency, the "100-Day" time clock began ticking, a benchmark that does more than commemorate the outpouring of legislation in 1933. It is used by journalists of all stripes to judge (and usually fail) the legislative leadership of a newly elected president. By that standard, President Bush was an abject failure, since no law cleared Congress for his signature during that period, not even a centerpiece of his election campaign—educational reform.

The most significant schooling measure since the Elementary and Secondary Education Act of 1965 was enacted on January 9, 2002, after President Bush brokered a deal with key Democrats Senator Edward M. Kennedy (D-MA) and Representative George Miller (D-CA). The major achievement before the crisis presidency unfolded was enactment of a $1.3 trillion, decade-long tax cut. After September 11, a new spirit of bipartisanship was reported on Capitol Hill. The *New York Times* editorialized that "Politics Is Adjourned" and reported that the "Gang of Five"—the Speaker of the House of Representatives plus the House and Senate majority and minority party leaders—were cooperating as never before. In a rare development, though late, all thirteen regular appropriations bills were cleared by Congress, most with huge majorities, and a fiscal year 2002 budget was approved before lawmakers ended the first session of the 107th Congress. Left undone were the energy plan, farm subsidies, the patients' bill of rights, campaign finance reform, and aid to religious charities. What was not left undone were the measures backed by President Bush to wage war abroad and maintain security at home: a resolution (which passed the House 420 to 1 and the Senate 98 to 0) authorizing use of force; $40 billion for domestic security and to rebuild New York City; an antiterrorism bill to expand surveillance and detention powers; $15 billion to compensate the airlines for lost business; and legislation to federalize thirty thousand airport screeners and baggage inspectors.

For presidency scholars, legislative leadership is one litmus test of the modern period, pertaining to whether and how presidents initiate new policy and influence the legislative process. There are empirical and normative overtones to this question. We want to know not only how presidents acted to shape legislation but, more importantly, whether their behavior was an accepted modus operandi long before Franklin D. Roosevelt dramatized legislative leadership during his One Hundred Days. Leadership of Congress presumes that the president has a policy agenda, which leads most contemporary scholars to expect that only a subset of "great" or "near-great" presidents would quality. Yet a closer reading of the intellectual history of the presidency may suggest that a range of incumbents have engaged in this behavior.

Does the organization of the executive branch service presidential leadership?
Richard Neustadt doubted that constitutional authority—what he dubbed *command*—was sufficient to convert a "clerkship" president into a leader. That argument lost some of its edge with Vietnam, and now some more

6

with the War against Terrorism. As with most military engagements, the decision to engage the enemy was Bush's, and he consulted only a few advisers—mainly National Security Advisor Condoleezza Rice, Vice-President Richard Cheney, Secretary of State Colin Powell, and Defense Secretary Donald Rumsfeld. Once that decision was made, President Bush relied on what the *New York Times* termed a "war troika" of his defense secretary, the chairman of the Joint Chiefs of Staff, and the military head of the U.S. Central Command, who daily assessed the war's progress, plotted the next move, and chose military targets—a model similar to what his father used during the Persian Gulf War. And as with the Persian Gulf War, military (if not political) success was achieved. It took a matter of months for the U.S. armed forces, with help from allies, to rout the Taliban forces and liberate Afghanistan. Can we imagine any better contemporary example of why Max Weber, the German sociologist, called the military chain of command the "ideal type" of bureaucracy because authority pyramids top-down?

Winning the war may be easier than keeping the peace at home. President Bush installed Pennsylvania governor Tom Ridge as the new director of homeland security, an important symbolic gesture for public consumption. But the bureaucratic reality is that Ridge had to coordinate the activities of localities, counties, states, and numerous federal agencies into a coherent plan for protecting Americans from bioterrorism (for example, anthrax); contamination of their water, food supply, and energy sources, including nuclear power plants; and attacks on the infrastructure, such as bridges and tunnels.

The growth of bureaucracy gave rise to the "institutionalized" presidency under Franklin D. Roosevelt, a presidential branch designed to help the chief executive "take care that the laws are faithfully executed." As our intellectual history shows, few observers before FDR viewed the federal bureaucracy in worrisome tones; even the young political scientist Woodrow Wilson advocated a "policy-administration" dichotomy in which political leaders formulate the policies that public administrators implement. The Executive Office of the President was established in 1939 on the advice of the famous Brownlow Committee, which declared in words equally famous that the president "needs help" to manage a bigger government. Yet Roosevelt's administrative burdens were manageable compared to what came later. Federal budgets were smaller; many federal employees were not protected by civil service (being patronage hires); important federal agencies were newly established, and Roosevelt appointed loyal New

Dealers to head them. In other words, he did not inherit a huge federal establishment, trillion-dollar budgets, and politically connected interests protective of their bureaucratic friends. FDR tamed his administration, but it is an open question whether any of his successors have been able to do so.

An Overview of the Book

In the ten chapters that follow, we discuss the major thinkers and presidential scholars in terms of historical position and philosophical leanings. For the first 150 years, it is readily apparent which thinkers should be included, but the choice becomes problematical in the contemporary era, dominated by new scholarly directions. Many more books are produced today, though our feeling is that only a relative few have so defined the essentials of this subfield as to warrant inclusion.

We begin our intellectual excursion by revisiting the celebrated debate between two ideological adversaries who seemingly defined the meaning of liberalism and conservatism in terms of presidential leadership during the 1950s and 1960s: James MacGregor Burns and Willmoore Kendall. But we review their arguments not to praise but to condemn them, because their ideas perpetuated a lasting myth that the Constitution mandated an ineffectual presidency. In retrospect, their debate did a disservice to our collective understanding of republicanism and executive energy. Burns mischaracterized James Madison, and Kendall gave Madisonianism a bad name, so we begin our argument with this misinformation as background for a more thorough and truthful rendering of Original Intent.

Chapter 2 discusses Original Intent with respect to Article 2 of the Constitution, mainly by laying bare the opposing arguments of Alexander Hamilton and Thomas Jefferson. Our review begins with the Founding, when the Federalists (who favored a strong executive coupled with a strong national government of limited scope) did ideological battle with the Anti-Federalists (who favored a weak executive coupled with a weak national government of limited scope).

Chapter 3 explores the Jeffersonian legacy and the advent of Whiggism. We begin with Supreme Court justice Joseph Story, who faithfully echoed Federalist arguments, and proceed to Alexis de Tocqueville's assessment of presidential decline during the Jefferson-Jackson era. To illustrate the extremes to which the Jeffersonian doctrine could reach, we touch on two commentators who defended the weak executive—Frederick Grimke and George Ticknor Curtis—before considering Lord James Bryce, whose highly celebrated *The American Commonwealth* presented a more positive view of presidential power. We conclude with another minor figure, Henry Clay Lockwood, whose strong Whiggish sentiments led him to advocate the abolition of the presidency.

Chapter 4 discusses the fundamental indictment of the constitutional presidency by the Progressives and their reconstruction of the American regime. We devote most of our attention to the seminal writings of a young political scientist named Woodrow Wilson, showing how his assessment of the presidency was fundamentally transformed between the years 1885 and 1908. A close reading is given to Henry Jones Ford, one of Wilson's closest advisers, and to Theodore Roosevelt, before concluding with brief attention to three highly influential intellectuals: J. Allen Smith, Charles Beard, and Herbert Croly.

The Progressive critique of the Founding led to a counterattack by constitutionalists early in the twentieth century. William Howard Taft penned his observations on the presidency to defend his own record as well as to disparage Teddy Roosevelt's, but arguably the best scholarly assessment of the origins of Article 2 was authored by Charles Thach in 1923. Although Thach did not challenge the Progressives by name, he did so implicitly by providing a powerfully detailed argument that Article 2 was crafted to allow executive energy to emerge unencumbered by Congress. The Progressives had argued that the separated-powers system posed an obstacle to effective government. Calvin Coolidge assumed the presidency in 1925 and subsequently published his autobiography, which included his personal statement about presidential leadership. Coolidge is informative not only because he was a constitutionalist but also because he is so regularly named as a wholly ineffectual president.

Almost every president seemed ineffectual in the wake of Franklin D. Roosevelt, according to the liberal academics who dominated the field of presidential scholarship during the post–World War II period: James MacGregor Burns, Richard Neustadt, Herman Finer, and Clinton Rossiter. But as early as 1940, this view was expressed by a British scholar, Harold Laski, who tied presidential leadership to the grandeur of class warfare and redistributive politics. These thinkers are covered in chapter 6.

Just as Progressivism fermented a defense by the early constitutionalists, so did liberalism prompt an intellectual backlash with vengeance by writers associated with the "anti-aggrandizement" school of thought. They are included in chapter 7: Edward Corwin, Alfred de Grazia, and C. Perry Patterson. However, our detailed look at their texts suggests that Corwin has been badly misrepresented. Although there are similarities among Corwin, de Grazia, and Patterson, these are outweighed by much more profound differences. Corwin needs to be revisited as one who held a more benign view of presidential leadership, which is applicable today.

Chapter 8 spans the 1960s and 1970s, when there were two discordant literatures on the presidency. One was provoked by the Vietnam excesses of Lyndon B. Johnson and was extended to Richard M. Nixon; the other is defined by the presidencies of Gerald R. Ford and James Earl Carter. Of all the historical eras chronicled herein, these two most blatantly represent political statements driven by the exigencies of the moment, not by any adherence to constitutionalism or historicism. For one group of authors, the presidency had grown monarchal: James David Barber, George Reedy, and Arthur Schlesinger Jr. They were followed in short order by another literature, which bemoaned ineffectual presidents, especially Jimmy Carter, whom both Charles Jones and Erwin Hargrove nonetheless tried to salvage with revisionist interpretations. During this period, when governance seemed implausible and presidential weakness intractable, Charles M. Hardin, Rexford Tugwell (a member of FDR's original Brains Trust), and James L. Sundquist advocated fundamental reform of the political system. Both of these schools of thought lasted barely longer than a decade, and both, despite their dissimilar diagnoses of the presidency, believed that the fundamental problem was with the incumbent, not so much with the office. For the most part, these groups of critics reflected the liberal persuasion that positive government was good so long as the right person inhabited the White House.

Chapter 9 identifies yet another strain of intellectual opinion, which we term the New Traditionalists. Traditionalism implies conservatism, but, unlike some previous thinkers who upheld constitutional principles in the name of limited government and a weak executive (such as Willmoore Kendall), these contemporary thinkers embrace strong presidents in the name of limited government: L. Gordon Crovitz, Jeremy A. Rabkin, Gordon S. Jones, John A. Marini, and Terry Eastland. Nothing explains their intellectual arrival more than the election of Ronald Wilson Reagan.

Chapter 10, covering the 1980s and 1990s and continuing today, argues that a "new realism, an old idealism" have captured the imagination of contemporary presidency scholars. The Founders' Constitution finds renewed support within mainstream scholarship, whether liberal or conservative. Theodore J. Lowi first articulated the values of this period; others equally sympathetic—but from differing vantage points—include Jeffrey

Tulis, Charles Jones, Stephen Skowronek, David Mayhew, and Sidney Milkis, to mention but a few. This period is marked by four core normative themes that are manifested in a variety of empirical and behavioral works on the presidency: the expectations gap, divided government, the ennobled Congress, and presidential constraints. In sum, presidency scholarship has come full circle to recognize the enduring principles of the Constitution for shared governance within a system of separated powers.

Yet the fact that the New Traditionalists are linked to the Reagan presidency begs an important question that must underlie our conclusions. At first glance, the ebb and flow of scholarly opinion about the presidency may be perceived simply as a function of whether your policy agenda is represented by the in-party of the White House or the out-party in Congress. Such an easy explanation seemingly accounts for the divergent views of Hamiltonianism versus Jeffersonianism, Progressivism versus Whiggism, New Deal Liberalism versus Conservatism, and obviously the writings of those alienated 1970s Liberals as well. The Conclusion looks through the lenses of constitutionalism, history, and politics to untangle the intellectual causes and effects in the evolution of presidential scholarship. None alone is sufficient to explain this evolution, just as all three in combination may lead to confusion. A final verdict will depend upon how we answer the six questions that are identified as defining the essential parameters of presidential leadership. Our summary judgment is that three overarching paradigms have shaped the ebb and flow of presidential scholarship over time: Hamiltonianism, Jeffersonianism, and Progressivism.

CHAPTER ONE

Constitutional Mythology
The Burns-Kendall Debate

During the 1950s and 1960s, no two scholars popularized the divergent opinions of "liberalism" and "conservatism" better than James MacGregor Burns and Willmoore Kendall. Burns was an unabashed Liberal Democrat and a biographer of Franklin D. Roosevelt and John F. Kennedy, who contested (but lost) a congressional seat from Massachusetts in 1958.[1] Kendall was a normative theorist, self-educated conservative, and southern agrarian, who did not welcome the growth of big government. This ideological divide colored their views of the presidency in the political system. To assert that Burns miscast Madison is less spectacular a claim than to chide Kendall for misreading the Founding, because many scholars in the Progressive-Liberal tradition doubted the efficacy of the separation-of-powers system. Compared to constitutionalists like Edward Corwin or contemporary conservatives like Terry Eastland, Kendall limited the president to a passive role in our system of government.

The opening volley in this intellectual confrontation came in 1960 when Kendall published his "two majorities" thesis. Three years later Burns penned his "deadlock of democracy" argument to formalize his understanding of presidential leadership and to lay the foundation for his 1965 book on "presidential government" (see chapter 6) as opposed to Woodrow Wilson's claim of "congressional government" (see chapter 4). Widely divergent views of majoritarianism led to their publication of a celebrated "debate" in 1964.

The "Two Majorities" Thesis

In 1960 Willmoore Kendall authored "The Two Majorities," truly a classic given the way events have transformed liberal and conservative opinion in the decades since.[2] In the stream of intellectual history, so well does Kendall's interpretation dovetail with that of Alfred de Grazia (see chapter 7) that he, like de Grazia, might rightly be characterized as a fervent "anti-aggrandizement" scholar fearful of presidential power. The title of his article telegraphs Kendall's arguments that the legislative and executive branches represent distinctive majorities in the body politic and that divergence explains the ongoing "tension" between the two popular branches of government.

Kendall posits eleven policies in which this tension was exhibited, with Congress generally more supportive of internal security, pork-barrel spending, trade protectionism, right-wing dictators, military spending, national and local (not international) interests, and restrictive immigration but less supportive of southern racial integration, deficits, and foreign aid.[3] The policy conflicts between the legislative and executive branches were, in modern jargon, zero-sum, because "either we move in *this* direction . . . or in *that* direction," with the result, Kendall argues, that "Congress pretty consistently gets its way" on these ideological disputes. Since conflict "between Executive and Legislature is normally a liberal-conservative tension," Kendall sees "an unexplained mystery" in American politics, namely that voters "elect to the White House a man devoted to the application of high principle to most important problems of national policy, and to the Hill men who consistently frustrate him."[4]

In addition, Congress was opposed to the "current program" of political scientists "for transforming the American political system into a *plebiscitary* political system, capable of producing and carrying through *popular mandates.*"[5] By the "current program" Kendall meant the various reforms aimed at achieving responsible partyism along the lines of a parliamentary regime, a theme typical of some leading presidency scholars in the Progressive-Liberal tradition.[6] Included in his inventory are these seven reforms (1) offer voters a "genuine" choice among candidates committed to the party program; (2) eliminate filibuster and the seniority system so nobody can frustrate the congressional majority; (3) eliminate the overrepresentation of rural populations and white southerners; (4) enact stronger civil rights laws to prevent white southerners from disfranchising Negro voters; (5) "streamline" the executive branch "to transform it into a ready and homogeneous instrument that the President . . . can use effectively in carrying out his mandate, and so as to 'concentrate' power and make it more 'responsible'"; (6) eliminate independent agencies; and (7) "glorify and enhance the office of President, and try to make of presidential elections the central ritual of American politics," thus enabling the president "with a popular mandate" to plead "against a recalcitrant Congress, that *his* mandate must prevail."[7]

Kendall challenges the view among liberals, and specifically Robert A. Dahl,[8] that the Framers intended to frustrate popular government. The liberal assumption is that majorities rule through presidential mandates, but Kendall believes that the Framers were intrigued with "the 'republican principle' as working precisely through the election of members to the two houses of Congress."[9] Kendall then sets the record straight:

> Taught as we are by decades of political theory whose creators have been increasingly committed to the idea of majority mandates arising out of plebiscitary elections, we tend to forget that the alternative, not having been invented yet, was *not* in the mind of the Framers at all; which is to say, we end up accusing the Framers of trying to prevent something they had never even heard of, and so cut ourselves off from the possibility of understanding their intention.[10]

Kendall wants us to consider "what we may call *two* popular majorities" and understand that the presidential majority was "*engrafted* on our political system," since "it was not intended by the Framers, not even present to their minds as something to be 'frustrated' and have 'barriers' put in its way."[11] In other words, the Framers were concerned about blocking majority tyranny, not frustrating popular mandates, though the congressional majority was designed to be the route by which public opinion is translated into public policy. The reason the intellectuals turned against the (conservative) Congress, alleges Kendall, is simply that they favored the presidential (liberal) policy agenda. Thus he asks that scholars "abandon the fiction" that "we have on the one hand an Executive devoted to high principle, and a Legislature whose majority simply refuse to live up to it, and confront the possibility that what we have is in fact two *conceptions* of high principle about which reasonable men may legitimately differ."[12]

Deadlock of Democracy

Writing political history with broad strokes, James MacGregor Burns claims that the "deadlock of democracy" resulting from four-party politics is a by-product of the constitutional system. His four-party thesis—that the "presidential wings" of both parties were liberal whereas their "congressional wings" were conservative—attracted few adherents among party theorists or presidency scholars and surely did not survive the test of time. Burns's not-so-hidden agenda was to graft both congressional wings into a minority "conservative" party and the two presidential wings into a dominant "liberal" party, thereby yielding the majoritarianism that Burns much preferred over the Madisonian system.

Pointing to the defeat of President Kennedy's policy initiatives, Burns declares that government could not effectively deal with national crises. The "main reason for our political futility and frustration" is the political system, and the prevailing view that is overly "entranced by the Madisonian model of government," which, alleges Burns, "is also the system of checks and balances and interlocked gears of government that requires the consensus of many groups and leaders" before the nation can act decisively. By "glorifying the Madisonian model we have undervalued—have even been frightened by—the great competing system of Jefferson" insofar as we "underestimated the powerful balances and safeguards that are built into a system of majority rule and responsible parties."[13] With these words, the die was cast between two polar opposites, Madison versus Jefferson (Hamilton was not recognized as a third presidential model until Burns published his 1965 book; see chapter 6).

Burns believes that two deeds of the Framers "would shape the strategy of American politics for decades to come," first the creation of the national government "at a price" of "a 'balance of checks' that prevented the government . . . from wielding too much power" and, second, the establishment of the presidency. Madison was the architect of the first governing principle, but with regard to the second, "[n]one of the Framers save Hamilton glimpsed the potential uses of executive power—and Hamilton, with his demand for a strong President in a strong national government, was about the least influential delegate in Philadelphia." In sum,

> The Framers saw the President as a wise magistrate who would carry out the laws of Congress, who would have a vague inherent power of his own, and who, with his modified veto, could defend his office against the power of the legislature and check any dangerous passions in the more popular branch. It is the great paradox of the Constitution—otherwise the world's foremost example of audacious and effective political planning—that what would turn out to be its most creative element, the Presidency, was one on which the Framers' grip was most unsure.[14]

Fear of majoritarianism was the paramount consideration, says Burns: "The key to Madison's thinking is his central aim to stop people from turning easily to government for help. Today, when many people want protection by or through government, and not just protection from government, the power of a minority to stop the majority from acting through government may be as arbitrary as majority rule seemed to Madison." Thus Madison "believed in a government of sharply limited powers," as "the new national government was supposed to tame and temper popular majorities —which some states had been unable to do."[15]

Burns thus argues that the separated and federated system is so fragmented that the Constitution cultivates rather than curbs the growth of factions around a myriad of local, state, and federal offices and thereby allows strategically positioned minorities ("veto groups" in the vocabulary of modern political science) to deny the majority will. He asserts that, because the system that Madison arranged was more effective at preventing laws than passing them, the way around the Constitution has to be through extraconstitutional devices—political parties.

Burns believes that "within fifteen years" of adoption, "the Madisonian model was suddenly overturned" in a "revolution" led by Thomas Jefferson. However, there are two Jeffersons: "[t]he Jefferson that feared national power and presidential tenure," whom Burns calls the "ideologist," and "Jefferson the politician, who grew up in the Virginia tradition of public service." Concludes Burns: "This second Jefferson, the politician and pragmatist, is, I think, as 'real' a Jefferson as the first, and far more relevant to the America of the 1960s."[16]

Burns chronicles the rise of the Jeffersonians, first as a congressional party under Madison and later as a grassroots organization supporting the presidential ambitions of Jefferson in 1800. Once elected, Jefferson transformed his party into a vehicle of majority rule, as evidenced by the Louisiana Purchase: "Here was the first Republican President saying in effect that his party should support his unconstitutional act because the voters would sustain the party at the next election." What is curious about this formulation is that Burns gives no credence to prerogative power—surely Hamilton and Washington would not have viewed negotiations with Napoleon as an unconstitutional act. Rather he emphasizes the after-the-fact support given to that purchase by the Republican majority in Congress. Yet, did not the Federalist majority under Washington support the controversial Jay Treaty, which involved the precedent-making assertion of presidential prerogative in treaty-making by the president? Burns proceeds to offer this characterization of Jefferson's legislative leadership:

> Above all, it was in his leadership of Congress that Jefferson upset old Republican notions of the executive-legislative balance. Considering himself the national head of the party, he gave close and constant leadership to his forces in Congress; he personally drafted bills and had them introduced into Congress; saw to it that the men he wanted took the leadership posts in

Congress; induced men he favored to run for Congress by holding out promises of advancement; made the Speaker and the floor leader of the House his personal lieutenants; changed the leadership as he saw fit; used Ways and Means and other committees as instruments of presidential control; dominated the Republican caucus in the House. In short, he took the machinery that the congressional Republicans had built up against Federalist Presidents and turned it to his own uses.[17]

We have no quibble with Burns's assertion that "Jefferson was the father of the first truly national Republican party" but wonder whether it would be equally applicable were Hamilton its subject, not Jefferson. Most observers agree that Hamilton upset the separated system by formal means (his personal intervention), whereas Jefferson did so by informal means (his intervention through partisans). Yet the effect was the same. Hamilton dominated the Federalist Congress just as Jefferson dominated the Republican Congress. In other words, the "deadlock" thesis argued that presidential leadership depends on political power, not prerogatives, and provided Burns with a rationale for responsible partyism via the Jeffersonian model.

Jefferson's strategy of majority rule had three elements, according to Burns. First, "[m]ajority rule in a big, diverse nation must be moderate." This tendency to moderation is Burns's answer to Madison's checks and balances. "Since 'tyranny of the majority' has long been a term to scare little children with, we must note again that the Jeffersonian system had internal checks and balances, just as Madison's formula had." Second, "[t]he Jeffersonian formula of majority rule allows more government action than the Madisonian model of checks and balances." On this point, Burns argues that Jeffersonianism is more conducive to positive government because Madison would require a virtual consensus. "In a sense the difference between the two systems was quantitative—the Jeffersonian formula required leaders to gain and keep the support of a simple majority of the people—say 55 per cent—behind federal action, while the Madisonians demanded clearance with a far larger proportion of the people (since any major group held a veto power)."[18]

And third, we finally arrive at Burns's policy agenda. "Jeffersonian majority rule had a more popular, egalitarian impetus than the Madisonian" because "[t]o win majorities a party leader must reach out to embrace new voters, while holding on to his present supporters; otherwise the opposition party might get the jump. It did not matter if the new voters were poor or ignorant, if they were aliens or even women—every effort must be made to enfranchise more voters and to get the warm bodies to the polls."[19]

Burns argues that, as president, "Madison [was] finally checkmated by his own formulas," and therefore "the supreme irony, for our purposes, was that the Madisonian system, which above all aimed at balance, moderation, adjustment, and a harmony of interests, was soon to be perverted by extremists into a caricature of itself, and to help produce a tragic disruption of government and breaking of the nation." In the end, however, Burns accommodates the "father" of our Constitution by relenting to this extent:

> [W]e must not dismiss Madison too cavalierly, [because, although] Jefferson turned his system upside down . . . not for many years, if ever, would any other President prove as effective as the great Virginian in organizing his party and Congress in defiance of the Madisonian formula. And even Jefferson, after all, had failed to take control of the judiciary—the final barricade erected by the Madisonian system against majority rule. In the years ahead the country would try to manage a strange hybrid of both majority rule and checks and balances, but Madisonian theory much more than Jeffersonian practice would dominate the strategy of American politics.[20]

One must wonder why such an ephemeral quality as charisma is required to bolster partisanship, since a political party is presumably built upon a more permanent foundation—principles and issues—than personalities. Burns is asking us to submit to his partisan game plan for America, having admitted that party is no cure-all for the deadlock he envisions. More to the point, Jefferson established no political legacy analogous to the one President Washington created based on prerogative power. Prerogative power adheres to the office and does not depend upon party, but nowhere does Burns acknowledge its existence in the arsenal of presidential powers. Why cannot prerogative power overcome any deficiencies in the Madisonian system? Two years later Burns does include Hamiltonianism as a possible model for presidential leadership (see chapter 6), but still he finds it deficient compared to Jeffersonianism.

Debating Constitutionalism

A formal debate between Kendall and Burns over the executive-legislative relationship was published in 1964. In his opening statement, Kendall says that he is the kind of conservative who is concerned about "how we are *going to make decisions* here in America about the kind of problem that lies so heavily upon Mr. Burns' heart." On deadlock, Kendall has "very little quarrel" with Burns, because "Congress does indeed . . . refuse in general to pass the legislative proposals rained upon it from the White House," though he takes issue with Burns about what the term *deadlock* implies. Kendall accuses liberals like Burns of having "a *program* . . . which they are *determined* to carry out" by having the president send it "over to one of his flunkies in Congress, who, one by one, drops the bills into the hopper." But Congress then proceeds to destroy or decimate that legislation, which is just fine with Kendall: "Mr. Burns wants to call that 'deadlock.' The majority of Congress, naturally enough, want to call it protecting the country against the extremist proposals of the liberal intellectuals. Mr. Burns wants to call Congress 'obstructionist.' We, the people, who biennium after biennium elect a Congress that *will do just what Mr. Burns says Congress does*, think of it as defending our way of life against those who would undermine and destroy it."[21]

Second, says Kendall, Burns talks about deadlock because "he does not want to face political reality." Burns implies "that the *trouble* is in Washington—that is, in the nation's political *machinery*" when in reality "[t]he deadlock . . . is not in Washington, but out in the country." Kendall continues: "I say, Political reality in America is that we Americans disagree profoundly on the *merits* of that program." Furthermore, "it is *not* just Congress that rejects your program, it is *we the people* as articulated through the Constitution that *we* ordain and establish. It is *we* who reject your program; and you, Mr. Burns, you and your friends are clearly powerless . . . to do anything about it! Political reality in America is that the liberals don't have the votes."[22] In sum, Congress is conservative because the American people are conservative.

Kendall's final point is that Burns wants "to *change* the rules so that he and his friends *can* win" and, toward that end, would go beyond the structural reforms of "his predecessors" in their advocacy of a "responsible party system" to accomplish "nothing less than a *coup d' etat*" by reconfiguring the two parties: "Let the liberals—he [Burns] calls them the Presidential Democrats and the Presidential Republicans . . . conspire together to capture *both* parties. Let us have, instead of a Liberal Party and a Conservative Party, *two* liberal parties (each of which will offer the electorate only liberal candidates)."[23]

In his brief rebuttal, Burns says that Kendall made a "serious concession to liberalism" by his "willing[ness] to base his concept of what is good for this nation on a question of public opinion, on a question of numbers, on a question of who has the most votes." Burns "believe[s] that majority rule is ultimately the way a democracy must be run and the only way it can effectively be run" and, in fact, that the majority has been voting liberal for several decades.[24] As evidence, he cites "the results of the last forty years of presidential elections," in which "it has been the candidate offering the liberal program who has won the election." And they "are the *national* decisions," in which "*all* the American people take part," unlike congressional elections, where, Burns observes, the total number of votes cast is many fewer compared to presidential elections.[25]

Kendall's retort begins with two points, that "conservatives are the voting majority of the Congress" and that the "historical bases of conservatism in America have to do with the American political system, and not with the content of the decisions that that political system produces." Burns, says Kendall, "is the liberal of liberals because it is he who challenges us conservatives *on our political system itself*. It is he who says that it is a bad political system; he who has the most ingenious plan for remaking it." Proceeding, Kendall calls Burns "a problem" because of his "blind devotion" to the majority principle. Essentially, Kendall equates Burns's majoritarianism with majority tyranny, not consensus-building, and suggests that the outvoted minority may not be so compliant. (Here Kendall mentions the South).[26] Pure majoritarianism is contrary to the "American understanding of majority rule," because, although "in a sense the numbers do prevail," more "[c]oncretely however, the majority of our elected representatives decide, *not* the majority of the electorate—but decide, in any case, subject to two clearly understood provisos."[27]

Those provisos are, first, that "the majority decides precisely with an eye to whether or not the minority *will* obey" and, second, that Americans can make some but not all decisions by majority rule, since we are "not a nation—but a federation of states in which majority rule has no status and no meaning. We have no tradition here in America for the kind of majority rule that is prepared to say to the minority (as Mr. Burns would not, I think, hesitate to say to the white Southerners on civil rights, or on the seniority principle), You are going to obey our policy directives *because* we are the majority. You are going to obey because if you do *not* obey, we are going to *make* you obey." At base, then, the Kendall rebuttal is that the system "was *never* intended for translating popular will into action" but rather was designed by Framers "who feared and disliked *above all things* the operation in politics of sheer, naked will." Instead they devised arrangements "to bring about amongst us a more perfect union . . . [but] not to divide us into majority and minority," "[t]o assure us the blessings of liberty . . . [but] not to keep us busy coercing one another," and "to reconcile the conflicting claims of *different* wills amongst us," that is, "to effectuate not the will of the people" but "rather . . . the deliberate sense of the community, the *whole* community, as to what ought to be done, and what policies ought to be adopted."[28] On the question of racial segregation, perhaps Kendall was too revealing of his sensitivities. There is always a danger to social stability when noncompliance by a determined minority is threatened, but Kendall's implication that majority rule applies within each state but seemingly cannot be imposed on any or all states by the national polity is a mischievous, if not dangerous, doctrine.

In his concluding remarks, Burns reveals his fundamental difference of opinion with Kendall on that issue facing the South. Burns "propose[s] majority rule in the area of economic and social change, but not majority rule in the area of civil liberties and the Bill of Rights," because he "want[s] those bill of rights in the nation and the states always to be there, always supported by a consensus. I never want them changed by a majority. They *do* represent a consensus," but then Burns adds that "I'm just a bit more sensitive (*perhaps* just a bit more sensitive) to the problem of those whom we're trying to help, especially in terms of their freedom and individual liberty." For blacks, in other words, the "consensus of Mr. Kendall doesn't seem to be working," since "[w]e waited for that consensus to work decade after decade, but it hasn't worked." Therefore, "[b]ecause these people are tired of waiting for that consensus to come . . . they want the government to move ahead under majority action," which seems to Burns like a "compromise position" between Kendall, "who will wait decades upon decades for action to take place, and those minoritarians who want to bring about action through direct struggle in the streets. Majority rule *is* a moderate system."[29]

As regards the "basic rules of the game," Burns thinks "[t]he majority *does* have a right . . . to change *those rules of the game that are not part of our original tradition.*" After all, the House Rules Committee, seniority rule, and the filibuster are "not part of our original system." Burns ends with a clarion call for majority rule, whatever the ideological stripe: "It is honestly because I want the conservatives of this nation (when their day comes, when they have persuaded a majority of the nation in a presidential election to their point of view—and perhaps this will be 1964) to have a right to rule in their day—when they have a majority behind them—that I want the liberals of the nations to have a right to rule in what I think is their day today."[30]

Conclusion

Does the president actively or passively engage the legislative process and promote a policy agenda? This question cuts to the heart of the Kendall-Burns policy debate. Obviously Burns believes that Congress should follow the president's lead and enact "liberal" policies, whereas Kendall argues that Congress is the natural home for "conservative" policies. Kendall's "two majorities" thesis reaffirms the legitimacy of Congress as the premier lawmaker by virtue of its "deliberative" role in consensus-building, just as Burns prefers presidential dominance as an agency for majoritarianism reflective of national electoral mandates. Kendall would reply that, because Congress is the rightful fount for representative government, the legislative branch can ignore the presidential legislative agenda, regardless of the election outcome.

Does presidential power derive from the prerogatives of office or from the incumbent? As will be seen in chapter 6, Burns undergoes a transformation: having ignored presidential prerogative in 1963, he acknowledges it (though disparagingly) in his 1965 writings. Burns talks more directly about the presidency than Kendall does, but the context of Kendall's comments speaks volumes about how a conservative of his stripe would view executive-legislative relations. For Burns, politics underlies presidential power. For Kendall, we cannot be sure that he would be any more comfortable with political or prerogative power, if the result is presidential leadership of Congress.

Does presidential influence depend upon the force of personality, rhetorical leadership, or partisanship? Intellectually the focus of the Kendall-Burns debate is ideological, but politically it hinges on the nature of two-party government. Burns believes that presidential leadership is best utilized through his ideal of two responsible parties, one conservative and one liberal. An electoral mandate legitimates presidential campaign pledges, and the congressional party stands ready to fulfill them. Kendall decries nationalized parties both for subverting policy preferences in the states and congressional districts and for disrupting consensus-building. Responsible parties would sacrifice local minorities to the national majority.

Does the organization of the executive branch service presidential leadership? Neither Burns nor Kendall makes mention of the federal bureaucracy, though Kendall disparages big government as much as Burns embraces it. Apart from the size of government, however, our concern is whether presidential leadership is augmented by bureaucracy, and no speculation can be gleaned from the Kendall-Burns encounter.

Does presidential leadership depend upon historical context, or is regime-building manifested through political, institutional, and constitutional developments? Kendall's concept of Original Intent is stuck in the eighteenth century, as he gives no ground to institutional developments (the rise of parties and democratized elections) in the following centuries. Since presidential majorities were not intended by the Framers—or even contemplated—and have been "engrafted" onto our political system, Kendall considers a national mandate as less legitimate than the majority viewpoint as filtered through Congress. Thus he rejects any benign understanding of regime-building, which suggests to us that Kendall properly belongs in the "anti-aggrandizement" school of thought (see chapter 7) and is philosophically isolated from such "conservatives" (we say constitutionalists) as ex-presidents William Howard Taft and Calvin Coolidge (see chapter 5) or Kendall's contemporary in the presidency studies, Edward Corwin (see chapter 7).

Burns complains that the Constitution did not mandate antimajoritarian devices within Congress. But neither did the Constitution preordain nor prohibit their use. To fill Burns's prescription would require a fundamental reordering of how Congress does business, but then complaining about the seniority system, filibuster, and the Rules Committee was standard fare for Liberals of that day.[31] Nonetheless, those antimajoritarian procedures continue today, with almost no Liberal commentators asking for their abolition (perhaps because the filibuster now is used as much by liberals as by conservatives).

Does presidential leadership vary between domestic and foreign affairs? Although both Kendall and Burns mention pressing foreign problems (e.g., the cold war), their programmatic differences center on domestic policy. The civil rights struggle is the powerful subtext of the Kendall-Burns debate, as shown by Burns's oblique reference to his greater "sensitivities" on the subject. Kendall's dogged belief that Congress is somehow inherently conservative was not clairvoyant given the turnabout of ideological conflict between the popular branches once Richard Nixon, Gerald Ford, Ronald Reagan, and both Presidents Bush succeeded to the White House. In fact, what made Congress conservative in the 1960s was that the "conservative coalition" of southern Democrats and Republicans were the governing majority. By the 1980s the congressional Democrats, especially in the

House of Representatives, became more unified and were as liberal as the Republicans are now conservative. Thus, the 1980s gave us heightened partisanship coupled with ideological purity within each congressional party.

Kendall and Burns were embroiled in a policy debate reflecting the politics of their time. Constitutionalism is largely irrelevant to how Burns views the American regime (other than his fealty to the Bill of Rights), whereas Kendall gives a reading of Original Intent with respect to representation that could well deny any president—liberal or conservative—much leverage over the legislative process. Kendall sees no constitutional grounding for legislative leadership in Article 2, a sharp contrast with today's conservatives; see chapter 9). This gives us reason to question whether Kendall's conservatism is something other than constitutionalism. To put into relief the one-sided interpretations of Kendall and Burns with respect to presidential leadership in our separated system, we revisit the Founding in the next chapter.

CHAPTER TWO

Original Intent and the Presidency
Hamilton versus Jefferson

Although the federal Constitution of 1787 had gained nearly universal acceptance by the early years of the next decade, the political divisions that had emerged during the debate over ratification between Federalists and Anti-Federalists lived on. The struggle reemerged in the Washington administration with the political contest between Secretary of the Treasury Alexander Hamilton and Secretary of State Thomas Jefferson. Nevertheless, the Federalists created a strong executive and established essential presidential prerogatives during the Washington administration. But Jefferson's election in 1800 largely reversed the Federalists' statecraft and redefined the presidency in new and ultimately destructive terms. Jeffersonian principles became the dominant paradigm for the nineteenth century and established the political and intellectual context for evaluating presidential performance. This paradigm created a minimalist view of constitutional power, which in turn diminished presidential power. Before considering Jefferson's popular, party foundation for the presidency, we will outline the office the Hamiltonians believed was safely codified in the newly ratified Constitution.

The Hamiltonian President

In the justly famous *Federalist*, Alexander Hamilton makes the most integrated and thorough analysis of the Founders' view of presidential power. Because the coauthors, John Jay, James Madison, and Alexander Hamilton, writing under the pseudonym Publius, wished to smooth out the controversial aspects of the new Constitution, Hamilton turned his attention to arguing that executive power was compatible with republicanism when he penned his Papers on the presidency (F, 67–77). In addition, James Madison is reported to have read all of Hamilton's contributions to the *Federalist* in advance, so Hamilton, writing as Publius, could not have been greatly at variance with the other leading members of the Constitutional Convention.

In the *Federalist*, Hamilton shows great interest in the presidency and appears to regard the office, in some sense, as the capstone of the new Constitution. If the presidency was the most difficult office to give a constitutional frame, it appears the most promising of the convention's creations. "There is hardly any part of the system," Hamilton writes, "which could have been attended with greater difficulty in the arrangement of it than this" (F, 452).[1] That promise springs from Hamilton's confidence that the new president would become an "energetic" national leader. Energy in the executive was as much a catchword for Hamilton as presidential "vigor" became for John Fitzgerald Kennedy. Absence of energy results in a feeble execution of presidential powers, and a "feeble execution is but another phrase for a bad execution: And a government ill executed, whatever it may be in theory, must be in practice a bad government" (F, 471–72). *Federalist* 70 summarizes the qualities necessary for energy: "The ingredients, which constitute energy in the executive, are first unity, secondly duration, thirdly an adequate provision for its support, fourthly competent powers" (F, 472). With these expansive qualities, Hamilton expects the new president to become the keystone or bulwark of the constitutional order, as George Washington proved to be in the Revolutionary War.

Hamilton immediately turns to the four criteria required for executive energy. First: "That unity is conducive to [executive] energy will not be disputed. Decision, activity, secrecy, and dispatch will generally characterize the proceedings of one man, in a much more eminent degree, than the proceedings of any greater number" (F, 472). As the Senate in ancient Rome limited executive power by electing dual consuls to check one another, the advocates of a weak American system sought to limit the president by making him subject "to the control and co-operation of others, in the capacity of counselors to him" (F, 473). But the Framers ultimately decided against creating any type of council with which the executive was required to consult or cooperate.

Having guaranteed energy through unity, the Framers wanted sufficient duration in office to achieve the same end. Rejecting a single term of seven years, the convention proposed a four-year presidential term capable of indefinite renewal. This shorter term guaranteed greater public oversight of the president, and indefinite renewal allowed him time to bring his projects to fruition. Duration, in other words, encourages the president to pursue the public good: "One ill effect of the exclusion [from reelection] would be a diminution of the inducements to good behavior. There are very few men who would not feel much less zeal in the discharge of a duty, when they were conscious that the advantages of the station, with which it was connected, must be relinquished at a determinate period, then when they were permitted to entertain a hope of *obtaining* by *meriting* a continuance of them" (*F*, 488). But after his practical experience with the new office, George Washington, with Hamilton's support, retired after two presidential terms. This practice continued until the Progressive-Liberal embrace of presidential power enabled Franklin Roosevelt to gain the presidency four times. But FDR's long reign proved the exception that confirmed the rule. The Twenty-Second Amendment limited presidential terms to two.

Duration in office supports a president's initiative and firmness in accomplishing his constitutional responsibilities. It also strengthens his position with Congress. Duration in office enables the executive to "be in a situation to dare to act his own opinion with vigor and decision" (*F*, 483). A long term also permits the president to exercise independent leadership when popular sentiment varies from the public good:

> When occasions present themselves in which the interests of the people are at variance with their inclinations, it is the duty of the persons whom they have appointed to be the guardians of those interests, to withstand the temporary delusions, in order to give them time and opportunity for more cool and sedate reflection. Instances might be cited, in which a conduct of this kind has saved the people from very fatal consequences of their own mistakes, and has procured lasting monuments of their gratitude to the men, who had courage and magnanimity enough to serve them at the peril of their displeasure. (*F*, 482–83)

Of particular importance is the stability that duration in office imparts "to the system of administration which may have been adopted under [the president's] auspices" (*F*, 481). Only in the twentieth century did Herbert Croly and the Progressives (see chapter 4) recognize that Hamilton was the Founder who most consistently emphasized the importance of good administration for good government. Hamilton wrote:

> The administration of government, in its largest sense, comprehends all the operations of the body politic, whether legislative, executive or judiciary, but in its most usual and perhaps in its most precise signification, it is limited to executive details, and falls peculiarly within the province of the executive department. The actual conduct of foreign negotiations, the preparatory plans of finance, the application and disbursement of the public monies, in conformity to the general appropriations of the legislature, the arrangement of the army and navy, the direction of the operations of war;

these and other matters of a like nature constitute what seems to be most properly understood by the administration of government. The persons therefore, to whose immediate management these different matters are committed, ought to be considered as the assistants or deputies of the chief magistrate; and, on this account, they ought to derive their offices from his appointment, at least from his nomination, and ought to be subject to his superintendence. This view of the subject will at once suggest to us the intimate connection between the duration of the executive magistrate in office, and the stability of the system of administration. (*F*, 486–87)

Hamilton feared that political alliances (or parties) would encourage wholesale changes in administration under each new president. Appointing new administrative officials benefits political allies and reflects the conviction of a new president "that the dismission of his predecessor has proceeded from a dislike to his measures, and that the less he resembles him the more he will recommend himself to the favor of his constituents" (*F*, 487). Seemingly forecasting the Jacksonians' motto "to the victor go the spoils" and their policy of "rotation in office," Hamilton warns: "These considerations, and the influence of personal confidences and attachments, would be likely to induce every new president to promote a change of men to fill the subordinate stations; and these causes together could not fail to occasion a disgraceful and ruinous mutability in the administration of the government" (*F*, 487). Because of the prevalence of Hamilton's view of administration, presidents before Andrew Jackson by and large considered the administrative officers nonpolitical and kept them in place based on merit, not party affiliation. Only after a half-century of Jacksonian-inspired "rotation in office" did civil service reform begin to establish a standard of professionalism.

The third element of executive energy "is an adequate provision for its support." Given the "propensity of the legislative department to intrude upon the rights and to absorb the powers of the other departments," the maintenance of executive independence from the "legislative vortex" is paramount (*F*, 494). The security of the president's "salary and emoluments" guards him against congressional manipulation, but his major defense against legislative "encroachment" is his qualified veto power over legislation. Indeed, Hamilton says: "The primary inducement to conferring the power in question upon the executive, is to enable him to defend himself" (*F*, 495). Even if the president must use the veto sparingly, given the greater popularity and power of the legislature, the veto threat makes him always the chief legislator, given the two-thirds majorities in both houses needed to overrule him. The Framers made the absolutist veto of the British monarch more republican by allowing Congress to override a presidential veto.

Hamilton argues that the president's use of the veto will be restrained by the power and prestige of Congress, as well as by the popular fear of such a "monarchical prerogative." He remarks that the king of England, with "all his train of sovereign attributes, and with all the influence he draws from a thousand sources, would at this day hesitate to put a negative upon the joint resolutions of the two houses of Parliament" (F, 496). Indeed, "a very considerable period has elapsed [in Great Britain] since the negative of the crown has been exercised" (F, 497). But, given the Framers' strong desire for executive energy and vigor, one may assume that they would prefer to have the veto actively used rather than to have the new republic fail because of a lack of executive resolve.

Another indication of Original Intent is the second argument that Publius advances for the necessity of a presidential veto: the need to prevent bad legislation. "The secondary [purpose of the veto] is to increase the chances in favor of the community, against the passing of bad laws, through haste, inadvertence, or design" (F, 495). Although it may appear that "haste, inadvertence, [and] design" are limiting qualifiers over the executive veto, a moment's reflection suggests they are not. Robert J. Spitzer's observation seems apt:

> [T]he founders' conception of the circumstances under which the veto could be applied, and the quality of the power itself, were substantially broader than is typically realized or acknowledged. This is important partly because of the subsequent conflicts over the circumstances of veto use, which in the minds of the founders were extremely broad. Essentially, the president was free, in constitutional terms, to veto any bill that crossed his desk, as long as he stated his reason for doing so and then returned the bill to the legislative chamber of origin. In a Committee of Detail Draft of the Constitution, written during the federal convention in July, the application of the veto was summarized by saying that a bill might be returned if "it shall appear to him [the president] improper for being passed into a Law." No other circumstances were specified. It is difficult to conceive of any piece of legislation not covered by this language.[2]

For Hamilton and the Framers, the veto made the president a legislative leader.

The Jeffersonians stoutly denied the president the authority to use the veto except on the narrowest grounds. As a result, the veto was used infrequently and reluctantly throughout the first quarter of the nineteenth century. Usually presidents before Jackson, bowing to the Jeffersonian demand for limited and mainly legislatively dominated government, were forced to defend their vetoes on the narrow ground of preventing unconstitutional acts. To veto legislation on policy grounds alone would appear to exercise the same prerogative power used by English monarchs over the colonial legislatures.

Hamilton next elaborates the areas of public life under executive control. The three great powers in Article 2 are these: (1) The president is "Commander in Chief of the army and navy of the United States, and of the militia of the several states *when called into the actual service* of the United States" (F, 464). (2) He is to have the power "by and with the advice and consent of the Senate, to make treaties, provided two-thirds of the Senators concur" (F, 467). (3) The president is "to *nominate* and by and with the advice and consent of the Senate to appoint Ambassadors, other public Ministers and Consuls, Judges of the Supreme Court, and all other officers of the United States, whose appointments are not otherwise provided for in the Constitution" (F, 509).

As chief executive officer, the president must enforce the laws and therefore needs both military power and control over administrative officials. He shares the treaty- and war-making power with the Senate, appoints ambassadors, and, as became established during the Washington administration, negotiates and interprets treaties. Hamilton gives due weight to the extraordinary and far-reaching nature of these powers. When combined with his command of the military, they make the president the leading figure in foreign and military affairs. Also noteworthy is that Hamilton passes over, virtually without comment, "the only remaining powers of the executive," those of "giving information to Congress of the state of the union; in recommending to their consideration such measures as he shall judge expedient" (F, 519–20). Out of this brief sentence eventually emerged the argument that the executive should set the legislative agenda for Congress and the nation. Long before this development, however, Hamilton argued that the president would be a major legislative figure: recommending bills to Congress for their consideration and using his veto power to shape legislation congenial to his view of the public weal.[3]

Not wishing to draw undue attention to the expansive powers of the new executive, the *Federalist* is silent about the brevity of Article 2, especially in comparison with the much longer exposition of legislative powers in Article 1. Hamilton later makes the case for the inferred prerogative power this brevity suggests in his *Pacificus Papers*. He argues that Congress has only the powers specifically granted to it. However, the broad and brief grant of executive authority gives the president every conceivable executive power, "subject only to the [very few] *exceptions* and *qualifications* which are expressed in the instrument [the Constitution]."[4]

A fundamental difference between the Federalists and the Jeffersonians concerns their view of implied powers. How should the Constitution be interpreted with reference to the enabling powers that permit the branches of government to complete the tasks assigned to them in the Constitution? The Federalists argue that any measure fulfilling constitutional ends is justified under the "necessary and proper clause." The Jeffersonians argue that the "necessary and proper clause" essentially contained no grant of power at all.

Federalist 23 takes the broadest view of implied powers. Hamilton frames his argument for essentially unlimited implied powers in the national government by focusing on the exigencies of national defense:

> The authorities essential to the care of the common defense are these—to raise armies—to build and equip fleets—to prescribe rules for the government of both—to direct their operations—to provide for their support. These powers ought to exist without limitation: *Because it is impossible to foresee or define the extent and variety of national exigencies, or the correspondent extent & variety of the means which may be necessary to satisfy them.* The circumstances that endanger the safety of nations are infinite; and for this reason no constitutional shackles can wisely be imposed on the power to which the care of it is committed. This power ought to be co-extensive with all the possible combinations of such circumstances; and ought to be under the direction of the same councils, which are appointed to preside over the common defense. (F, 147)

Beyond national defense, Hamilton broadens the claim to include all possible power necessary to secure "those objects which are intrusted to its [the national government's] management."

> Every view we may take of the subject, as candid enquirers after truth, will serve to convince us, that it is both unwise and dangerous to deny the Federal Government an unconfined authority, as to all objects which are intrusted to its management . . . For the absurdity must continually stare us in the face of confiding to a government, the direction of the most essential national interests, without daring to trust it with the authorities which are indispensable to their proper and efficient management. Let us not attempt to reconcile contradictions, but firmly embrace a rational alternative. (F, 150–51)

In Hamilton's view, the crucial decision is what ends the people ought to *"delegate to any government."* In other words, the government should have limited areas of responsibility, but when it is decided that responsibilities such as defense and currency regulation have been given to it, all the powers necessary for their execution are implied by logical and political necessity. Once the limited ends of government are granted, "the co-incident powers may safely accompany them" (*F*, 150). In *Federalist* 33, Hamilton interprets the "necessary and proper" clause to the same effect, asking rhetorically: "What is a power, but the ability or faculty of doing a thing? What is the ability to do a thing but the power of employing the *means* necessary to its execution? What is a LEGISLATIVE power but a power of making LAWS? What are the *means* to execute a LEGISLATIVE power but Laws? What is the power of laying and collecting taxes but a *legislative power*, or a power of *making laws*, to lay and collect taxes? What are the proper means of executing such a power but *necessary* and *proper* laws?" (*F*, 204–5). In sum, the government should enjoy strong means but constitutionally limited ends.

During the Washington administration, Hamilton used presidential power expansively by making far-reaching claims in both domestic and foreign matters. With Hamilton as secretary of the treasury and Jefferson as secretary of state in a national unity cabinet, Washington appears to have sought a position above the political fray that engulfed his two secretaries, even while employing Hamilton to carry out necessary initiatives. Hamilton's leadership was notable in passing an expansive economic program: the first national bank, the repayment of existing public debt, and policies to benefit the development of commerce and industry. As secretary of the treasury, Hamilton drafted these bills and their extensive rationales or defenses, while personally lobbying Congress to promote their passage. Hamilton's actions had the intended effect of demonstrating that the president could be a leader in legislative matters.

In foreign affairs, Hamilton played a similar role in the Proclamation of Neutrality in 1793, which established the president as the emphatic leader in this area as well. Both the Federalists' economic policy and their interpretation of neutrality were strenuously, but unsuccessfully, opposed by Thomas Jefferson. Whether acting independently or at the behest of Washington, Hamilton quickly demonstrated the practicality of the arguments he had made earlier in the *Federalist*. Legislative leadership and a strong foreign policy could be asserted largely on presidential prerogative alone.

So complete was the Federalists' view of presidential power that at least one scholar has described George Washington as the first modern president.[5] In truth, modern presidents have gained enormous power as a result of the Progressive reinvention of the science of politics and administration.[6] Washington, who pursued no broad modernist agenda like the Progressives, never had cause to avail himself of the full panoply of modern powers.[7] Yet, a careful review of the Federalists' approach to presidential leadership in foreign affairs, with at least equal participation in legislative matters, illustrates a powerful executive suitable for any age.

The Jeffersonian Executive

Even as the secretary of state in the cabinet of George Washington, Thomas Jefferson—increasingly with the support of James Madison, the leader of the House of Representatives—became the locus of opposition to the Federalists' strong national government and energetic executive. Fearing the loss of political liberty and social equality in the nation, the Jeffersonians argued for ever-more-limited national power against the Hamiltonian "monocrats," who, they claimed, were using the government to acquire wealth and station. Whereas Hamilton had argued in the *Federalist* for all powers necessary to realize the ends given the new government by the Constitution, the Jeffersonians argued that unless the means are as explicit as the ends, they cannot be considered to exist, much less be considered as "implied" under the "necessary and proper" clause. In the *Kentucky Resolutions*, for example, Jefferson repeatedly invoked the Tenth Amendment as a declaration of the states' constitutional independence from political tyranny. Objecting to the Alien and Sedition Act, Jefferson wrote:

> *Resolved*, That alien friends are under the jurisdiction and protection of the laws of the State wherein they are: that no power over them has been delegated to the United States, nor prohibited to the individual States, distinct from their power over citizens. And it being true as a general principle, and one of the amendments to the Constitution having also declared, that "the powers not delegated to the United States by the Constitution, nor prohibited by it to the States, are reserved to the States respectively, or to the people," the act of the Congress of the United States, passed on the ____ day of July, 1798, instituted "An Act concerning aliens," which assumes powers over alien friends, not delegated by the Constitution, is not law, but is altogether void, and of no force.[8]

Apart from the constitutionality of the Alien and Sedition Act, it is revealing that Jefferson relegated the power of regulating aliens to the states alone, seemingly an absurd restriction on national power.

Hamilton sought to strengthen the economic and social resources of the largely middle-class businessmen and the professionals found in the meritocratic northern states. Jefferson, on the contrary, rhetorically appealed to those farmers, especially on the western frontier and in the South, who sought greater social equality. In Jefferson's mind social equality would come primarily from reforms within the states and localities, not from a strong national government. By its very conservative nature, Jefferson believed, the Constitution would inevitably move the country backward toward the hierarchical institutions of European despotism.

Jefferson brought the complaints and fears of the Anti-Federalists into the American political mainstream. He repeatedly accused the Hamiltonians of empowering the national government in order to maintain the social classes of the *old regime* and to increase the wealth of the grandees who benefited from high taxes, the promotion of industry, and the regulation of the currency. In addition, Jefferson argued that "administration [should] be vested in the unit of government nearest the individuals to be served."[9] As a result, the federal government should only be given authority that could not be placed elsewhere. According to Jefferson, "this was primarily the power over foreign relations."[10]

Weak governments, in contrast, permit and encourage the ongoing revolutions that Jefferson sought. Commenting on Shay's Rebellion, which he endorsed, Jefferson warned: "God forbid we should be twenty years without such a rebellion . . . If [the people] remain quiet under such misconceptions, it is a lethargy, the forerunner of death to the public spirit."[11] If the Federalists were building a new nation that would create new jobs and new wealth in a stable and prosperous political society, Jefferson wanted a weak government in which average Americans, especially farmers—"the chosen people of God, if ever he had a chosen people"[12]—would gain wealth, social opportunity, and political power. If America was the new promised land for God's chosen people, a strong government would, as in the old world, be the source of new snakes slithering over her verdant beauty. Jefferson's first inaugural address captures this libertarianism:

> Kindly separated by nature and a wide ocean from the exterminating havoc of one quarter of the globe; too high-minded to endure the degradations of the others; possessing a chosen country, with room enough for our descen-

dants to the hundredth and thousandth generation; entertaining a due sense of our equal right to the use of our own faculties, to the acquisitions of our industry, to honor and confidence from our fellow citizens, resulting not from birth but from our actions and their sense of them . . . what more is necessary to make us a happy and prosperous people? Still one thing more, fellow citizens—a wise and frugal government, which shall restrain men from injuring one another, which shall leave them otherwise free to regulate their own pursuits of industry and improvement, and shall not take from the mouth of labor the bread it has earned. This is the sum of good government, and this is necessary to close the circle of our felicities.[13]

Jefferson then addresses the Federalists' fear that weak governments threaten the safety of citizens:

[S]ome honest men fear that a republican government cannot be strong; that this government is not strong enough. But would the honest patriot, in the full tide of successful experiment, abandon a government which has so far kept us free and firm, on the theoretic and visionary fear that this government, the world's best hope, may by possibility want energy to preserve itself? I trust not. I believe this, on the contrary, the strongest government on earth. I believe it is the only one where every man, at the call of the laws, would fly to the standard of law, and would meet invasions of the public order as his own personal concern.[14]

In other words, political power should not rely on the constitutional principles established by those who sought greater energy in government, because energy can always be found in the people in arms.

Jefferson's reliance on the people's revolutionary and patriotic spirit was amply displayed in the Kentucky Resolutions. Among many interesting aspects of this portentous document is that John C. Calhoun later claimed it as a theoretical basis for the doctrines of nullification and secession. The resolutions called upon the states to interpose between the national government and their citizens, because whenever "the General Government assumes undelegated powers, its acts are unauthoritative, void, and of no force." In addition, Jefferson claimed that "as in all other cases of compact among powers having no common judge, each party has an equal right to judge for itself, as well of infractions as of the mode and measure of redress."[15] Although Jefferson eventually acceded to the Supreme Court's claim of judicial review on constitutional matters, many of his southern followers, including John C. Calhoun, did not.

Jefferson was suspicious of the executive power that was found in the

Constitution and realized in the administrations of George Washington and John Adams. Of course, Jefferson used presidential powers expansively, notably in the Louisiana Purchase, and agreed with Secretary of the Treasury Albert Gallatin "[t]hat the United States as a nation have an inherent right to acquire property." However, for party and public consumption, Jefferson argued that he was "forced" by an imperative necessity to act unconstitutionally in making the purchase.[16] Jefferson was also suspicious of the legislative veto, considering it a prerogative or monarchical power, and he did not use it while in office.[17] Jefferson developed the view, which became widespread among his followers, that the veto was given to the executive to block unconstitutional legislation, and for little else.[18] "[U]nless the president's mind on a view of everything which is urged for and against a bill is tolerably clear that it is unauthorized by the Constitution; if the pro and con hang so even as to balance his judgment, a just respect for the wisdom of the legislature would naturally decide in favor of their opinion."[19]

The *Federalist* had sought to make the president the chief legislator, mainly through his veto power. In Publius's view the president should veto or threaten to veto bills that in his judgment are adverse to the public interest. Although George Washington vetoed only two bills, one is of interest. By vetoing a military bill, Washington forced Congress to restore funding for two military units that he considered militarily indispensable. On another occasion, he used the threat of a veto to negotiate with Congress. Washington withdrew his veto threat against a tariff bill that he thought discriminated unwisely against the "good friends" of the United States "when he was informed that Congress was already considering a revision that would satisfy many of his objections."[20]

This sharp difference over the veto is illustrative of the gulf separating Hamilton's and Jefferson's views of the executive. Hamilton regarded the president, much as we do today, as the essential actor on the political stage, one who must play an indispensable role in domestic as well as foreign policy. Through his power of appointment, the president shapes the direction of the Supreme Court; as chief law enforcement officer, he plays a vital part in how Court decisions are enforced.

Jefferson understood that the agrarian interests, especially the slaveholders, feared federal interventions in their local institutions and economies. The majority of the electorate wanted as little government, especially national government, as possible. Jefferson agreed that the people should be left alone to be "free to regulate their own pursuits of industry and improvement." Indeed the majority remained satisfied with a national government so weak that Tocqueville found it nearly invisible.[21] For this reason, the Hamiltonians believed the national government could not depend directly on the popular will alone. Effective government needed to be rooted in the prerogative powers of the new Constitution, whose officeholders, though elected, were, once in office, capable of effectively governing the reluctant states and semisettled territories. The Jeffersonians, on the contrary, embraced the economic interests of the farmer and the liberty of the states, which sought wide autonomy in their domestic and economic arrangements, including the "peculiar institution" of slavery.[22] As political scientists Sidney Milkis and Michael Nelson explain:

> Washington and Adams [following Hamilton] believed that some distance from the people was required if presidents were to perform their task properly, which was to moderate the clash of parties and interests that inevitably would occur in Congress. But Jefferson felt that the most effective and responsible way for the president to lead the government was through the very institutions that were rooted most firmly in a popular base, the House and the Senate. Rather than stand apart from the developments in the legislature, he sought to direct them. Thus, in contrast to Hamilton's conception of a strong presidency, which emphasized the need for independent executive initiatives, Jefferson assumed the mantle of party leader in an effort to unite the separate branches of American government.[23]

As president, Jefferson was effective in creating a disciplined party apparatus in Congress, with the "president relying on his floor leaders in the House and Senate to advance his program."[24] Jefferson also perfected the party caucus originally initiated by the Federalists. Democratic-Republican leaders personally chosen by Jefferson coordinated policies, thus politically circumventing the separation of powers. Jefferson's populism extended even beyond his deference to Congress to cultivate direct popular approval. In deference to Congress, he reversed Washington's practice of presenting his Annual Addresses to the Congress in person: he presented them in writing instead. This was "a calculated political act, designed to . . . reduce the 'relics' left by Federalists and underline the return to sound republican simplicity."[25] Similarly, Jefferson abandoned Washington's practice of riding in a coach with liveried outriders, and rode around the new capitol on his own horse. If Washington dressed up, Jefferson dressed down. Jefferson's republican rusticity often seemed beneath that required for a head of state, or even a respectable gentleman farmer.[26] But Jefferson's appeal to popular opinion created the first dominant political party in American history. The Democratic-Republican Party won every presidential election but two from 1800 until 1860.

Although Jefferson successfully maintained his power by using the rhetoric of democracy and control over congressional party leaders, his successors became weaker as the political tides turned against them. Jefferson gained power over Congress by ensuring that all key posts in the House were occupied by his party followers. When Jefferson's successors lost control of the caucus, they found they had burned their bridges to the "monarchical" prerogative powers that their party eschewed but presidents required. John Marshall had predicted this dangerous politicization of the presidency in a letter to Alexander Hamilton. Marshall wrote: "Mr. Jefferson appears to me to be a man who will embody himself with the House of Representatives. By weakening the office of the president, he will increase his personal power. He will diminish his responsibility, sap the fundamental principles of government, and become the leader of that party which is about to constitute the majority of the legislature."[27]

Thus the congressional caucus, which strengthened Jefferson personally, left the presidency bereft of power and influence when the caucus turned against his successors and followed its own political lights. Congressional ascendancy was completed when Henry Clay became Speaker of the House of Representatives in 1811. Working with his powerful lieutenants, John C. Calhoun, who was a congressman from 1811 to 1815, and John Quincy Adams, Clay seemed to take control of the Madison administration. Apparently the caucus made Madison's commitment to the War of 1812 a condition of his renomination for office.[28] The Monroe administration was not as blemished by its deference to Congress, compared to its predecessor, but Monroe exercised even less power over Congress. Wilfred Binkley summarized presidential decline under the Jeffersonians in this way:

> Thus in the first quarter of the century Congress, by direct election or through the caucus, had chosen every president. So weak was the opposition of the Federalist party that the electoral college had done little more than ratify the choice of the Republican caucus. The constitutional framers had considered the election of the executive by the legislature and had rejected it but a chain of circumstances had come to pass that practically reversed their decision. Such a long trend in the actual process of choosing the President must inevitably have left its mark upon the office. Jefferson, through the force of his personality, delayed the effect but Madison and Monroe offered no such resistance to congressional influence on the presidency.[29]

John Quincy Adams, one of the National Republicans who sought a stronger domestic program than the southward-leaning Jeffersonians, recommended a comparatively far-reaching domestic agenda. Adams's first annual message to Congress proposed a "broad array of internal improvements, a national university, an observatory, scientific exploration, and voyages of discovery."[30] Although his two predecessors "Madison and Monroe [had] followed Jefferson in believing that a constitutional amendment was needed before anything could be done . . . Adams boldly rejected the narrow construction of the Constitution and deference his predecessors had shown to Congress."[31] To stop such heresy, Senator Andrew Jackson rallied the loyal Jeffersonians against the National Republicans. He blocked passage of Adams's program, and his followers swept the elections of 1826 on his way to the presidency in 1828. The "Democratic-Republican era ended with Congress, not the president, at the center of government power."[32] The Framers' strong but limited president remained the constitutional standard, but the success of Jefferson's rhetoric and party inexorably weakened the national government and the president. Arguably, it was because of presidential weakness that the regional differences festering over slavery were never adequately addressed.

As the French political observer Alexis de Tocqueville argues (see chapter 3), the immense popularity of the Democratic-Republican Party permitted the rule of their presidents as party leaders. The party broke apart, however, making it ineffective as a governing body, when its major southern wing demanded total autonomy for its "domestic" institutions. To the southerners, the union of states created by the Constitution was little different in character from that created by the Articles of Confederation. Therefore, secession was constitutional. Popular opinion in the South, manifest and therefore exaggerated by its influence on the nation's major political party, welcomed the collapse of national power. As a consequence of these developments, the president was subordinated to the legislative and judicial branches and, finally, to the decisions of the state governments in deciding the Union's future. James Bryce argues that after the presidency of Andrew Jackson (see chapter 3), the office became moribund, its weakness marked by the ineffectual rule of eight presidents in twenty-four years.

Unwilling to shape opinion or policy or to defend "the constitutional rights of their place," in Madison's famous phrase, the last two Democratic presidents were eager to see others assume the initiative in solving the sectional crisis.[33] First, Senator Stephen A. Douglas, the "Little Giant from Illinois," offered the Kansas-Nebraska Bill as a solution. Subsequently, the

Democratic-appointed Supreme Court attempted another solution in its Dred Scott decision. The failure of these congressional and Court initiatives illustrates the depth of the wound, inflicted by the party and regionalism, which had emasculated the presidency. The last two Jeffersonian Democratic presidents, Franklin Pierce and James Buchanan, became passive observers of the disintegration of the Framers' "more perfect union." Only with Lincoln's radical invocation of the constitutionality of emergency prerogatives did the presidency begin to escape from the wilderness of the Jeffersonians' embrace of a congressionally based party populism, strict constitutional construction, and administrative decentralization as the only legitimate bases of democratic political power.

Conclusion

Does presidential power derive from the prerogatives of office or from the incumbent? A summary judgment would be: Hamilton embraces prerogative and Jefferson embodies politics. Hamilton and the Founders were constitutionalists. From their perspective the powers of the office were sufficient to make any capable individual, popular or unpopular, a powerful president. Alexander Hamilton believed that the very principle of a strong executive was anathema to the Anti-Federalists, and therefore presidential power had to be constitutional and prerogative or it would become subject to constantly changing, and generally hostile, public opinion. For the Federalists, presidential power was firmly established in foreign affairs. In domestic affairs, the president's power was also extensive, relying on the veto especially. The Hamiltonians cultivated public opinion in order to guarantee support for the new Constitution and prestige for the president. President George Washington made public speeches to increase respect both for the office of the president and the new government, never for any narrow, political or partisan advantage.

Does presidential leadership depend upon historical context, or is regime-building manifested through political, institutional, and constitutional developments? For Jefferson, the fact that the realigning election of 1800 ended Federalist viability and inaugurated an era of one-party rule made possible the partisan governing style of President Jefferson. Although Hamiltonianism was facilitated by Federalist dominance of all three branches, hardly could the treasury secretary openly extol the political virtues of partisanship in light of how the Framers feared faction.

Does presidential leadership vary between domestic and foreign affairs?

Diplomacy during the period of belligerency between revolutionary France and Great Britain demonstrated that President Washington, and not Congress, made foreign policy. Yet domestically, Washington and Hamilton also sought control over the national finances. The *Federalist* argued that the national government had been explicitly empowered in this area.

Does the president actively or passively engage the legislative process and promote a policy agenda? The Federalist confidence in prerogative power extended to legislative leadership, as President Washington desired to strengthen the Constitution's executive by careful precedent building. For example, Washington decided to give the State of the Union message to Congress in person, dramatically associating his person and office with his formal legislative proposals. As secretary of the treasury and chief adviser to President Washington, Hamilton took the lead in creating the essential policies and institutions for a strong economy, and he used his considerable personal influence to bring this about. Hamilton's use of presidential influence to secure passage of major economic legislation demonstrated executive power, but power limited to clear constitutional ends. However, the Jeffersonians considered this use of presidential prerogative a violation of their desired legislative sovereignty. Thomas Jefferson later suspended Hamilton's practice, choosing to send a written statement, to avoid any hint of the Washington administration's "regal" precedent.

Does the organization of the executive branch service presidential leadership? There was no administrative presidency, since the organization of the executive branch was rudimentary by modern standards. Washington established the first cabinet, comprised of the secretaries of war, state, and treasury, plus the attorney general, all of whom were friends and eminent politicians personally chosen by him. These formal advisers, truly a cabinet government by all accounts, were never displaced by informal confidants (like the "kitchen cabinet" employed by Andrew Jackson). Administrative control was direct and immediate under Washington.

Does presidential influence depend upon the force of personality, rhetorical leadership, or partisanship? The Federalists opposed political parties as factions and viewed rhetorical leadership as demagoguery. Although the president should cultivate public opinion to maintain the prestige of his office, he should govern by energetically employing his strong constitutional powers, with the understanding of the legendary Chicago mayor, Richard J. Daley, that "good government is good politics." Moreover, the relatively nonpartisan first years of the Washington administration are widely considered as an extension of the Constitutional Convention. Both

President Washington and the first Congress consciously set precedents and passed legislation, such as "The Bill of Rights," designed to complete and implement the Constitution. In fact, a majority of Congress had been delegates to the Constitutional Convention. The nearly unanimous Federalist Congress voted the measures necessary to complete and vivify the Constitution. But since they preferred prerogative power, although enjoying overwhelming majorities in Congress, the Federalists never encountered or considered the importance that popular opinion and political parties would soon play in American politics under the new Constitution. They failed to foresee the place of democratic politics as an independent variable capable of limiting or enhancing presidential power. Thus, Hamiltonianism did not long survive, because the nineteenth century proved to be a difficult period for the presidency. The Jeffersonian embrace of populism and congressional supremacy that would dominate the century encouraged few strong presidents and produced little effective policy. This is the lesson of chapter 3.

CHAPTER THREE

Jeffersonianism Sustained
Nineteenth-Century Thinkers

In the nineteenth century, Thomas Jefferson, not Alexander Hamilton, exercised the greatest influence over the theory and practice of the presidency. Rejecting the Federalists' desire to secure American independence by making the nation an economic and military power, the Jeffersonians were content to let the oceans serve in place of a formidable military establishment. Agrarian pursuits were preferred to industry and trade, and political liberty and regional control to national and presidential power. As a view of governing, the "Jeffersonian model" employed congressional dominance in domestic affairs, administrative decentralization, and reliance on political parties, rather than the president, to maintain the direction of national affairs.

In recent decades presidency scholars have discovered in Andrew Jackson the beginning of a genuinely democratic and populist leader able to tame the congressional power that had waxed as a result of the Jeffersonian antagonism to presidential monarchy.[1] Through his use of the veto power, control of his cabinet and administrative offices, and strengthened party organization, Jackson became the "tribune of the people" and the leader of a great democratic nation. His personal power and the patriotism he encouraged enabled President Jackson to successfully challenge the first Southern movement toward secession in the Nullification Controversy of 1832–33.

Nevertheless, there was almost universal agreement among Jackson's contemporaries that he built his personal presidency on such questionable principles that he further eroded his high office and the national government. Alexis de Tocqueville, who toured the United States during Jackson's first term, was one of many critics of Jackson's personality and policies:

> Far from wanting to extend federal power, the current president [Jackson] represents, on the contrary, the party that wants to restrict the power to the clearest and most precise terms of the Constitution, and does not ever accept any interpretation favorable to the government of the Union; far

from presenting himself as the champion of centralization, General Jackson is the agent of provincial jealousies . . . The power of General Jackson constantly increases, therefore; but that of the president diminishes. In his hands, the federal government is strong; it will pass to his successor enfeebled.

Either I am strangely mistaken or the federal government of the United States [under President Jackson] tends to weaken daily; it successively withdraws from affairs, it contracts the sphere of its actions more and more. Naturally weak, it even abandons appearances of force. On the other hand, I believe I saw in the United States that the sentiment of independence became more and more lively in the states, the love of provincial government more and more pronounced.[2]

Tocqueville enumerates many more examples of national decline under Jackson (and the Jeffersonians generally) and concludes: "Far from the federal government's gaining force with age and threatening the sovereignty of the states, I say that it tends to weaken each day and that the sovereignty of the Union is in peril."[3]

President Abraham Lincoln's powerful use of emergency prerogatives was the exception that proved the old Jeffersonian rule. For Lincoln's prerogative approach was not considered exemplary of good peacetime practice and was not followed by his successors. But change was in the air. The stupendous American industrialization after the Civil War, coupled with the growth of strong modern bureaucratic European nations, initiated a torrential reappraisal by century's end of the "national weakness" that was now seen as the true Jeffersonian legacy.

This chapter begins with Joseph Story's *Commentaries on the Constitution* (1833), which reacted to the Jeffersonian and Jacksonian populist view of the presidency with a reassertion of Hamilton's defense of strong presidential prerogative. Then we analyze Alexis de Tocqueville's view of presidential decline in the Jeffersonian era in *Democracy in America* (1835, 1842). After these two "Federalists," we turn to two theorists of Jeffersonian democracy, Frederick Grimke and George Ticknor Curtis. Grimke, a southern Democrat, argues for the necessity of a weak executive in *The Nature and Tendency of Free Institutions* (1848). Turning to the postbellum period, we will see that George Ticknor Curtis, James Buchanan's biographer, also defends presidential weakness, in his *Constitutional History of the United States* (1889). In his monumental classic *The American Commonwealth* (1888), Lord Bryce describes the postwar development of presidential power in positive terms, although he still finds a weak presidential office. Finally, in *The Abolition of the Presidency* (1884), Henry C. Lockwood offers one of the first radical critiques of the constitutional system. He argues that executive power has always tyrannically dominated the popular will of the House of Representatives. Lockwood seeks an American version of English cabinet government to replace the elective American "monarchy."

Joseph Story

Joseph Story, a member of Jefferson's Democratic-Republican Party in New York, was appointed to the Supreme Court by President James Madison in 1811. If Madison expected Justice Story to support his party's goal of limiting national power by restraining the influence of the great Federalist chief justice, John Marshall, he was soon disappointed; Story became a major luminary of the Marshall Court. Like Marshall, Story thought the Jeffersonians' doctrines injurious to the new nation and found in the federal courts a logical counterweight to right the sinking fortunes of the Framers' more perfect Union.

Both Marshall and Story considered Alexander Hamilton the greatest intellect among the Founders and the Hamilton-inspired *Federalist* the authoritative guide to the Constitution. Although Story had a half-century of constitutional development to supplement the *Federalist's* original defense of the Constitution, his *Commentaries on the Constitution* is consistent with the Framers' view of constitutional powers and purposes. Like the *Federalist's* rhetorical dialogue with the Anti-Federalist opponents of ratification, Story's *Commentaries* engages the constitutional criticism of John C. Calhoun and other radical Jeffersonians. Indeed, the *Commentaries'* great popularity helped counteract, at least among informed northerners, what Abraham Lincoln later called the constitutional "sophisms" of the Southern heralds of nullification and secession.

Like the *Federalist*, Story argues that the executive is in an important sense the first among constitutional equals. He dismisses the view, held by both Jeffersonians and Whigs, "that a vigorous executive is inconsistent with the genius of a republican government." On the contrary, an important objective of government is "to secure energy in the executive, and safety to the people." Energy in the executive is "essential to the protection of the community against foreign attacks . . . to the steady administration of the laws, to the protection of property . . . and to the security of liberty against the enterprises and assaults of ambition, of faction, and of anarchy."[4] Story cites *Federalist* 70 in support of his view that "a feeble execution is but another phrase for a bad execution; and a government ill executed, whatever may be its theory, must, in practice, be a bad government." Fortunately, the essential criteria for an energetic executive—"unity, duration, and adequate provision for its support, and competent powers"—are provided for in the Constitution.[5]

Duration in office is a key element of presidential energy. Long duration encourages energetic administration. "If [presidential plans are] perpetually falling into new hands before they are matured . . . Who will plant, when he can never reap?" Four-year terms with the possibility of reelection are sufficient to give presidents power and responsibility. Addressing presidential selection, Story voices dissatisfaction at the failure of prevailing constitutional practice to free presidents from a dependency on party for their election. "In no respect have the enlarged and liberal views of the framers of the Constitution . . . been so completely frustrated, as in the practical operation of the system, so far as relates to the independence of the electors in the electoral college. It is notorious, that the electors are now chosen wholly with reference to particular candidates, and are silently pledged to vote for them."[6] In other words, mere partisanship has replaced the electoral college's meritocratic function in selecting the best individual for the presidential office.

For Story, as for the Founders, the power of the presidency results from the prerogative powers of the Constitution. Although subject to congressional consent through its power to appropriate, ratify, and confirm presidential actions, the president has sufficient constitutional power to shape the direction of both foreign and domestic policy. The president's power of judicial appointment also contributes to the direction of judicial decisions. Because the unitary executive acts with secrecy and dispatch, "the executive department is a far better depositary of the [treaty-making] power, than Congress would be."[7] For example, in giving the president the power of nomination in the executive and judicial branches, the Founders escaped the rule of "selfish interests of individuals and cabals" found in all numerous public bodies like Congress. Citing *Federalist* 76, Story argues that "one man of discernment is better fitted to analyze and estimate the peculiar qualities, adapted to particular offices, than any body of men of equal, or even of superior discernment."[8]

Story elaborates the extent of presidential prerogative. Presidential power to "advise and inform Congress" has quickly developed into the "State of the Union Message." Because of "the nature and duties of the executive department, he [the president] must possess more extensive sources of information, as well as in regard to domestic and foreign affairs, than can belong to Congress." Therefore there is wisdom "in requiring the president to lay before Congress all facts and information, which may assist their deliberations; and in enabling him at once to point out the evil, and to suggest the remedy."[9]

Similarly, the president's ability to receive ambassadors is tantamount to the power to recognize new nations: "the exercise of this prerogative . . . is therefore . . . an executive function of great delicacy." Story remarks, "it is surprising, that the Federalist should have treated the power of receiving ambassadors and other public ministers, as an executive function of little intrinsic importance."[10] The power to appoint the heads of the state department and the military, to negotiate treaties, and to receive ambassadors makes the executive the preponderant power in foreign affairs.

Story next discusses the veto, the greatest presidential prerogative with respect to Congress. The veto power makes the executive the nation's first legislator, although he is weaker than the kings of England, who have an absolute veto power. Like Publius, Story argues that an absolute veto, even a three-quarters veto, would so remove the executive from the more popular Congress that it would weaken executive influence: "It is true, that in England an absolute negative is vested in the king, as a branch of the legislative power; and he possesses the absolute power of rejecting, rather than of resolving. And this is thought by Mr. Justice Blackstone and others, to be a most important, and indeed indispensable part of the royal prerogative, to guard against the usurpations of the legislative authority. Yet in point of fact this negative of the kings has not been once exercised since the year 1692."[11]

Story defends the veto on two grounds. First, without it the president would surely lose his other powers to Congress: "There is a natural tendency in the legislative department to intrude upon the rights, and to absorb the powers of the other departments of government . . . If the executive did not possess this qualified negative, he would gradually be stripped of all his authority, and become, what it is well known the governors of some states are, a mere pageant and shadow of magistracy."[12]

In addition to the veto's prophylactic virtues, the veto encourages good legislation by forcing Congress to deliberate with the branch that must enforce policies, once they are enacted:

> The [veto] power is important, as an additional security against the enactment of rash, immature, and improper laws. It establishes a salutary check upon the legislative body, calculated to preserve the community against the

47

effects of faction, precipitancy, unconstitutional legislation, and temporary excitements, *as well as political hostility* . . . He [the president] will have an opportunity soberly to examine the acts and resolutions passed by the legislature, not having partaken of the feelings or combinations, which have procured their passage, and thus correct, what shall sometimes be wrong from haste and inadvertence, as well as design. His view of them, if not more wise, or more elevated, will, at least, be independent, and under an entirely different responsibility to the nation, from what belongs to them. He is the representative of the whole nation in the aggregate; they are the representatives only of distinct parts; and sometimes of little more than sectional or local interests.[13]

In addition to preventing "bad laws," the veto checks "[t]he great evil of all free government . . . a tendency to over-legislation. The mischief of inconstancy and mutability in the laws forms a great blemish in the character and genius of all free governments."[14]

Although the legislative branch has more contact and control over public opinion, the president, with a four-year term and numerous prerogatives, is given the institutional means to be energetic and farsighted with or without congressional support. Like the Framers, Story believes the presidential office is well equipped to be highly effective: "I think it will be impossible to [with]hold from [Article 2] of the constitution a tribute of profound respect, if not of the liveliest admiration. All, that seems desirable, in order to gratify the hopes, secure the reverence, and sustain the dignity of the nation, is, that the office should always be occupied by a man of elevated talents, of ripe virtues, of incorruptible integrity, and of tried patriotism, one who shall forget his own interests, and remember, that he represents not a party, but the whole nation."[15]

Alexis de Tocqueville

Tocqueville is probably the greatest political philosopher ever to write about the American presidency. A sensitive political observer, Tocqueville offers anything but a theoretical or unhistorical understanding of the office. Indeed, he argues that political developments since the Founding have weakened and diminished the president's strong prerogative powers. "The president of the United States possesses almost all royal prerogatives, which he has no occasion to make use of, and the rights which, up to now, he can use are very circumscribed; *the laws permit him to be strong, circumstances keep him weak*."[16]

Tocqueville visited the United States for nine months in 1831–32. Volume 1 of *Democracy in America*, which includes his analysis of the presidency, appeared in 1835, volume 2 in 1842. Tocqueville's American sojourn coincided with the height of Jacksonian/Jeffersonian democracy, convincing him that Thomas Jefferson had fundamentally altered American politics. Under Jefferson's leadership America became a populist democracy, although Tocqueville observed that "the federal constitution, which still subsists in our time, is a lasting monument to their [the Federalists'] patriotism, and their wisdom." The Constitution has some residual effect on Jeffersonian populism.[17] But Jefferson's election to the presidency in 1800, which permanently reversed the Federalists' political fortunes, marked a true revolution in American politics: "When [Jefferson's] Republicans arrived in their turn [to power], the opposing party [the Federalists] was as if enveloped in the midst of a sudden flood. An immense majority declared itself against it, and right away finding itself so small a minority that it immediately despaired of itself. Since that moment, the Republican or Democratic Party has advanced from conquest to conquest, and taken possession of society as a whole."[18]

Jeffersonianism, by democratizing public life and increasing the influence of public opinion, inevitably weakened the executive, even in foreign affairs. The Jeffersonians' desire to found an empire of liberty oceans away from the world's tyranny and corruption, a policy eventually realized in the Monroe Doctrine, left the president the commander in chief of a continental army of only six thousand troops. American isolation became so complete that "one could almost say that no one has need of them and that they have need of no one. Their independence is never threatened."[19] Therefore, even in the conduct of foreign and military policy, where presidents should gain political prestige, America's isolation only further undermines their power. "It is principally in relations with foreigners that the executive power of a nation finds occasion to deploy its skill and force. If the life of the Union were constantly threatened, if its great interests were mixed every day with those of other powerful peoples, one would see the executive power grow larger."[20]

In domestic policy, De Tocqueville argues that the president is wholly overshadowed by the legislative branch: "In America, the president cannot prevent the forming of laws; he cannot escape the obligation to execute them. His zealous and sincere cooperation is doubtless useful, but it is not necessary to the working of the government. In everything essential that he does, he is directly or indirectly subject to the legislature . . . It is therefore his weakness, and not his force, that permits him to live in opposition to the legislative power." The power of the presidential veto is more than outweighed by the weakness of American political parties. The fact that the president can remain in office without a majority in Congress, impossible in the European monarchies that enforce the laws at their pleasure, demonstrates the weakness of the independent American executive. Comparing the president with the constitutional European monarchs, Tocqueville observes that the latter exercise "a real part of sovereignty, for the laws cannot exist if he refuses to sanction them."[21] But the American president is constitutionally compelled to enforce legislation that he opposes.

American federalism also restricts presidential power. The executive of a united nation has considerably more political patronage than the American president. Vast patronage power gives a national executive ample clout to influence votes and create legislative majorities. Moreover, federalism isolates the president from local life. Compared with congressmen, who are well known to their constituencies, the president is mainly invisible to the electorate.

According to Tocqueville, frequent elections also undermine presidential power by causing an interruption in public affairs. Every presidential plan is endangered by the timing and uncertainty of his reelection and possible removal from office: "At the approach of an election, the head of the executive power thinks only of the conflict being prepared; he no longer has a future; he can undertake nothing and pursues only feebly what another is perhaps going to complete."[22] Re-eligibility weakens presidents by making them too responsive to public opinion. With only a single term, the president would be free to use his prerogatives to implement policies boldly without compromising the public interest for future political advantage. Tocqueville also thought the manner of presidential election dangerous. He feared that the complexity of the electoral process encouraged ambitious candidates to pursue victory through partisan attacks and to take legal advantage of the laws' complexity.

As we have seen, Tocqueville accepted Thomas Jefferson's view of the revolutionary character of his election in 1800. For Tocqueville, the consequence of Jefferson's association of power with privilege, and true democracy with weak political institutions, meant that the more populist the politics and the more powerful public opinion, the weaker the president would inevitably become. Certainly, the power and prestige of the national government and the presidency declined in the nineteenth century under the Jeffersonians' party rule.

Public opinion is so powerful in democratic societies that it trumps the legal and constitutional powers of elected officials. The public clamor for weak, inactive government permits the Jeffersonian party to "sweep all before it." Therefore, whereas Story describes an energetic president deploying his extensive prerogative powers, Tocqueville sees the exact opposite: a once powerful constitutional officer now enslaved by a Lilliputian democracy. Given the new populist nature of American democracy, the powers of the executive are essentially political, highly dependent on changes of party philosophy and popular opinion. Presidents cannot rely on their constitutional powers or prerogatives to sustain them when in conflict with a popular Congress. To maintain his power, the executive must continually shape public opinion using the political and populist means at his disposal; he cannot rely on constitutional prerogatives for his support.

On the subject of presidential power, Tocqueville's historical sociology too easily dominates his prudent political philosophy. In attributing the most radical populism to democracy in general, and American representative democracy in particular, Tocqueville is guilty of the kind of fatalism he generally condemns. Given the novelty and power of Jeffersonian democracy in the new world, Tocqueville may perhaps be excused for confusing the politically powerful, but transient, with the enduring American faith in the Constitution. But concern with the politically transient reaches new heights in the thought of the Jeffersonian stalwarts Frederick Grimke and George Ticknor Curtis.

Frederick Grimke

Frederick Grimke was from a prominent South Carolina family. His father had served as an officer in the Continental Army and was a member of the South Carolina convention that ratified the federal Constitution. Two of his sisters, Sarah and Angelina Grimke, became leading abolitionists, and Angelina authored the popular abolitionist pamphlet *An Appeal to the Christian Women of the South* (1836). Frederick Grimke followed his older brother to Yale. After a legal career in Charleston, he moved to Ohio in 1819 as the protégé of the state's first governor, Thomas Worthington. Grimke was elected to the Ohio Supreme Court in 1836 but resigned in 1842 to write the first of several editions of his magnum opus, *The Nature and Tendency of Free Institutions* (1848). This work is highly influenced by the sociological method and democratic argument of Alexis de Tocqueville. Grimke pursues the Jeffersonian argument that executive authority is essentially regal in character and thus dangerous, if not tyrannical, in practice. Like Tocqueville, Grimke develops his argument historically.

Originally all government was executive and absolute. But as civil society develops, "public affairs become so unwieldy and complicated that it is physically impossible for one mind to preside over them, much less to administer them in person." The prince must communicate his authority to subordinate agents in order to relieve himself from the burden of rule. In doing so, the prince slowly diminishes his influence, loses his prerogatives, and prepares the way for more regular democratic institutions. He needs to appoint judges and administrative officers to do thoroughly what he is imperfectly able to perform. As a consequence, "a legislative body soon after makes its appearance . . . it ultimately acquires a considerable influence over the crown itself" (NT, 518–19).[23]

The legislative and judicial power "wrested" from the crown permits the development of a commonwealth where public opinion rules. The more diffuse public opinion and power become, the greater the stimulus for the development of political parties. Although parties historically have been divisive defenders of rival classes, with the creation of a politically effective middle class, truly free and responsible popular party government became possible. The middle class, as a "universal class," does not need to concentrate power against its rivals; middle-class governments should be inactive and decentralized, the opposite of either monarchical governments or regimes with ongoing class conflicts.

Because the middle-class American system always makes public opinion the basis of policy, it is the beau ideal of politics: "The American system has answered the desired purpose, and it may be termed the 'beau ideal' in politics. It has demonstrated that all the great ends for which civil government is established may be attained without the employment of those curious and artificial contrivances which render men unfit for self-government simply because they hide government from their observation. By rendering men free, by satisfying their wants, so far as it is in the power of human institutions to do, it has removed out of the way the prime cause of all public discontent" (NT, 562–63). Similarly, Alexis de Tocqueville had argued: "The people reign over the American political world as does God over the universe. They are the cause and the end of all things, everything comes out of them and everything is absorbed into them."[24] Whereas Tocqueville condemned the "tyranny of the majority" and Jeffersonian democracy, Grimke welcomes both. Writing in 1848, little more than a decade before secession and Civil War, Grimke argues that weak leaders of national parties will pacify sectional controversies, permitting the North and the South to adjust their differences peacefully, even if such adjustment requires Southern secession.

Whereas Tocqueville condemned the emasculating effect of populism and party government, particularly on the president, Grimke elaborately defends the Jeffersonian transformation of the Framers' Constitution: "Parties, whatever may be the exterior form which they wear, almost always contain the elements of great improvement. They are among the instruments which are appointed to push the race of mankind forward. The heated passions and fierce disputes through which they sometimes cause themselves to be heard are the means . . . by which any signal change in the public policy of the state or the condition of the people can be attained." Given the key role that parties play in the progress of public opinion, "it [is] very important that the president of the United States be chosen by a party" (*NT*, 523).

The majority of Grimke's analysis of "The Executive Power" is dedicated to public opinion and parties. Since a fundamental antagonism exists between democracy and executive power, only a strongly democratic, populist society like the United States can limit executive influence.

According to Grimke, the success of the American system has had a salutary effect on the presidency; the office has been reduced to virtual insignificance. In foreign and military affairs, where presidential power and prerogative was nearly universally acknowledged, the president is merely a congressional agent, in Grimke's view: "To declare war and to make treaties are the exclusive prerogatives of the king in a monarchical government. In the United States, the war-making power belongs to the legislature, and the treaty-making power is under the control of the Senate" (*NT*, 569). In domestic policy, Grimke discovers an important, democratic function for the executive. As leader of the larger of the two political parties, it is natural that he should share in the legislative process in support of his party's goals. "The president is altogether the creature of public opinion. He has no prerogatives. His authority consists in exercising the power which the majority of society conferred upon him. His ambition is to represent and to give effect to the will of that majority" (*NT*, 564).

The veto is key to the president's legislative power. Because it is subject to a legislative override, it is not a dangerous power or equal to the absolute veto of the English monarch. Moreover, because of the importance of public opinion and frequent elections, the president is unwilling to use the veto in a bad cause or to be overridden in an unpopular one. The veto allows him to represent effectively those who cast their votes for him and his party.

The one abuse of office that Grimke alleges is that of the patronage power. Patronage is an unwelcome carryover from the excesses of regal prerogative; the American abuse of this power is most clearly seen in the naming of postmasters. To reform this abuse, the Jeffersonian Grimke recommends even further administrative decentralization. National offices, such as postmasters, should be elective in the localities where they serve (*NT*, 547).

The president cannot abuse his powers because "the real and effective business of the state is transacted by the legislature and judiciary, there, accordingly, has the active authority of the state been deposited" (*NT*, 562). Grimke argues that Congress controls foreign policy through its treaty- and war-making power (*NT*, 569). The president's power to appoint is limited by strict constitutional control. Even in the area of administration, the president's power is divided: "The executive power is distributed between the president and the thirty state governors . . . This arrangement, while it causes all public business to be conducted with a greater degree of exactness and regularity, imposes numerous and powerful checks upon the exercise of power" (*NT*, 534).

The president is, in the main, the powerless, symbolic leader of a successful self-governing machine that runs by itself. The wisdom and morality of the middle-class electorate and the near perfection of the populist American political system make the president a calming peacemaker devoted to smoothing over difficulties. His real power comes not from the prerogative powers of his office but from his ability to mobilize national public opinion based on his leadership of a national political party. In his capacity as party leader, the president must be a skillful compromiser. Grimke recognizes and welcomes the fact that this pedestrian political activity attracts men of mediocre talent and goals to the presidential chair: weak presidents are the willing servants and handmaids of public opinion. The absence of a great political reputation prevents presidents from exercising any independent political leadership, especially that which could increase regional divisions:

> In the United States there has been a marked disposition of late years to elevate men of moderate talents to the presidency. And this has been regarded as a circumstance of deep omen to the future and as indicating a retrograde movement in society. But there is no reason why we should take

this view of the matter. The election of such men, where there is no question of their integrity and patriotism, may not only be very consistent with
the public welfare but it may have a distinct and very important meaning
which it is our duty to decipher . . . The man of commanding talents is not
sought after because he represents too faithfully one part of society and, by
so doing, fails to represent all other parts. On the other hand, the man of
moderate abilities, the man who has no very strong and salient points of
character, by failing to represent any one part exclusively succeeds more
fully in representing the whole. (*NT*, 570–71)

Grimke's formulation of the compromising president is in total opposition to Alexander Hamilton's energetic executive who shoulders a leading
responsibility for the well-being of society. A radical Jeffersonian, Grimke's
president is emphatically not the national leader. Instead, he is the compromiser, consoler, and healer of the Union. As such, the president takes
on the function of the least dangerous branch that the *Federalist* reserved
for the Supreme Court. For Grimke, the executive is not the solver but the
assuager of crises.

George Ticknor Curtis

Like Frederick Grimke and Thomas Jefferson, George Ticknor Curtis
(1812–1894) argues that a strong president poses more a threat than a promise to the nation. Curtis was a major writer on political affairs, authoring
biographies of Daniel Webster and James Buchanan in addition to his
major history of American politics, *A Constitutional History of the United
States from Their Declaration of Independence to the Close of the Civil War*
(1889). Curtis, a Northern Democrat, is an example of the intellectual
partisanship of the Jeffersonians throughout the nineteenth century.

Curtis argues that Northern abolitionists, and Abraham Lincoln in particular, provoked the Civil War by denying the Southern states the right to
determine their own domestic arrangements and institutions. Lincoln's
"House Divided Speech," which proclaimed that the country could not
remain "permanently half slave and half free," began a political and constitutional war on the Southern states' right to maintain their freedom.
"When it came to a popular cry in the North that the whole of the republic
was to be either slave-holding or non-slaveholding [the thesis of 'A House
Divided'], it was inevitable that rational methods should give place to a trial
of strength between the two sections, first at the polls, and secondly by the
arbitrament of civil war."[25]

To illustrate his commitment to decentralization, Curtis quotes with approbation James Buchanan's denial of any presidential emergency power over the secession crisis in his address to Congress of January 8, 1861:

> I certainly had no right to make aggressive war upon any state, and I am perfectly satisfied that the Constitution has wisely withheld that power even from Congress . . . But the dangerous and hostile attitude of the states towards each other has already far transcended and cast in the shade the ordinary executive duties already provided for by law, and has assumed such vast and alarming proportions as to place the subject entirely beyond executive control. The fact cannot be disguised that we are in the midst of a great revolution. In all its various bearings, therefore, I commend the question to Congress, as the only human tribunal, under Providence, possessing the power to meet the existing emergency. To them exclusively belongs the power to declare war, or to authorize the employment of military force in all cases contemplated by the Constitution.[26]

It would be difficult to exaggerate or overstate the difference between the views of Abraham Lincoln and James Buchanan on presidential emergency powers. A comparison of the Buchanan speech quoted above with Lincoln's Special Address to Congress of July 4, 1861, offers a study in the extremes of constitutional interpretation. Lincoln invoked the inherent prerogative power for national self-preservation.

> [Secession and the attack on Fort Sumter] embraces more than the fate of these United States . . . It presents the question, whether discontented individuals, too few in numbers to control administration, according to organic law, in any case, can always, upon the pretenses made in this case, or on any other pretenses, or arbitrarily, without pretenses made in this case . . . break up their government, and thus practically put an end to free government upon the earth . . .
>
> So viewing the issue, no choice was left [to the president] but to call out the war power of the Government; and so to resist force, employed for its destruction, by force, for its preservation.[27]

But Frederick Grimke and George Ticknor Curtis were probably closer to the mainstream of presidential thought of this period than was Abraham Lincoln. Defending his political position, Lincoln consistently agreed with the major concern of these authors for the right of slaveholding states to maintain their domestic institutions. Lincoln said the federal government had no power to regulate slavery where it already existed. (He also argued that the government did have the right to put slavery on the road to ultimate extinction by prohibiting the introduction of slavery into federal territories.) In any case, Abraham Lincoln's rhetorical endorsement of Thomas Jefferson as a statesman and a democratic theorist was a wise concession to the prevailing opinion about the sanctity of liberty and local rights. Lincoln agreed that Jefferson was "one of greatest teachers of freedom and free labor."[28] Lincoln's presidential acts, in contrast, were directed to the renewal of the Union and the Constitution from their near-total neglect by the Jeffersonians. Although Lincoln was revered as a great president, his peace-time successors were unaffected by his wartime precedents.

James Bryce

The Englishman James Bryce is best known to political science for his two-volume compendium on American politics, *The American Commonwealth* (1888). Like Tocqueville, Bryce was a serious student of American political history, but, unlike the Frenchman, he was seemingly indifferent to the major theoretical disagreements between the heirs of the Federalists and the Jeffersonians, which continued to shape American political thought and practice. The remarkable changes in American society, however, did not escape him. Bryce argues that these changes, especially territorial expansion and economic development, necessitate a larger and more active national government than what Americans were accustomed to. Greater activity could already be seen in Congress: "In the Thirty-seventh Congress (1861–63) the total number of bills introduced was 1,026 . . . In the Fifty-first Congress (1889–91) the number had risen to 19,646" (AC, 138).[29] Moreover, since the Civil War the reputation of Congress has declined while the president's has advanced. People now approve of the executive's use of his veto power:

> So far from exciting the displeasure of the people by resisting the will of their representatives, a President generally gains popularity by the bold use of his veto power. It conveys the impression of firmness; as it shows that he has a view and does not fear to give effect to it. The nation, which has often good grounds for distrusting Congress, a body liable to be moved by sinister private influences, or to defer to the clamor of a noisy section outside, looks to the man of its choice to keep Congress in order, and has approved the extension which practice has given to the [veto] power. (AC, 59)

Bryce explains the "expansion" of the veto power in this way: "The President's 'qualified negative' was proposed by the Convention of 1787 for the sake of protecting the Constitution, and in particular, the executive, from Congressional encroachments. It has now come to be used on grounds of general expediency, to defeat any measure which the Executive deems pernicious either in principle or in probable results" (AC, 59). The rise of the veto power is the surest basis of presidential influence over legislation. "The real strength of the executive therefore, the rampart from behind which it can resist the aggressions of the legislature, is in ordinary times the veto power. In other words, it survives as an executive in virtue not of any properly executive function, but of the share in legislative functions [the veto] which it has received; it holds its ground by force" (AC, 226).

James Bryce argues that leadership in foreign and military affairs also contributes to the president's strength. Even these prerogatives are subject to congressional checks: "He [the president] cannot declare war, for that belongs to Congress . . . Treaties require the approval of two-thirds of the Senate . . . The House of Representatives has no legal right to interfere, but it often passes resolutions enjoining or disapproving a particular line of policy." Moreover, "as some treaties, especially commercial treaties, cannot be carried out except by the aid of statutes, and as no war can be carried on without the votes of monies, the House of Representatives can sometimes indirectly make good its claim" (AC, 54).[30]

The president is even weaker in the conduct of domestic than of foreign affairs. "The direct domestic authority of the President is in times of peace small, because the larger part of law and administration belongs to the State governments, and because Federal administration is regulated by statutes which leave little discretion to the executive" (AC, 54). All of this changes in war, when the president acquires emergency powers. "Both as commander-in-chief of the army and navy, and as charged with 'the faithful execution of the laws,' the president is likely 'to assume all the powers which the emergency requires'" (AC, 55).

For Bryce, the surest source of the president's power, in addition to his command of the veto, is his ability to maintain the support of his party through his "elevated stature as a great man" and his skills as a politician and a president. Without party support, presidents have little direct influence over public opinion: "The President has the right of speaking to the nation by addresses or proclamations, a right not expressly conferred by the Constitution, but inherent in his position"; however, the "occasions requiring its exercise are uncommon." Presidents give the inaugural address and the annual "state of the union" (in writing), but after these they may usually speak only on ceremonial and nonpartisan occasions. Partisan speeches, unless to the president's own party, are considered highly inappropriate. "It is thought bad taste for the President to go round on a political stumping tour, and Andrew Johnson injured himself by the practice" (AC, 56). Since the two major political parties are so equally balanced, public opinion is more reliably addressed through the party apparatus than through direct presidential addresses.

Lord Bryce is known for his ranking of presidents in a chapter famously titled "Why Great Men Are Not Chosen President." Bryce's presidential rankings reveal as much about the stature and conduct of the office over time as they do about the criteria of greatness that Bryce uses for his selection. Of the twenty presidents elected to office from 1789 to 1900, the first six—those before Andrew Jackson—were "statesmen in the European sense of the word, men of education, of administrative experience, of a certain largeness of view and dignity of character" (AC, 83).

Following this line of notables from George Washington to John Quincy Adams, presidents in the second period were comparative nonentities: "In the second period . . . the Presidents were either mere politicians, such as Van Buren, Polk, or Buchanan, or else successful soldiers, such as Harrison or Taylor, whom their party found useful as figureheads. They were intellectual pygmies beside the real leaders of that generation—Clay, Calhoun, and Webster" (AC, 83). Bryce believed Jackson's presidential strength resulted from his ultrademocratic program and the vehemence of his character (AC, 66, 269). The presidents of the third period, from Lincoln through McKinley, were more distinguished than their "pygmy" predecessors: "Even the less distinguished Presidents of this period contrast favorably with the Polks and Pierces of the days before the war, if they are not, like the early Presidents, the first men of the country" (AC, 83).

Bryce concludes by comparing American presidents with eminent English prime ministers: "If we compare the twenty Presidents who were elected to office between 1789 and 1900 with the twenty English prime ministers of the same period, there are but six of the latter, and at least eight of the former whom history calls personally insignificant, while only Washington, Jefferson, Lincoln, and Grant can claim to belong to a front rank represented in the English list by seven or possibly eight names" (AC, 83–84). The discrepancy in the number of great executives in the two systems results from their political differences: "It would seem that the . . . English parliamentary system . . . had more tendency to bring the highest gifts to the highest place than the more artificial selection of America" (AC, 83). Bryce's comparison of the two executives parallels his argument for the superiority of parliamentary over congressional democracy. Although friendly to American democracy, he contributes to the view he shares with Woodrow Wilson and many others, that the reformed British constitution of the late nineteenth century should serve as a model for the reform of America's rigid (because written) and thus outdated Constitution.

America does not produce great presidents because great men are *not* needed in the American system. Executives may occasionally become powerful in war, but "four-fifths of [the president's] work is the same in kind as that which devolves on the chairman of a commercial company . . . choosing good subordinates, seeing that they attend to their business, and taking a sound practical view of such administrative questions as require his decision" (AC, 80). The system discourages statesmanship and thus does not select statesmen as presidents.

Bryce is also critical of the effect of American electoral procedures on presidential quality. The party's demands for political balance, ethical spotlessness, and absolute loyalty always make the safe candidate preferable to the best candidate. Nevertheless, the process selects competent and honest, if not great, presidents. Moreover, the skillfulness of the constitutional design has stood the test of time. Since the administration of Abraham Lincoln, the presidential standard has been a consistently high one.

In Bryce's view the president's power is not only prerogative: "a particularly able or energetic president may exert" considerable additional personal influence (AC, 66). "His power to affect legislation largely depends on his personal capacity for leadership" (AC, 65). To supplement his weak prerogative powers, an able executive can become truly effective by mobilizing popular and party opinion. Finally, it can be seen that although presidents were more active and the presidency attracted better men after the Civil War, the president's office Bryce describes is still limited by the continuing Jeffersonian belief in congressional supremacy.

But the Jeffersonian legacy, still central to Lord Bryce's description of the presidency, was undergoing more radical attacks as the nineteenth century drew to a troubled close. The end of that century witnessed a newly powerful commerce and industry. National magazines and newspapers in the developing urban centers, especially New York, Chicago, and San Francisco, inspired reform movements; considerable reform legislation was eventually proposed and passed. But reformers argued that these successes were too few and hard won and only exposed the deeper defects and misrule under the present system. The constitutional breakdown that preceded the Civil War, the abject failure of postwar Reconstruction, and the graft, corruption, and economic crisis of the Gilded Age all suggested that the true legacy of the American Constitution was systemic political failure. In contrast, European nations, notably Germany and England, were seen to be successfully reforming along lines suggested by the new social sciences. As a result, by century's end a new Progressive Liberalism was born. It took root in a confident belief in the social perfection made possible through the development of the new social sciences. To bring those sciences into the mainstream of American life, the Progressives argued for a new modernist agenda for the nation.

Before the new Progressive president became the major focus of reformers, moderates like Lord Bryce and the early Woodrow Wilson argued for institutional modifications replicating the English model of parliamentary government. As shown in the next chapter, Wilson wished to strengthen the president by making him a party leader and, with his cabinet as members and leaders in Congress, to guarantee his direction of national affairs. In contrast to Wilson, who was truly a Progressive, Henry C. Lockwood was both the last Jeffersonian and the first Progressive in his desire to strengthen and modernize Congress as the proper vehicle of reform, eliminating the president altogether.

Henry Clay Lockwood

In the last quarter of the century, moderate reformers found in the English parliamentary system the popular control and the modern welfare and regulatory policies missing in America. One of the most original and lucid of these early reformers was Henry Clay Lockwood, a New York lawyer and author of eclectic works of history . He is best known (even Edward Corwin mentions him) for his distinctive argument in *The Abolition of the Presidency* (1884).

Like the Progressives, Lockwood believes that the Founders—especially Hamilton—were covertly antidemocratic monarchists. While professing themselves true democrats, they invented a supermajoritarian Constitution (requiring three-fourths of the states for ratification of amendments) to perpetuate the most anachronistic characteristics of the British monarchical system. According to Lockwood, British politics in 1787 were already more republican than the backward-looking American Founders understood or desired. Moreover, in the century following 1787, the flexible "living English constitution" became even more thoroughly democratic, while the rigid American Constitution, presided over by its monarchical president, became more anachronistic and out of touch with democratic developments. "That which stands out more prominently than anything in American history is the great similarity of our fundamental law with the ancient and obsolete theories of the Constitution of Great Britain."[31]

The Senate and the president were created by the Framers, and preserved in immutable constitutional law, to overawe the popularly elected House of Representatives. Of these two retrograde institutions, the president, through his prerogative power, most thoroughly dominates the government and fulfills the Framers' conservative expectations. Lockwood argues that the president's veto power, command of the armed forces, patronage power, and long fixed term of office—protected by the near impossibility of impeachment—have in combination created a monarchy within a putative republic. Moreover, the president's selection by the party caucus and the electoral college eliminates any real popular influence on him.

Lockwood offers a selective analysis of the presidents since the Founding to demonstrate the tyrannical rule resulting from prerogative power. Of the presidential tyrants, Andrew Jackson is placed in the most lurid and uncompromising light: "[Jackson] went blindly on until he approached the verge of absolutism. And he did all this while he was the Executive of the Government of the United States. His stubborn and perverse nature was the cause of the pronounced and rapid development of all the defects of the Presidential system. An usurper, he claimed that he was acting within constitutional limitations; a creature of the [electoral] colleges, he asserted that he was the true representative of the people."[32] While the American president was perfecting the arts of constitutional absolutism, Britain successfully reformed, moving from a monarchical to a parliamentary government.

With a single exception, Lockwood does not share the economic concerns of the Progressives. Although he condemns President Garfield's sympathy "with the great monopolies and corporations of the vast, growing commonwealth,"[33] Lockwood generally associates presidential self-interest with personal vanity and honor. The Founders had increased presidential power to maintain their own aristocratic social order, not to participate in capitalism's new wealth.

Although not an economic reductionist like the Progressives, Lockwood shared the Progressives' utopian expectations for a radically new democratic society: "Never before in the history of the world have the masses possessed such a favorable environment for the development of the highest and purest forms of citizenship, as it exists at the present day. Those who advocate the rights and powers of the people are no longer required to prove that the rule of the 'many' is a better form of government than that of the 'one' or the 'few.'"[34] The perfection of modern education fosters optimism about the future of society:

> It [popular education] is the foundation-stone upon which this whole superstructure of republican government rests. It is only through the diffusion of education that the people will be able to form correct opinions upon the financial, governmental, economical, and even ethical questions, that must necessarily be submitted to them for their decision. All grades of the people must associate in the common schools, in order to acquire common ideas and aspirations, and get rid of the heart-burnings of caste . . . [Then] all issues will be understood and controlled by the people, who will require the temporary power-holder to respect their rights and opinions in matters of legislation, and finally to render account of his stewardship before his electors.[35]

Lockwood's recommendations for reform are in the same utopian spirit. He proposes a purified parliamentary government in which the problem of party and faction will vanish. The presidency, the Senate (along with the state governments), and the current court system will all be abolished and replaced by a unicameral legislature and the executive council it elects: "This [reform establishes] the principle of responsible Council government . . . In its essential properties, it would be the same as the English Cabinet system."[36] Like Roger Sherman's proposal at the Constitutional Convention, in Lockwood's system "Congress shall appoint . . . [an executive council], who shall execute, under the direction and control of Congress, all the laws of the United States."[37]

Members of the executive council would head the six departments of state, treasury, war, navy, interior, and the combined postmaster general–attorney, and they would serve at the pleasure of Congress. If Congress rejected its decision, the council would have the right to dissolve Congress and call for new elections. Moreover, the members of the executive council would be members of Congress and would be expected to defend their policies in that chamber. The council would prove more permanent than the British cabinet. A new election would result in a new Congress and a new council. During the term of Congress, the council would remain in place unless individually removed by Congress. Even then "it may be observed, that the proposed plan places it in the power of the remaining members of the council to refuse to submit to the removal of any one of its number, and appeal to the people [by forcing the election of a new Congress]. This course would seem both wise and salutary."[38] Lockwood thus proposes a model of the British cabinet system, perfected by direct representation and the elimination of political parties. Given Lockwood's educated electorate and the "professional and skilled service" in the six departments, he expects that his executive council would become the servant of the science of administration, escaping the current government's "partisan warfare."[39]

As we will see, the young Woodrow Wilson also made the (reformed) British system the model of his reforms. But Wilson more clearly belongs to the Progressive era than Lockwood in his understanding that the new problems confronting American government result from the crisis of industrial capitalism. Even in his early *Congressional Government* (1885), Wilson argued against Lockwood. Whereas Lockwood understood the existing Constitution to be too strong to guarantee popular rule, Wilson understood it to be too weak, or "Whiggish," to do so. Also against Lockwood, Wilson thought that Congress had proved to be too strong, preventing the president from becoming the effective administrator of a modern, scientific society. Of course, Wilson later became intrigued by the decisive role political parties might play in strengthening the power of the executive over the legislative branch.

Conclusion

The presidential practice of the nineteenth century should be seen in light of the Jeffersonians' argument for a limited president whose powers originated in a popular political party. Alexis de Tocqueville turned out to be a prophetic critic of the populist Jefferson's abnegation of the Framers' strong government—which Tocqueville incorrectly feared, reflected the inevitable weakness of all political democracies. The decentralized, legislative-centered model that the Jeffersonians imposed on the constitutional system slowly eroded presidential power until the last two antebellum Democratic presidents became passive observers of secession and civil war. Only in foreign affairs did the Democratic presidents maintain a modicum of constitutional prerogative. In retrospect, their few successes in foreign affairs contrast all the more starkly with the fatal drift in slavery policy that finally turned their weakness in this decisive domestic policy area into rivers of native blood spilling onto native soil.

James Bryce took up the Tocquevillean theme near the end of the century. He attributed the mediocrity of the antebellum presidents to the popular, antimonarchical liberalism of the Jeffersonians that the Whigs were forced to emulate as the minority party. But the press of new national business was already making the post–Civil War presidents into larger men and stronger presidents. Presidential leadership, including the veto power, was now politically popular, and Congress increasingly was thought to be parochial, out of touch, and corrupt. Most reformers believed the Founders' conservative oligarchs *and* their Constitution too weak to become the vehicle of serious political and social reform. Since the Constitution was weak (too subject to Jeffersonian populism and decentralization of power) and oligarchic (the Founders created a rigid Constitution to protect existing elite interests), the reformers agreed that reform must achieve a radical transformation of the constitutional politics of both Thomas Jefferson and Alexander Hamilton.

Does presidential power derive from the prerogatives of office or from the incumbent? The Jeffersonians rejected presidential prerogative for reasons of principle and politics, arguing that the presidency as developed by the Hamiltonians was based on monarchical prerogatives offensive to true democrats.

Does presidential influence depend upon the force of personality, rhetorical leadership, or partisanship? Instead of prerogative power, therefore, the president should use the political power deriving from his party leadership to strengthen the existing democracies in states and local communities. For Jeffersonians, presidential influence depended almost exclusively on partisanship, not personality or rhetorical leadership.

Does presidential leadership depend upon historical context, or is regime-building manifested through political, institutional, and constitutional developments? The Jeffersonians have almost nothing to say about political culture or historical context, other than that advanced democracies are based on enlightened social mores. The development of party government, had it been realized after Jefferson, would have represented a form of regime-building that deviated from Original Intent. However, the fact that the Jeffersonians repudiated certain practices initiated by Washington and Hamilton retarded the legitimation of executive energy. Thus, whereas Hamiltonianism stood for a strong but limited government, the weak and limited government of the Jeffersonians, so influenced by the ideal of agrarian freeholders, could not and did not serve the nation during the original onslaught of industrialization. In their view, advanced middle-class societies, as Grimke argued, do not require the "monarchical" authority of strong presidential leadership.

Does presidential leadership vary between domestic and foreign affairs? Although the president has limited powers in foreign affairs, the important domestic issues and the control of the political parties, which truly represent the people, should be left to Congress. The Jeffersonians preferred a weak president who ruled, insofar as he ruled at all, through his leadership of the party that nominated and, given its influence in the electoral college, usually elected him as well.

Does the president actively or passively engage the legislative process and promote a policy agenda? The president should not promote a policy agenda for the sovereign and popularly elected Congress. Andrew Jackson punished President John Quincy Adams for trying to do so. The president engages the legislative process only through his party leadership.

Does the organization of the executive branch service presidential leadership? Being opposed to presidential power, the Jeffersonians were mainly indifferent to organizing or mobilizing the president's executive staff. If anything, they tried to downsize the national government, especially the military establishment. The same rationale found the radical Jeffersonians urging that administrative power be decentralized; an example was the view of Southern Jeffersonian Frederick Grimke that federal postmasters should be locally elected.

Chapter 4 addresses the Progressives, who were radically different both intellectually and politically from the Hamiltonians and the Jeffersonians. Although many intellectual histories have described these great differences, their impact is largely unappreciated by scholars in related fields. Only recently have presidency scholars begun to dig into the Progressive Era for clues to the origins of the modern presidency. In terms of our historical analysis, the Progressives offer the third great paradigm for understanding the presidency, one still animating most contemporary analysis of the means and ends of presidential power.

Indictment of Constitutionalism
The Progressive Reconstruction

The Civil War marked a turning point in the growth of the American republic. The impassioned rhetoric and wartime sacrifices for the Union and the Constitution were consummated in the powerful Civil War Amendments, which ended slavery throughout the nation (the Thirteenth) and made the rights and liberties of republican government nationally protected (the Fourteenth and Fifteenth). Abraham Lincoln, who carried the embattled Union through the crisis, demonstrated after the failures of the two previous Jeffersonian Democrats, Franklin Pierce and James Buchanan, the flexibility and power of the presidency in the darkest hour of national peril. But with the end of the war, Lincoln's consistent use of wartime emergency prerogative power obscured any significance his precedents might have had for the presidency in times of peace. Moreover, the failure of radical Reconstruction, the South's new internal secession, and the Supreme Court's emasculation of the Civil War Amendments all suggested that the war-forged dedication to the national government, presidential power, and racial justice did not long survive the Union's hour of struggle and sacrifice.

Of greater significance than the Civil War in creating an appreciation of the presidency was the new American age of coal and steel that the war ushered in. If antebellum America was graced by Thomas Jefferson's agrarian ideal and Stephen Foster's mythic southern gentility, by the 1870s a new spirit of commerce, industrialization, and science—the ingredients for the conquest of nature and man—had produced a new social paradigm: social Darwinism. The extreme changes brought by this new industrial age apparently made the antebellum agrarian Constitution obsolete. The young Woodrow Wilson offered an early version of what came to be the Progressive mantra. "We are the first Americans," Wilson averred, "to hear our own countrymen ask whether the Constitution is still adapted to serve the purposes for which it was intended; the first to entertain any serious doubts about the superiority of our institutions as compared with the systems of Europe" (*CGAP*, 27).[1] Following Wilson, the Progressives would come to argue that new social conditions produced by new economic realities had rendered the Framers' horse-and-buggy Constitution wholly obsolete. To quote Wilson again: "The evident explanation of this change of attitude towards the Constitution is that we have been made conscious by the rude shock of the war and the subsequent developments of policy, that there has been a vast alteration in the conditions of government, that the checks and balances which once obtained are no longer effective; and that we are really living under a constitution essentially different" (CGAP, 28). Later, Wilson is even more explicit:

> Unquestionably, the pressing problems of the present moment regard the regulation of our vast systems of commerce and manufacture, the control of giant corporations . . . and many other like national concerns, amongst which may possibly be numbered the question of marriage and divorce; and the greatest of these problems do not fall within even the enlarged sphere of the federal government; some of them can be embraced within its jurisdiction by no possible stretch of construction; and the majority of them only by wrestling the Constitution to strange and as yet unimagined uses. Still there is a distinct movement in favor of national control of all questions of policy which manifestly demand uniformity of treatment and power of administration such as cannot be realized by the separate, unconcerted action of the States; and it seems probable to many that, whether by constitutional amendment, or by still further flights of construction, yet broader territory will at no very distant day be assigned to the federal government. (CGAP, 54–55)

By including marriage and divorce, Wilson may be signaling that the evolution of society will soon bring everything under national control.

All Progressives believed the Constitution was hopelessly inadequate for the new industrial and urban world, which, they argued, was the harsh reality that now followed America's loss of agrarian innocence. They differed, however, in their diagnosis of the causes of the constitutional crisis and the solution to it. Their one shared conviction was that the weak, Jeffersonian presidency required radical improvement to make the national government competent to meet the exigencies of the new social wars of Darwinian America.

To the Progressives the new industrialization was only the clearest manifestation of the radical advances in science. In addition to the great wealth promised by new industrial technologies, improvements in medicine promised equally great advances in public health. Of paramount importance were the new social sciences, which promised a new rational beginning for all modern societies. Together, these new sciences revealed the historical, evolutionary origin of societies as well as of species. Whereas the Founders spoke of universal philosophical principles of good government, the Progressives speak of organic growth in societies. Woodrow Wilson warns against those beguiled by traditional theory into believing in chimeras like natural rights and separation of powers: "The trouble with *theory* is that government is not a machine, but a living thing. It falls, not under the *theory* of the universe, but under the theory of organic life. It is accountable to Darwin, not to Newton. It is modified by its environment, necessitated by its tasks, shaped to its functions by the sheer pressure of life. No living thing can have its organs offset against each other as checks, [as in checks and balances], and live."[2] In sum, "[l]iving political constitutions must be Darwinian in structure and in practice."[3]

Accepting this evolutionary view of the organic growth of all things, the Progressives wrote political science as a form of social history. For example, Wilson believes that "the government of the United States has had a vital and normal organic growth and has proved itself eminently adapted to express the changing temper and purposes of the American people from age to age."[4] As followers of Georg Hegel and Charles Darwin, the Progressives thought that since the modern Constitution and the presidency were the result of the historical development of American society, all constitutional "principles" were subject to change.[5]

Different Progressives took different positions regarding how extensively science could perfect society. The radical Herbert Croly believed the president should become merely an administrator of national, uniform social scientific public policy, whereas moderates like Woodrow Wilson and Henry Jones Ford accepted that the president would remain a political leader, reconciling opposing views of the public good.

In this chapter we discuss the major Progressive writers on the presidency: Woodrow Wilson, Henry Jones Ford, Theodore Roosevelt, J. Allen Smith, Charles Beard, and Herbert Croly. Woodrow Wilson and Theodore Roosevelt were both Progressive presidents and theorists of the Progressive presidency. Henry Jones Ford, a prominent political scientist, was a close adviser to Woodrow Wilson during most of Wilson's political life, and his theory of the presidency resembles Wilson's. Teddy Roosevelt offers a dynamic model of the heroic president who calls forth the nation to Progressive greatness. J. Allen Smith, Charles Beard, and Herbert Croly were famous public intellectuals. Herbert Croly was an adviser to Presidents Roosevelt and Wilson and founding editor of the *New Republic*. Croly was a supporter of the heroic president and the new nationalism, but he had a more radical view than either Roosevelt or Wilson of the need for widespread reform. Although the Progressive-Liberal political era ended with President Harding's election in 1920, the intellectual influence of Progressive modernity extended at least through the administration of Lyndon B. Johnson.

Woodrow Wilson

Woodrow Wilson, a Virginian, taught political science at Bryn Mawr, Wesleyan, and Princeton, before becoming president of Princeton in 1902. He was elected governor of New Jersey in 1910 and president of the United States in 1912. Wilson's major writings, *Congressional Government: A Study in American Politics* (1885) and *Constitutional Government in the United States* (1908), offer similar views of the Framers' intention and the subsequent failure of their Constitution. But his view of the presidency changes profoundly.

In *Congressional Government*, Wilson argues that the Constitution was conceived along Newtonian lines as a finely balanced machine to protect the interests and liberties of the elites. "The government of the United States was constructed upon the Whig theory of political dynamics, which was sort of an unconscious copy of the Newtonian theory of the universe." Following Whig theory, the Founders sought to "make Parliament (the Congress) so influential in the making of laws . . . the king (the President) could in no matter have his own way."[6] Thus the Constitution leans in the direction of congressional government in which the committees, and their chairmen, become the arbiters of policy. In the course of the nineteenth century, the committee chairs succeeded in subordinating the president to their influence. Their new power transformed the original constitutional design: "The noble charter of fundamental law given us by the Convention of 1787 is still our Constitution; but it is now our *form of government* rather in name than in reality, the form of the Constitution being one of nicely adjusted, ideal balances, whilst the actual form of our present government is simply a scheme of congressional supremacy" (*CGAP*, 28).

Those unaware of the Constitution's historical evolution are blinded by their faith in eternal truths. These traditionalists have usually been influenced by Alexander Hamilton and James Madison's *Federalist*: "Their thoughts are dominated, it would seem, by those incomparable papers of the 'Federalist,' which, though they were written to influence only the voters of 1788, still, with a strange, persistent longevity of power, shape the constitutional criticism of the present day, obscuring much of that development of constitutional practice which has taken place. The Constitution in operation is manifestly a very different thing from the Constitution of the books" (*CGAP*, 30).

But Wilson's analysis of the presidency differs radically between 1885 and 1908. In *Congressional Government* he argues that the early presidents' personal decisiveness allowed them to amass political power: "Washington and his Cabinet commanded the ear of Congress, and gave shape to its deliberations; Adams, though often crossed and thwarted, gave character to the government; and Jefferson, as President no less than as Secretary of State, was the real leader of his party. But the prestige of the presidential office has declined as the perfection of selfish party tactics has advanced" (*CGAP*, 47). Congress became strong enough to take even the administration of government into its orbit: "It [Congress] has entered more and more into the details of administration, until it has virtually taken into its own hands all the substantial powers of government" (*CGAP*, 48). "Because the power of Congress had become predominant," after Thomas Jefferson the presidency attracted, with the exception of Abraham Lincoln, men of poor character. "[T]he prestige of the presidential office has declined with the character of the presidents. And the character of the presidents has declined as the perfection of selfish party tactics has advanced" (*CGAP*, 49).

Since the separation of powers has allowed Congress to balkanize and corrupt executive administration, some measure must be found to restore effective government. Wilson's solution is to make the already powerful Congress more responsible. An admirer of the British political system, Wilson suggests that American politics should be reformed to imitate British cabinet government. With no hope for a renewed executive, Wilson proposes extraconstitutional means to overcome the Framers' original mistake in dividing power in their Whig fashion. "It is quite safe to say that were it possible to call together again the members of that wonderful Convention to view the work of their hands in light of the century that has tested it, they would be the first to admit that the only fruit of dividing power had been to make it irresponsible" (*CGAP*, 187). The literary theory of the checks and balances prevents both power and responsibility by parceling out power and confusing responsibility for its use and results.

Wilson seeks to empower Congress so it can guarantee the administration of government. To overcome separation of powers, extraconstitutional political parties must be strengthened to bridge the separation between the executive and legislative branches created by the Framers:

If the signs of the times are to be credited, we are fast approaching an adjustment of sovereignty quite as "simple" as need be. Congress is not only to retain the authority it already possesses, . . . [it] is to have ever-widening duties and responsibilities thrust upon it (CGAP, 205) . . . Our Constitution, like every other constitution which puts the authority to make laws and the duty of controlling the public expenditure into the hands of a popular assembly, [should] practically set that assembly to rule the affairs of the nations as supreme overlord. But, by separating it entirely from its executive agencies, [the Constitution] deprives it of the opportunity and means for making its authority complete and convenient. (CGAP, 203)

The British have shown us the way by successfully reforming their politics through the creation of "responsible party leadership" (CGAP, 209). Unlike the United States, the British were able to reform their system because "its [constitution's] growth has not been hindered or destroyed by the too tight ligaments of a written fundamental law" (CGAP, 202–3). To imitate the British, Wilson's Darwinian-styled organic politics requires the strong temporal and extraconstitutional parties to replace the weak rule of constitutional law and congressional statute. The government must derive its power from existing political arrangements (party government) and not from constitutional principles or mere parchment declarations.

Congressional Government has comparatively little to say about the office of the president, because Congress has usurped presidential powers. But Wilson's vision of strong party government enhancing the powers of Congress allows Congress, not the president, to regulate American society. Moreover, the organic constitution that Wilson embraces eliminates any constitutionally based doctrine of explicit and implied congressional powers, which is central to both the Hamiltonians and the Jeffersonians, in favor of the broad accretion of political power. Wilson argues that "the times seem to favor a centralization of governmental functions such as could not have suggested itself as a possibility to the framers of the Constitution" and will require "still further flights of [Constitutional] construction" (CGAP, 54–55).

In contrast to the earlier *Congressional Government* (1885), Wilson's *Constitutional Government in the United States* (1908) offers a more conventional Progressive case for presidential greatness. As in the earlier work, Wilson argues that the United States is now a national community: "Our life has undergone radical changes since 1787, and almost every change has operated to draw the nation together, to give it the common consciousness, the common interests, the common standards of conduct, the habit of concerted action, which will eventually impart to it many more aspects of the character of a single community."[7] The vital needs of the new national community reveal the Framers' Whig Constitution to be dangerously abstract and weak: "It is difficult to describe any single part of a great governmental system without describing the whole of it. Governments are living things and operate as organic wholes. Moreover, governments have their natural evolution and are one thing in one age, another in another. The makers of the Constitution constructed the federal government upon a theory of checks and balances which was meant to limit the operation of each part and allow to no single part or organ of it a dominating force; but no government can be successfully conducted upon so mechanical a theory."[8]

In *Congressional Government* Wilson argues that Congress had become the central and dominant force in the national government. He now suggests that the president is the true center of "our complex system": "Greatly as the practice and influence of Presidents have varied, there can be no mistaking the fact that we have grown more and more inclined from generation to generation to look to the President as the unifying force in our complex system, the leader both of his party and of the nation."[9] To defend his thesis, the scholarly Wilson, like the other Progressive thinkers, offers a new version of American history to demonstrate (this time) that the president, not Congress, has been the determining political force in the nation's history.

The only unequivocal and useful political power granted the president by the Constitution is in foreign affairs, where executive power is almost absolute:

> The initiative in foreign affairs, which the President possesses without restriction whatever, is virtually the power to control them absolutely. The President cannot conclude a treaty with a foreign power without the consent of the Senate, but he may guide every step of diplomacy, and to guide diplomacy is to determine what treaties must be made, if the faith and prestige of the government are to be maintained. He need disclose no step of negotiation until it is complete, and when in any critical matter it is completed the government is virtually committed. Whatever its disinclination, the Senate may feel itself committed also.[10]

Wilson's overestimation of presidential power in foreign affairs may account for his later failure with the League of Nations. Perhaps Wilson failed to see how Teddy Roosevelt's political dynamism gave him the muscle to dictate foreign affairs to Congress, a dominance Wilson wrongly judged to be the norm. In any case, in domestic matters Wilson went to the other extreme and personalized the basis of presidential power. Except for the veto, the president's powers are independent of enabling constitutional provisions.

Throughout, Wilson speaks of individual presidents. Because the Constitution, as a result of its Whiggish separation of powers, is politically weak, strong presidents are necessarily self-created, political personalities strong enough to conquer their historical eras. The man makes the office; the office does not make the man. The true power supporting the president is his political party, not the prerogative powers conferred by Article 2 or by presidential precedents. Parties do more to promote presidential governance than any other institution, because they tie together the geographic divisions of American politics and overcome the Whig-inspired separation of powers. Using his party skillfully, Wilson's president, like Machiavelli's prince, can heroically dominate his historical moment with only his personality and political skill. Good presidents are forced to overstep the limited constitutional role assigned to them and create their administrations through the force of personality. Fortunately, the people now recognize the president as the natural leader of the nation and support the growth of presidential power.

In our new national community, the president draws power from public sentiment expressed through the parties. His party leadership gives the president leverage over Congress in enacting measures he deems "necessary and proper." Even though the rules of engagement between president and Congress are defined by political power, and not by the Constitution, Wilson adopts the rules of the Marquis of Queensberry and not the bare-knuckle approach of Roosevelt's stewardship. TR argued that the president should employ all means that are not clearly unconstitutional in order to advance the public good. For Wilson, "The President is at liberty, both in law and conscience, to be as big a man as he can. His capacity will set the limit; and if Congress be overborne by him, it will be no fault of the makers of the Constitution,—it will be from no lack of constitutional powers on its part, but only because the President has the nation behind him, and Congress has not. He has no means of compelling Congress except through public opinion."[11]

A great president must become a leader of Progressive reform. Although Wilson suggests that he is recovering the Founders' "original" view of executive power, his Progressivism requires a still further accretion of presidential power. Wilson succeeded in passing Progressive proposals for economic regulation in the first few years of his administration. However, he failed to gain popular support for his reformist foreign policy initiatives, notably the League of Nations treaty. His failure to mobilize the country to achieve a new internationalism was interpreted by Wilson as a personal failure.

Henry Jones Ford

Like his political mentor, Woodrow Wilson, the political scientist Henry Jones Ford offers a sociological account of the Founding in his major work, *The Rise and Growth of American Politics: A Sketch of Constitutional Development* (1898). According to Ford, American elites separated from England to escape royal tyranny, and not from a fondness for democracy. Therefore the elites broke their attachment to the English king "without breaking their attachment to the English constitution" (*RG*, 33).[12] As a result, their new Constitution maintains the class rule of the American gentry. The first presidential administration of George Washington continued the American monarchical/aristocratic tradition. When Washington spoke to Congress, "the Representatives went to the senate chamber to hear him, as the Commons proceed to the House of Lords on similar occasions. The tone was personal, such as a king might use" (*RG*, 73). Similarly, Washington's chief minister, Alexander Hamilton, entered "into direct relations with Congress . . . From the first, he assumed the functions of a crown minister to the fullest extent which circumstances would allow, and his example was soon followed by all other members of the Cabinet" (*RG*, 81).

Political parties were invented to overcome the Constitution's separation of powers, which was intended by the Founders to protect elite rule. Andrew Jackson was the first president to use executive patronage to strengthen his party and the veto to strengthen the presidency. After Jackson used the veto to gain ascendancy over Congress, the presidency for the first time became an institution of popular democracy. Through Jackson's vetoes a "remarkable transformation has taken place in the constitution of the presidency, and instead of an embodiment of prerogative, it has become a representative institution" (*RG*, 186). With this development, the president began to overshadow Congress in popularity and power. Moreover, President Jackson established the authority of the party platform, permitting him to set the political agenda for the nation. After Jackson, the once powerful House of Representatives came to represent the people's "passing moods rather than their settled habits of thinking . . . [because] the popular mandate is [now] delivered at the presidential elections" (RG, 194–95).

The newly developed national party conventions also moved the constitutional system in a popular direction. The conventions liberated presidential selection from the restraints of the electoral college and the House of Representatives. These "restraint[s] had been avoided by transferring the selection of Presidents and the initiative of administration to an extraconstitutional body [the political party and the party convention], free from all restriction, save such as public opinion might impose" (RG, 211). During the president's rise, Congress remained beguiled by private interests and powerful committee chairs.

Ford credits the modern executive with sufficient powers to run government effectively: "It is the business of other branches of the government to condition the operation of the executive department in accordance with the constitutional principles on which the government is founded; but to take care of the government, to attend to its needs, to shape its policy, and to provide for its responsibilities is the special business of the President" (RG, 275). Presidential power and responsibility rest on several interlocking functions, institutions, and constitutional habits. Patronage power gives him independence and influence over Congress. The executive is representative of all the people, since "the machinery of the electoral college passed under the control of a system of popular election," which further increased his influence over Congress (RG, 276–78). The veto power cements the president's control over the legislative program. "It is impossible for a party to carry out even a purely legislative programme unless it embodies a policy accepted by the President and sustained by the influence of his office" (RG, 279). The president's control over his party's members makes him the true voice of public opinion (RG, 283). The president can command congressional compliance. Congress cannot resist an "issue which [the executive] insists upon making." Moreover, if Congress is unable to decide a certain policy issue, "[t]he existence of a separate responsible authority to which questions of public policy may be resigned opens to Congress an easy way out of difficulty when the exercise of its own jurisdiction would be troublesome . . . The [Congress] goes only as far as it is compelled to go in obedience to a party mandate, and is apt to leave as much as possible to executive discretion." Congress's tendency to delegate its power "stimulates the development of presidential authority" and extends "the scope of federal duty powerfully" (RG, 284).

Taken together, these developments have made the presidency incredibly strong. The office is so powerful that even weak presidents cannot harm it. "Men have been raised to the presidency who never would have been thought of as a candidate for that office; but its powers have sustained no permanent loss thereby" (RG, 288). Although the presidential office makes the man, its strength derives in part from its elective character. "The truth is that in the presidential office, as it has been constituted since Jackson's time, American democracy has revived the oldest political institution of the race, the elective kingship" (RG, 293).

In Ford's sanguine view, recent political reforms have helped secure popular political control and effective public policies. The political parties, in particular, are now able to support a strong presidency. These new developments reveal the weakness of parliamentary government, which Ford argues is "a transitory phase of political participation" (RG, 371). Unlike the early Woodrow Wilson, Ford argues that England has "yet to make terms with democracy," whereas every advance in America is "based upon democratic foundations." He anticipates that as the "Grand Elector," the American president will eventually embody national unity and "comprehend every element of majesty and strength" (RG, 373).

The Founders' original timidity has been overcome through the growth of the centers of strong democracy, the parties and the nominating conventions, which both concentrate power in the executive. Ford's confidence in the constitutional system is related to his indifference to the oftentimes radical social agenda of the other Progressives. Satisfied with the reforms of recent administrations, he does not envision a new social revolution requiring the national government's leadership in uprooting traditional views of human nature and religion and substituting the discoveries of social science. As we will now see, Theodore Roosevelt's extensive political and social agenda requires a stronger executive than even Ford's "elective kingship."

Theodore Roosevelt

Theodore Roosevelt offers a more radical Progressive view of the presidency than did Henry Jones Ford or Woodrow Wilson. Roosevelt thought American political "backwardness" demanded major new reforms and regulations. As tribune or Rough Rider, the president is the best agenda-setter for progress. In his *Autobiography* (1925), TR grandly describes his new view of the constitutional principles supporting strong presidential leadership. Roosevelt contrasts two inherent paradigms of presidential action: the narrow legalistic approach of James Buchanan and William Howard Taft, and the prerogative-driven presidencies of Andrew Jackson and Abraham Lincoln. The first paradigm argues that the executive should follow existing law and constitutional precedent, ceding decisions to the courts and Congress when there is any constitutional ambiguity.

Roosevelt's view of the second strong paradigm is best represented by Abraham Lincoln's use of prerogative power. Lincoln combined two essential qualities, a great humanitarian vision of equality and an expansive use of presidential prerogative. Lincoln sought to redeem the nation both from the sins of slavery and from its excessive economic inequality. As the secular redeemer of America, Lincoln proved himself a "stout adherent of the rights of the people" (A, 64)[13] and the leader of that Republican party, "which in the days of Abraham Lincoln was founded as the radical progressive party of the Nation" (A, 350–51). Lincoln was the "great radical democratic leader of the [18]60's . . . who put human rights above property rights when the two conflicted" (A, 385). Of equal importance, Lincoln used presidential power aggressively to pursue his policies: "[M]en who understand and practice the deep underlying philosophy of the Lincoln school of American political thought are necessarily Hamiltonian in their belief in a strong and efficient National Government and Jeffersonian in their belief in the people as the ultimate authority, and in the welfare of the people as the end of the Government" (A, 423).

But TR takes Lincoln and Hamilton's "belief in a strong and efficient National Government" out of the political universe that they shared and Roosevelt did not. Whereas these earlier statesmen believed in limited government, Roosevelt argued that a powerful president devoted to new social policies was the only effective means to overcome the forces of reaction, including traditional constitutionalism. Roosevelt appeals more to Abraham Lincoln than Alexander Hamilton, because Lincoln justified his major decisions and policies as war measures not subject to congressional action. But Roosevelt went far beyond Lincoln by invoking emergency prerogative power in a country at peace by merely declaring that warlike conditions prevailed. Referring to his intervention in the anthracite coal strike, Roosevelt said, "it is not too much to say that the situation which confronted Pennsylvania, New York, and New England, and to a less degree the States of the Middle West, in October, 1902, was *quite as serious as if they had been threatened by the invasion of a hostile army of overwhelming force*" (A, 465).

The source of the war that TR describes was not a hostile army but the inevitable conflict between past and future, reaction and progress, capitalists and workers. Because violence was inevitable along these philosophical and class divisions, a Progressive president must resolve such revolutionary conflict in the direction of progress to save the reactionaries from themselves: "I have always maintained that our worst revolutionaries to-day are those reactionaries who do not see and will not admit that there is any need for change . . . It is these reactionaries, however, who, by 'standing pat' on industrial injustice, incite inevitably to industrial revolt, and it is only we who advocate political and industrial democracy who render possible the progress of our American industry on large constructive lines with a minimum of friction with a maximum of justice" (A, 484–85). Convinced of the justice and revolutionary power of Progressive scientific and egalitarian ideals, TR sees the Progressive state as a conservative response to inevitable revolutionary violence, especially industrial warfare.

A Darwinian, TR recognizes that everything involves war: nation against nation, reaction against progress, worker against capitalist, generation against generation, race against race, and women against men. In the war of man versus man and man versus nature, the president is the ultimate Machiavellian lion who must act in a constant state of war. For this reason, TR adopts what he calls Lincoln's view of presidential prerogative: great actions can only be taken in a emergencies. But Roosevelt knew that an emergency may also be a state of mind. If the public only believes they have been saved from disaster, the presidential savior will be as liberated from constitutional constraints as if the emergency had been real.

Roosevelt operates at the opposite extreme from Thomas Jefferson. Jefferson argued that only explicitly granted powers were permitted the president. Roosevelt believes that whatever the Constitution and Congress do not explicitly forbid, they permit:

> The executive power was limited only by specific restrictions and prohibitions appearing in the Constitution or imposed by the Congress under its Constitutional powers. My view was that every executive officer, and above all every executive officer in high position, was a steward of the people bound actively and affirmatively to do all he could for the people . . . I declined to adopt the view that what was imperatively necessary for the Nation could not be done by the President unless he could find some specific authorization to do it. My belief was that it was not only his right but his duty to do anything that the needs of the Nation demanded unless such action was forbidden by the Constitution or by the laws. (A, 357)

TR's theory of presidential prerogative had positive results: "Under this interpretation of executive power I did and caused many things not previously done by the President and the heads of the departments. I did not usurp power, but I greatly broadened the use of executive power. In other words, I acted for the public welfare, I acted for the common well-being of all our people, whenever and in whatever manner was necessary, unless prevented by direct constitutional or legislative prohibition" (A, 357).

Roosevelt applied his stewardship theory of presidential prerogative across the board: in the anthracite coal strike, the creation of the national parks, the treaty with Santo Domingo, the acquisition of land for the Panama Canal, and the decision to send the Great White Fleet around the world. In each case, Roosevelt concedes that his actions might have been considered unconstitutional under a more restrictive view of executive power than his own. About Santo Domingo he says: "The Constitution did not explicitly give me power to bring about the necessary agreement with Santo Domingo. But the Constitution did not forbid my doing what I did. I put the agreement into effect, and I continued its execution for two years before the Senate acted; and I would have continued it until the end of my term, if necessary, without any action by Congress" (A, 510). Similarly, TR justifies his controversial decision to send the fleet around the world: "I determined on the move without consulting the Cabinet, precisely as I took Panama without consulting the Cabinet. A council of war never fights, and in a crisis the duty of a leader is to lead and not to take refuge behind the generally timid wisdom of a multitude of councillors" (A, 548).

Roosevelt's notion of executive prerogative is unusual, if not singular and unique. It is clearly at variance with the two models he cites: Alexander Hamilton and Abraham Lincoln. Although it is impossible to know how Lincoln's treatment of Congress would have differed if the country had not been at war, the fact is that it was. Lincoln's earlier writings, especially those directed against Polk's conduct of the Mexican War, suggest that he had a much more limited view of presidential power than did Roosevelt. Even Alexander Hamilton, the great monarchist among the Framers, was in favor of implied powers derived from the broad responsibilities granted in Article 2. In *Federalists* 23 and 33, Hamilton argues that if a power is given to the executive, as it is over military matters and national defense, the executive is implicitly given all the powers necessary to carry out this responsibility. Hamilton makes a similar case for the powers given to Congress. Since Congress has the power to regulate the currency, the creation of a national bank is an extension of Congress's explicit power. But Hamilton observes that neither Congress nor the president has the authority to operate in policy areas where the Constitution is silent. Although Congress and the president are nearly omnipotent in the areas of their constitutional responsibility, they have no power to do what they are not constitutionally authorized to do.

Roosevelt's new stewardship theory of executive prerogative is a doctrine of nearly unlimited constitutional power easily surpassing the Framers' strong, but limited, view. TR's doctrine should also be understood against the background of his constant attacks on Congress and the Supreme Court for conservatively interpreting the Constitution. Since increased presidential power is necessary for progress, strict constitutional construction is a defensive strategy for economic elites and social reactionaries. TR's expansive constitutionalism puts the other branches on the defensive, having to reclaim through statutory law and slow judicial remedy what a popular Progressive president has already declared indispensable and constitutional—and made a fait accompli through executive action.

Roosevelt's stewardship view of executive power has a major ideological component. The Progressives sought to replace existing social practices, and eighteenth- and nineteenth-century beliefs about human nature and religion, with a fully modern, egalitarian society. Roosevelt's executive leadership is geared to radical social change. He praises the Progressive Party, which he had helped make the most successful third party in American history. He invokes the party as "the four and a half million Progressive voters, who in 1912 registered their solemn protest against our social and industrial injustices" (A, 484). He believes that Progressive scientism will inform successful parties of the future. Labor unions especially will become fundamental institutions in the new American society: "I also think—and this is a belief which has been borne upon me through many years of practical experience—that the trade union is growing constantly in wisdom as in power, and is becoming one of the most efficient agencies toward the solution of our industrial problems, the elimination of poverty and of industrial disease and accidents, the lessening of unemployment, the achievement of industrial democracy and the attainment of a larger measure of social and industrial justice" (A, 480–81).[14]

The extraordinary expansion of presidential power in the twentieth century results from a deliberate effort by the Progressives and Liberals following Teddy Roosevelt and Woodrow Wilson to use the executive to create new social and political realities. The president is a revolutionary leader in the fight for a modern scientific society dedicated to social equality. Indeed, contemporary liberalism continues to search for a public philosophy like TR's Square Deal and Wilson's New Freedom capable of renewing the Progressives' commanding political vision.

J. Allen Smith, Charles Beard, and Herbert Croly

The Progressive era was unique in American public life, because for the first time a new scientific approach to human nature and politics challenged the view of the Founders. Professors J. Allen Smith, Charles Beard, and Herbert Croly were the most influential of the new public intellectuals who articulated the implications of the new sciences of politics and economics. They profoundly affected public opinion and the convictions of some presidents. Wilson's new confidence in the social sciences seems to account for the remarkable difference in tone and policy between *Congressional Government* and *Constitutional Government*. The new social sciences seemed to guarantee the practical success of all kinds of social and political reforms, which earlier had only the elusive status of ideals. Certainly this sentiment influenced TR's Progressive campaign in 1912.

J. Allen Smith was an early Progressive. From his chair in history and political science at the University of Washington, Smith contributed a rationale for the new reform agenda. After the reformers' failure in the 1890s to achieve any tangible successes, Smith concluded that the obstacles to reform lay deeper than what could be explained by the political process or party ideology. According to Cushing Strout, Smith proved what Progressives had long before come to believe: the Constitution was designed to create an antidemocratic political and economic order. "Smith was the first scholar to develop this theme in an extensive analysis made in the spirit of a bitter protest against what he felt to be a continuing betrayal of the democratic vision first glimpsed in the American Revolution. His passionate critique contrasted sharply with the mainline of American historians, who had written with Federalist-Whig-Republican sympathies."[15] According to Strout, Smith laid the foundation and general lines of argument that Charles Beard and Vernon Parrington turned into Progressive orthodoxy in the areas of politics and American literature in *An Economic Interpretation of the Constitution* (1913) and *Main Currents in American Thought* (1927). Parrington also took note of Smith's *Spirit of American Government*: "It provided the leaders of the La Follette 'Insurgent group' with an interpretation of American constitutional history congenial to their temper; it gave them a convincing explanation of the reasons for the failure of democracy in American political practice; and it was drawn upon freely in Congressional debates."[16]

In many respects Smith's argument is anticipated in Henry Lockwood's *Abolition of the Presidency* (see chapter 3). The genuine populism of the American Revolution was subverted in the Constitutional Convention by conservative elites seeking to protect themselves from further social revolution. But whereas Lockwood's "Thermidorian reactionaries" were looking backward to the glories of "throne and altar," Smith's reactionaries are capitalists or protocapitalists. For Smith, the strong executive, independent judiciary, rigorous amendment provision, and all the other constitutional devices that the Framers thought necessary for liberty and prudence were designed to thwart the democratic will of the House of Representatives. Moreover, the contemporary Supreme Court continues to "unfairly advantage the capital-owning class preserving property rights and corporate privileges which the unhindered progress of democracy would have abridged or abolished."[17] The presidency is another reactionary creation of the Framers. The president's election through the electoral college guarantees "a president acceptable to the conservative and well to do classes by guarding against the choice of a mere popular favorite."[18] Moreover, "in conferring the veto power on the president, the members of the Convention were actuated by the desire to strengthen a conservative branch of the government."[19]

Like Lockwood and the Progressives generally, Smith expresses an absolute confidence that the universal progress of the natural and social sciences guarantees the creation of a modern democratic nation wherever and whenever they are applied. Progressive science will universally replace "the crude political superstitions upon which the old governmental arrangements rested . . . The blind unthinking reverence with which [man] regarded it in the past is giving way to a critical scientific spirit . . . Democracy owes much to modern scientific research."[20] Confidence in the progress of science and democracy strengthens society, enabling it to "discourage and repress all individual activities not in harmony with the general interests of society."[21]

The historian Charles Beard was probably the Progressives' leading public philosopher. His extraordinary literary productivity over a long life was remarkable by any standard. Of his myriad histories, *An Economic Interpretation of the Constitution of the United States* (1913) was singularly influential. Here Beard claimed to prove what the other Progressives, including J. Allen Smith, had merely argued or surmised: the Fathers of the

American Constitution had a common economic interest. Nearly all of the Framers had large holdings in depreciated public securities.[22] Moreover, through the Society of the Cincinnati, the Founding elites had organized themselves into a powerful political faction.[23] In their oligarchic Constitution, the presidency was made into a major obstacle to democratic progress. Beard quotes selectively from the *Federalist* and from Max Farrand, *The Records of the Federal Convention of 1787*, to demonstrate that the Founders were committed to class-based government. The independent executive was to be one of the principal bulwarks, along with the judiciary, against the leveling propensities of the democratically elected legislature. He quotes the moderate William Livingston because Livingston best exemplifies the Founders' conservative approach to the executive: "As prejudices always prevail, more or less, in all popular governments, it is necessary that a check be placed somewhere in the hands of a power not immediately dependent upon the breath of the people, in order to stem the torrent, and prevent the mischiefs which blind passions and rancorous prejudices might otherwise occasion. The executive and judicial powers should of course then be vested with this check or control on the legislature; and that they may be enabled fully to effect this beneficial purpose, they should be rendered as independent as possible."[24]

Charles Beard most clearly articulates the core principle of Progressivism: true modernism demands the scientific transformation of society as well as of politics. "Yet the fact remains that political democracy and natural science rose and flourished together . . . More than that, science pointed the way to progressive democracy in its warfare against starvation, poverty, disease, and ignorance, indicating how classes and nations long engaged in strife among themselves might unite to wring from nature the secret of security and the good life. It was science, not paper declarations relating to the idea of progress, that at last made patent the practical methods by which democracy could raise the standard of living for the great masses of the people."[25] Science should set the social agenda for a modern nation. Social science can prove what the good life, or human happiness, is, philosophy and religion having failed to do so.

Herbert Croly, our third Progressive intellectual, provided a defense of Roosevelt's presidency and of the Progressive party and movement in *The Promise of American Life* (1909) and *Progressive Democracy* (1914). As the founder and editor-in-chief of the *New Republic* from 1914 until 1930, he defended the modernist agenda of the Progressives. Unlike J. Allen Smith, Croly was convinced that the presidency was the most Progressive branch of the government. And compared to J. Allen Smith and Charles Beard, with their class-oriented, radical democracy, Croly better understood the conservative implications of a great deal of nineteenth-century Jeffersonian populism. He also understood that progress in his own time depended on a powerful president who could lead the people against what he argued were the entrenched oligarchic and socially conservative congressional and judicial branches of government. Thus, he lauded Alexander Hamilton for recognizing that progress required energy in the executive.[26] For Croly, the energetic American president would provide the leadership for the creation of a modern administrative state. Everything should be done to empower the president to become the leader of rapid social progress.[27]

Croly provided the theoretical arguments for the mainstream of Progressive political reform. The administrative state offers the means to reform traditional societies into modern scientific and egalitarian ones. Since Congress represents the conservative economic interests and regions of the country, the president must stand against it and fight for progress. As *the* agent of modern revolution, the presidency must be greatly invigorated to complete the herculean tasks of social revolution. The Progressive president should be judged only by his success in reforming society through new programs and policies, rather than by how well he has fulfilled the electoral and constitutional responsibilities of his office. Indeed, for both Croly and his "student" TR, the president was truly the ruler of the country-to-be, the shining megalopolis on the hill. He was the heroic, visionary messenger of a perfect future.

Conclusion

The Progressives were the nearest to presidential absolutists of any theorists and practitioners of the presidency. To create a rational, egalitarian society, the Progressive president marshals public opinion while forcefully leading the political and social agencies of scientific progress. For both tasks he needs the great rhetorical power provided by the Progressives' intellectual vision. This linking of modern industrialization with the pure antitraditionalism of contemporary social science promised, at least for the first two-thirds of the twentieth century, a great leap forward in the United States and the entire world. Fortunately, the American democratic tradition limited the modern Caesarism of the Progressives to that of a relatively benign heroic president.

The Progressives offer the third major presidential paradigm after the

Founders' Hamiltonianism and the nineteenth century's Jeffersonianism. A major difference between the Progressives and the two earlier paradigms is that the Progressives are postconstitutional. Their belief in the evolutionary or historical nature of scientific knowledge convinced them that the Founders' epistemology and politics were time-bound and no longer relevant to an enlightened age, although both Herbert Croly and Theodore Roosevelt appreciated the Hamiltonian prerogative-based executive. Because the Constitution was so popularly venerated and protected by special interests, it was virtually impossible to amend. So the Progressives sought to interpret the Founders' supramajoritarian Constitution as capable of amendment by legal statute and judicial decision.

The Progressives were also a minority political movement that had to fight for a revolution in popular opinion. Unlike the Hamiltonians and Jeffersonians, who enjoyed immediate political success, the Progressive minority had to rely on the arguments and appeals of the new intellectual classes located in the public media and the universities, because politicians in both political parties reflected the public skepticism toward many aspects of Progressive utopianism. Even the Progressive presidents, TR and Woodrow Wilson, found the Progressive vision politically difficult to embrace in its totality. Although the Progressives' political success in 1912 (foreshadowed in the election of 1904) started to narrow the gap between public and Progressive opinion, only the Great Depression gave the Progressive forces the popular and political support the Hamiltonians and Jeffersonians had enjoyed with their initial political victories.

The president was the centerpiece of the Progressive-Liberal social revolution, because collectively the Progressives and Liberals despaired of ever controlling Congress. The latter was firmly in the grip of economic and local interests. Presidential power was the sine qua non of revolutionary change, and the president's policy victories were landmarks in the war for a modern egalitarian society. New policies regulating retirement, education, labor, and agricultural and rural life were the building blocks of a new republic that was later realized by FDR. If the Progressives were like the Jeffersonians in viewing the Founders as oligarchs and nouveau aristocrats, the Progressives differed from Jeffersonians in believing the Constitution too weak to promote the sweeping kind of modern democracy they envisioned. The Progressive solution to its original political weakness was to reduce the influence of partisan politics by increasing executive influence over the administrative agencies that the president had under his direct control. Later Franklin D. Roosevelt created new administrative bureaucracies to modernize American life, expecting to gain patronage for himself and his party.

Does presidential power derive from the prerogatives of office or from the incumbent? Progressives relied more on political than prerogative power, seeking to exploit the constitutional system to acquire more power than was envisioned by even the Hamiltonians. For example, they rhetorically championed the presidencies of Andrew Jackson and Abraham Lincoln because in their view both creatively misused the Constitution to serve egalitarian and humanitarian ends. Presidential prerogative was used when it served their modernizing agenda, and extraconstitutional parties and public interest groups were used to mobilize public opinion when prerogative power proved insufficient. Similarly, the Progressives' approach to the political party was the reverse of the Jeffersonians' approach. The latter had used the party to empower Congress and local politicians to thwart national and presidential power. Progressives sought to make the national party an agent of presidential government, reducing the influence of Congress and the state parties.

Does presidential influence depend upon the force of personality, rhetorical leadership, or partisanship? The Progressives relied more upon political partisanship and the mobilization of public opinion than upon the cult of personality. The Progressive president became the locus both of national politics and of the world, the cause of social mobilization and modernization (Wilson's League of Nations). The president assumed responsibility for the modern new republics to be born around the globe. Because they believed these goals were constrained by the Founders' deliberately weak and antidemocratic Constitution, Progressive presidents looked to new democratic political forces to invigorate their few constitutional prerogatives. Once the national media made mobilization of mass opinion feasible, the president could directly appeal to the people over the heads of the other political branches on behalf of specific reforms and policies. As we have seen, both Herbert Croly and Theodore Roosevelt supported new reform groups and movements capable of mobilizing public support. Both supported labor unions as instruments of Progressive policy. Both also supported the new Progressive Party, and Croly founded the intellectual journal *The New Republic* to further the Progressive revolution.

Does presidential leadership depend upon historical context, or is regime-building manifested through political, institutional, and constitutional developments? The Progressives believed their vision of a new society would create a new political culture permitting the powers of the presidency to be made anew. They had greater confidence in scientific positivism leading to rational reform than was ever envisioned by the Hamiltonians or Jeffersonians. Mankind makes itself as it advances. It does not need, and so can forgo, historical precedents and antiquarian parchments like the Constitution, which were based only on out-of-date historical conditions and ideas. As the agent of social progress, the president must lead public opinion. Neither precedent nor the Constitution should constrain the Progressive president.

Does presidential leadership vary between domestic and foreign affairs? The Progressives were almost exclusively interested in domestic matters in their creation of a modern egalitarian society. Nevertheless, Theodore Roosevelt understood that a strong foreign policy increased popular confidence in the national government, enabling it to become a greater force for domestic reform. Whereas the Hamiltonians and the Jeffersonians considered foreign policy the major area of presidential activity, the modernizing Progressives thought the opposite.

Does the president actively or passively engage the legislative process and promote a policy agenda? For the Progressives, every means should be employed to strengthen the president's domestic policy, including actively engaging the legislative process and promoting a policy agenda. If the Hamiltonians focused on the policy initiatives that they could constitutionally pursue, while the Jeffersonians had initially no domestic legislation, the Progressive modernists had new policy initiatives in every area of American life. In the Progressive view, the president both proposed legislation and assured that Congress did as he wished.

Does the organization of the executive branch service presidential leadership? The Progressive view of presidential power required a powerful office of the president. The president's active leadership of Congress, of his political party, and of other popular institutions, particularly the media, made the organizational apparatus of the presidential staff of paramount importance. Most functions that have developed within the institutionalized presidency are consistent with the new tasks the Progressives assigned to the modern president.

CHAPTER FIVE

Critics of Progressivism
The Early Constitutionalists

During the Progressive Era and its aftermath, there were three advocates of the constitutional presidency who took issue with the assumptions of those scholars who followed in the intellectual footsteps of Woodrow Wilson. Two were American presidents—William Howard Taft and Calvin Coolidge—and the third, Charles C. Thach Jr., wrote a dissertation that was destined to become the definitive statement of Original Intent with respect to Article 2. Published in 1923, Thach's study was reissued in 1969 with an introduction by the eminent University of Chicago theorist Herbert J. Storing. The Thach study was published midway between the Taft (1916) and Coolidge (1929) autobiographies. But let us begin by comparing the philosophies of high office held by these two ex-presidents.

William Howard Taft

Most accounts of the intellectual standoff between Presidents William Howard Taft and Theodore Roosevelt portray Taft as formalistic and legalistic as compared to TR, the defender of an expansive reading of presidential prerogatives.[1] Is this commonly accepted view of Taft accurate, especially in terms of the executive-legislative relationship? Like other political conservatives (e.g., Coolidge), Taft sees the "great problem" confronting the American people as "restraining the extravagance of legislatures and of Congresses." Thus, in championing the need for executive budget reform, Taft believes that the president, by virtue of his "method of choice" and "range of duties" has "direct relation to the people as a whole and the government as a whole" and therefore "is most likely to feel the necessity for economy in total expenditures."[2]

In *The President and His Powers*, Taft appears to agree that a parliamentary government "offers an opportunity for greater effectiveness in that the same mind or minds control the executive and the legislative action," whereas the president "has no initiative in respect to legislation" except "mere recommendation" and cannot engage in legislative debate other than through a "formal message or address." While in office he thought this situation "a defect," but "I am inclined now to think that the defect is more theoretical than actual." That is to say: "It usually happens that the party which is successful in electing a President is also successful in electing a Congress to sustain him. The natural party cohesion and loyalty, and a certain power and prestige which the President has when he enters office, make his first Congress one in which he can exercise much influence in the framing and passage of legislation to fulfil party promises. The history of the present administration [Wilson's] and that of many administrations bear me out in this."[3]

In other words, during his term Taft does not conceptualize the president's legislative leadership as going beyond the formal authority of his office—not in terms of popular rhetoric, personal bargaining and logrolling, or party leadership—although he later realizes the value of unified party government to presidential legislative success. Despite his legalistic approach, Taft upholds Jackson's view that the veto power is not limited to reasons of unconstitutionality, since "[i]t cannot be said . . . the Constitution implies any such limitation." However, after noting the "partial veto" exercised by some governors over appropriations, Taft is "not entirely sure it would be a safe provision."[4] Especially telling is Taft's rejection of a personalized legislative role by the president in favor of the indirect approach of using members of the cabinet to lobby Congress. For that reason, Taft recommended in his Annual Message of December 19, 1912, that cabinet members "should be given access to the floor of each House to introduce measures, to advocate their passage, to answer questions, and to enter into the debate as if they were members, without of course the right to vote."[5]

Taft also praises Wilson for returning to "the old practice of a personal address to both Houses," because "[o]ral addresses fix the attention of the country on Congress more than written communications, and by fixing the attention of the country on Congress, they fix the attention of Congress on the recommendations of the President." Taft could have, but did not, resurrect that original practice, fearing that the "faithful followers of Jefferson" would have denounced "'such a royal ceremony in a speech from the Throne,'" whereas "a member of the Jeffersonian Party [namely Wilson] has some advantages in the Presidential chair."[6]

Later chapters of *The President and His Powers* give a highly legalistic interpretation of constitutional powers (laced throughout with supportive judicial precedents). Not only the explicit appointive power but also the inherent removal power can be traced back to the Constitution (a view formalized by Chief Justice Taft in *Myers v. United States*): "They [Framers] gave him the power of absolute removal, and they placed in his hands the control of the action of all those who took part in the discharge of the political duties of the executive department."[7]

Although only Congress can declare war, "the President can take action such as to involve the country in war and to leave Congress no option but to declare it or to recognize its existence." The Prize Cases during the Civil War are referenced to argue that it is "only in the case of a war of our aggression against a foreign country that the power of Congress must be affirmatively asserted to establish its legal existence." So Taft could defend the deployment of our military forces in Central America, which "grows not out of any specific act of Congress, but out of that obligation, inferable from the Constitution, of the government to protect the rights of an American citizen against foreign aggression."[8]

In conducting foreign affairs, Taft views the treaty-making power as "a very broad one" insofar as "[e]verything . . . that is natural or customarily involved in such foreign relations, a treaty may cover." Beyond that, the president "has a very large authority outside of treaty-making," to include his appointing and receiving ambassadors that "gives him necessarily the duty of carrying on foreign negotiations between ourselves and foreign countries." Echoing another Hamiltonian refrain, Taft agrees that the president "alone is the representative of our nation in dealing with foreign nations. When I say he alone, I mean that it is he to whom the foreign nations look." Yet Taft stops short of fully embracing the kingly prerogative, believing that the president cannot "annul or abrogate a treaty without the consent of the Senate unless he is given that specific authority by the terms of the treaty."[9]

Taft's final chapter asserts yet another presidential prerogative—executive privilege—which he traces back to Washington's dispute with the House of Representatives over Jay's Treaty. The fact that the Constitution requires him to give Congress information on the state of the Union and to recommend measures that he judges necessary and expedient "does not enable Congress or either House of Congress to elicit from him confidential information which he has acquired for the purpose of enabling him to discharge his constitutional duties, if he does not deem the disclosure of such information prudent or in the public interest."[10]

Taft concludes by joining his intellectual debate with Theodore Roosevelt. Although the separation of powers "mark[s] out the exclusive field of jurisdiction of each branch of the government," Taft says "there must be cooperation of all branches"; otherwise "there will follow a hopeless obstruction to the progress of the whole government." In the final analysis, the "life of the government . . . depends on the sense of responsibility of each branch in doing the part assigned to it in the carrying on of the business of the people in the government, and ultimately as the last resource, we must look to public opinion as the moving force to induce affirmative action and proper team work."[11]

Taft recalls that Theodore Roosevelt classified "Lincoln Presidents" and "Buchanan Presidents" with "himself [placed] in the Lincoln class of Presidents, and me in the Buchanan class." But Taft does not think the Lincoln analogy holds, pointing to TR's intervention in a threatened anthracite coal strike. Although Taft admires his efforts to mobilize public opinion and to bring the contending parties to the bargaining table, he objects to Roosevelt's threat to take over the mines. To seize private property is a "lawless" action, and only an extremist would "seize the needed mines without constitutional amendment or legislative and judicial action and without compensation." To justify such action pursuant to Lincoln's view of prerogative during the Civil War, Taft counters that "Lincoln always pointed out the source of the authority [in the Constitution] which in his opinion justified his acts, and there was always a strong ground for maintaining the view which he took." Taft enumerates some extraordinary actions by Lincoln but concludes that he "never claimed that whatever authority in government was not expressly denied to him he could exercise."[12]

In sum, executive power is "limited, so far as it is possible to limit such a power consistent with that discretion and promptness of action that are essential to preserve the interests of the public in times of emergency, or legislative neglect or inaction." Therefore the Constitution "does give the President wide discretion and great power, and it ought to do so. It calls from him activity and energy to see that within his proper sphere he does what his great responsibilities and opportunities require."[13]

Calvin Coolidge

He may have been Ronald Reagan's favorite president, but Calvin Coolidge was no favorite of scholars in the Progressive-Liberal tradition. Like Taft, his reputed passivity was characterized as being a unique "style" of presidential behavior that contrasted sharply with the heroic achievements of Lincoln or FDR.[14] However, in one sense Coolidge sounds modern, because he too believed that, though a president must "get all the competent advice possible . . . [n]o one can make his decisions for him. He stands at the center of things where no one else can stand."[15] And rather than take sides in the Taft-Roosevelt debate, *The Autobiography of Calvin Coolidge* advocates prudence: "The Constitution specifically vests him with executive power. Some Presidents have seemed to interpret that as an authorization to take any action which the Constitution, or perhaps the law, does not specifically prohibit. Others have considered that their powers extended only to such acts as were specifically authorized by the Constitution and the statutes. This has always seemed to me to be a hypothetical question, which it would be idle to attempt to determine in advance. It would appear to be better practice to wait to decide each question on its merits as it arises." For one, Jefferson "entertained the opinion that there was no constitutional warrant for enlarging the [U.S.] territory," but when faced with that prospect, "he did not hesitate to negotiate the Louisiana Purchase" on his own. Yet, says Coolidge, "[f]or all ordinary occasions," the powers "assigned" to the president "will be found sufficient to provide for the welfare of the country. That is all he needs."[16]

Coolidge elsewhere invokes Jefferson's "faith in the people and his constant insistence that they be left to manage their own affairs" as well as "[h]is opposition to bureaucracy," but Coolidge contends that "[t]he trouble with us is that we talk about Jefferson but do not follow him. In his theory that the people should manage their government, and not be managed by it, he was everlastingly right."[17] But Jefferson was wrong to hold "the opinion that even the Supreme Court should be influenced by his wishes and that failing in this a recalcitrant judge should be impeached by a complaisant Congress."[18] For his part, Coolidge allowed his own administrators to "make their own decisions," and especially "[w]herever they exercise judicial functions, I always felt that some impropriety might attach to any suggestions from me."[19]

Coolidge's deference does not extend to Congress. He notes that White House breakfasts were attended by fifteen to twenty-five members of the House and Senate and, moreover, "I invited all the members of the Senate, all the chairmen and ranking Democratic members of the committees of the House, and finally had breakfast with the officers of both houses of the Congress." The gatherings, though not "to discuss matters of public business," were nonetheless "productive of a spirit of good fellowship which was no doubt a helpful influence to the transaction of public business."[20] Going beyond social niceties, Coolidge engaged in personal lobbying. Members of both congressional parties he found "willing to confer with me and disposed to treat my recommendations fairly," to the point where most "differences could be adjusted by personal discussion." Occasionally President Coolidge even resorted to "going public," as he explains: "Sometimes I made an appeal direct to the country by stating my position at the newspaper conferences. I adopted that course in relation to the Mississippi Flood Control Bill . . . The press began a vigorous discussion of the subject, which caused the House greatly to modify the [Senate] bill, and in conference a measure that was entirely fair and moderate was adopted."[21]

Regarding a 1928 tax bill, Coolidge recalls that he "appealed to the country more privately, enlisting the influence of labor and trade organizations upon the Congress in behalf of some measures in which I was interested." The House-passed bill cut revenues too much, so "[b]y quietly making this known to the Senate, and enlisting support for that position among their constituents, it was possible to secure such modification of the measure that it could be adopted without greatly endangering the revenue." On going public, however, Coolidge urges caution because "a [p]resident cannot, with success, constantly appeal to the country. After a time he will get no response." In other words, people are too busy and "can not give much attention to what the Congress is doing." As proof, Coolidge claims that most "policies set out in my first Annual Message have become law, but it took several years to get action on some of them."[22]

Coolidge wrote about an "unorganized, formless, and inarticulate" public opinion as existing "[a]gainst a compact and well drilled minority," but nevertheless public opinion will be "the court of last resort and their [the public's] decisions are final." Here the White House is very different from Congress: "It is because in their hours of timidity the Congress becomes subservient to the importunities of organized minorities that the President comes more and more to stand as the champion of the rights of the whole country." Laws enacted to benefit organized minorities, says Coolidge, are "not entirely bad" but "excessively expensive," meaning that his guardianship of the public good was obviously linked to government frugality.[23]

The president "is not only the head of the government" but "also the head of his party." Coolidge perceives "a decline in party spirit and a distinct weakening in party loyalty" but nonetheless finds it "necessary under our form of government to have political parties." Whereupon Coolidge ends with an eloquent defense of responsible partyism. Congress "is organized entirely in accordance with party policy," insofar as the parties "appeal to the voters in behalf of their platforms," and voters "make their choice on those issues." In sum, "[u]nless those who are elected on the same party platform associate themselves together to carry out its provisions, the election becomes a mockery."[24] Sometimes congressional party lines are disregarded, but "if there is to be a reasonable government proceeding in accordance with the express mandate of the people . . . on all the larger and important issues there must be party solidarity. It is the business of the President as party leader to do the best he can to see that the declared party platform purposes are translated into legislative and administrative action." Coolidge admits that he often got support from the opposition party and opposition from his supporters in his efforts to redeem platform pledges, but that situation "is entirely anomalous" insofar as "[i]t leaves the President as the sole repository of party responsibility." This is one reason why "the Presidential office has grown in popular estimation and favor, while the Congress has declined. The country feels that the President is willing to assume responsibility, while his party in the Congress is not."[25]

Coolidge never tried to "coerce Senators or Representatives, or to take reprisals," but still "[u]nder our system it ought to be remembered that the power to initiate politics has to be centralized somewhere. Unless the party leaders exercising it can depend on loyalty and organization support, the party in which it is reposed will become entirely ineffective." Ineffectual parties will be discarded, so "[i]f party is to endure as a serviceable instrument of government for the country, it must possess and display a healthy spirit of party loyalty. Such a manifestation in the Congress would do more than anything else to rehabilitate it in the esteem and confidence of the country."[26] Such was Coolidge, the constitutionalist as partisan.

Charles C. Thach Jr.

In his introduction to the 1969 reissue of Thach's classic, *The Creation of the Presidency, 1775–1789*, Professor Herbert J. Storing calls his book "so useful and so sound as to be indispensable" and notes "how well good scholarship directed to important questions holds up over the years."[27] Experience is key to Thach's understanding of Article 2, as he downplays the impact of abstract theorizing on the Framers. The revolutionaries of 1776 became the conservatives of 1787 because, during the interim, the Revolutionary War showed that "[t]he patriot cause was saved time and time again by the patience and resourcefulness of a single man [George Washington]. American successes flowed from governmental and military vigor, and this vigor came from the exercise of power. On the contrary, American difficulties, of which there were myriads, and American reverses flowed from lack of power" (*CP*, 15). Events subsequent to the war, notably Shay's Rebellion, depreciated democracy, because "leaders of the country, rightly or wrongly, felt that they were confronted by a crisis of the first magnitude. Confiscation of property, anarchy, military dictatorship, foreign intervention seemed only just around the corner. The only remedy was to strengthen the central government" (*CP*, 20–21). In sum, it was not the Framers' philosophy that shaped the Constitution but rather their experiences. "To take the Constitution from its historical setting is to fail to comprehend its meaning or that of its separate parts" (*CP*, 22).

Thach's treatise is historicist, not theoretical, and Thach proceeds to discuss executive power during the periods of colonial and state rule. The royal governor was viewed "in much the same relation to the local assemblies as that in which the Stuart kings had been to the Commons," and consequently "[i]n these struggles the popular assemblies were the bulwark of popular liberties, the executive departments the instrumentalities of British control," a fact that profoundly "affect[ed] the original American concept of republican executive power." After Independence, with the exception of New York, state constitutions "included almost every conceivable provision for reducing the executive to a position of complete subordination" (*CP*, 26–28). Thach believes that the example of New York had tremendous influence on the shaping of Article 2, because "all the isolated principles of executive strength in other [state] constitutions were here brought into a new whole. Alone they were of slight importance; gathered together they gain new meaning. And, in addition, we have new elements of strength utilized for the first time on the American continent." New York's influence was seen not only in its constitution but also in its Governor George Clinton, who, "[f]rom the standpoint of executive vigor, . . . could not have been . . . better," since "Clinton was able at the same time to rise to the position of dominating the political life of the whole State, and this despite the fact that he lacked the support of the most influential leaders of the State, such as Schuyler, Hamilton, Jay and Morris" (*CP*, 37, 39). Says Thach, "here was a strictly indigenous and entirely distinctive constitutional system, and, of course, executive department, for the consideration of the Philadelphia delegates" (*CP*, 43).

How the exigencies of Revolutionary War were handled by the Continental Congress is the other step in the evolution of national executive power. It is commonly understood "that this system failed, and failed lamentably." The "causes of the general administrative debacle" pointed to the necessity for three reforms: "personal separation of powers, unitary departmental control and integration" (*CP*, 62). Like New York governor George Clinton, George Washington served as an important counterexample for the Framers: "The example of Washington was a host in itself. Energy, probity, disinterestedness, and a magnificent tactfulness in avoiding even the semblance of advancing his personal interests are written large on almost every one of his official acts." Moreover, "[w]hat was even more important, Washington afforded the country an example of the national leader *par excellence*. In the troubled days that followed peace, thoughts of how his personality had ridden the storm of separatism and failure recurred, with the inevitable conclusion that it was only through the same agency that orderly government could be restored" (*CP*, 65).

Misconceptions exist about Original Intent regarding public administration, says Thach, because "the frequent assertion that administration in the modern sense was not considered as an executive function is incorrect." As he explains, "[t]he impetus for a separate executive so far as national affairs was concerned was furnished primarily by the desire to free Congress from the necessity of concerning itself with the details of administrative business" (*CP*, 73). On this score Thach implicitly is attacking the Progressive critique of the Founding (and perhaps Woodrow Wilson, since he authored a seminal article favoring a "politics-administration" dichotomy, in which the legislature would make policy but not interfere in its implementation by professional administrators).[28] This "modern" view was contrary to what the Framers intended in terms of how the Progressives characterized the men of 1787, but Thach implies that the Progressive critique is more myth than real. The Framers had come to understand the need to separate legislative from executive functions.

In sum, Thach claims that "national experience duplicated the teachings of state experience," insofar as "executive efficiency and responsibility vary inversely in proportion to the size of the executive body; that the power to appoint and remove subordinates is essential to control and responsibility on the part of the real head; that military efficiency is directly dependent on unification of command; and that a legislative body should not concern itself with the details of administration." Unlike the Progressive critique that separation of powers yielded enfeebled government, the counterargument by Thach is that "the principle of separation of powers, as interpreted to mean the exercise of different functions of government by departments officered by entirely different individuals, also seemed insistently demanded as a *sine qua non* of governmental efficiency" (*CP*, 74).

But the problem that remained was that "the tendency in the national field was more towards separation than equality," so Thach turns his attention to how "the new frame of government would settle the matter" of making the executive separate from and not subordinate to the legislature (CP, 75). At the Constitutional Convention, the "most difficult problem to be solved" was "lack of power, not lack of functions," and "[t]he delegates' chief concern was thus to secure an executive strong enough, not one weak enough" (CP, 76–77). Madison was not an architect of Article 2 because to his "contemplative, unassertive mind the executive problem was not particularly attractive," and, moreover, "his ideas on the subject of executive power were no more complete in 1787 than in 1785" (CP, 83). And "the executive of the Constitution is not traceable to Hamilton's recommendations" either (CP, 94). Rather it was James Wilson, the "nationalist of the nationalists," who "conceived the executive as a part of a governmental whole, which, deriving its powers from the general body of the nation, would supplant separatism and reduce the States to a position of practical and legal subordination to the nation." To achieve those ends, Wilson visualized the president as one man, without an advisory council, and directly elected by the people. But, says Thach, "the force of anti-democratic sentiment was too strong," and Wilson retreated from that extremely populist position (CP, 85–86).

Yet Madison was not exactly irrelevant to the outcome, since, on the key issue of presidential election, Madison shifted from his original position favoring legislative selection to declare it "essential . . . that the appointment of the Executive should either be drawn from some source, or held by some tenure, that will give him a free agency with regard to the Legislature. This could not be if he was to be appointed from time to time by the Legislature."[29] Thach claims that the early victories for executive unity and independence were "due to the devoted efforts of a small group of active proponents of executive independence and strength, at whose head stood Wilson and Morris, and their convert, Madison" (CP, 104).

The heart of the presidential article was crafted by three committees, a five-man committee of detail, an eleven-man committee on unfinished business, and a five-man committee on style. On the first was James Wilson, who was charged with drafting the committee report. Wilson's "choice of language, especially as concerns the vesting clause," which vested the "executive power" in the president, "was a matter that might have, and in fact did have, most momentous consequences." Wilson sought to emulate the executive provision of the New York constitution, and Thach contends that "[t]he greatest result of the committee's work was thus the inclusion of one main element of the Wilson executive plan—an independent possession by the executive department of its powers by direct grant of the people."[30]

Thach attributes special significance to a complete organizational plan for the administrative departments that Gouverneur Morris and Charles Pinckney proposed after the committee on detail reported its work. Although their organizational plan was never accepted, Thach reasons that two critically important lessons can be learned from that document. First, the Morris-Pinckney plan "serves strongly to confirm the opinion that the chief magistrate was regarded, by its authors at least, as the active chief of administration. The department heads were certainly conceived as completely subordinate to the chief executive, since they were to be appointable by the President alone and to hold office at his pleasure." Second, the Morris-Pinckney "proposed council is instructive. Executive influence on legislative measures is very generally spoken of as a modern development, entirely unforeseen by the framers of the Constitution, pictured as bound hand and foot by the doctrine of separation. And yet we see that the idea of executive preparation and report of plans of legislation was very much alive" (CP, 122, 124). Here again Thach seeks to correct the excesses of the Progressive critique of the separation of powers, asserting that the Framers did anticipate a legislative leadership role for the president.

The committee on unfinished business was the venue where "the second element of the Wilson plan, namely, choice by an organ independent of the legislature and somewhat approaching popular election, obtained its place in the Constitution." Also important was the final definition of the Senate role, insofar as the committee compromise "confined the participation of the Senate in foreign affairs entirely to treaties. Its control over ambassadors was now placed on the same basis as its control over any other officer, rather than on that of general senatorial control over their field of activity." Therefore, "[s]ince nothing was said concerning the general management of foreign affairs, the way was left clear for its exercise as a normal executive function with results that are well known" (CP, 133–35).

The committee on style, whose membership included Gouverneur Morris, Hamilton, and James Madison, was supposed to arrange the articles agreed to by the convention, but its work was entrusted to Morris. According to Thach, Morris "could do much by leaving the vesting clause as it stood." Thach emphasizes that the clauses that vested authority in the legislative and judicial branches did so by specifying their powers, "[b]ut the executive power was vested in the old way: 'the executive power shall be vested in a President of the United States of America.'" This was probably quite deliberate, as "this phrase was to prove a 'joker.' That it was retained by Morris with full realization of its possibilities the writer [Thach] does not doubt. At any rate, whether intentional or not, it admitted an interpretation of executive power which would give to the President a field of action much wider than that outlined by the enumerated powers" (CP, 138–39). This very issue was manifested in the newspaper debate between *Pacificus* (Hamilton) and *Helvidius* (Madison) over the legality of President Washington's Proclamation of Neutrality in 1793.

Thach says the work of the Founding continued with the first session of the First Congress, for three reasons. First, by its organization of the administrative departments, "it was sitting as a constitutional convention . . . just as certainly as the Convention, *par excellence*, was." Second, Thach points out that eighteen former members of the Convention now sat in Congress. The eight in the House included James Madison, and the ten in the Senate comprised nearly one-half of its membership. Third, "the political environment . . . of this first session of Congress was the same as that of the Convention," because "in 1789 the former delegates to the Convention brought to New York the same political beliefs and political prejudices that they had carried with them from Philadelphia" (CP, 141–42).

The cutting issue for Thach is the presidential removal power, and Madison's position was unambiguous: "He urged strongly the necessity of administrative integration in order to secure full executive responsibility, in words that leave not a shadow of a doubt that he thought of the President as the responsible head of administration" (CP, 146). The floor debate led Thach to conclude that "[t]he majority who opposed joining the Senate in removals were thus as one in considering the President as the head of administration with full power to superintend, direct and control all subordinates." However, they disagreed about the legal basis of that authority, with one group claiming that the Constitution conferred that power on the chief executive and another group arguing that Congress could vest that power where it chose pursuant to the "necessary and proper" clause of Article 1. Thach believes that Madison initially relied "on the legislative grant idea" but ultimately embraced the view that presidential authority flowed from the "executive power" clause of Article 2. In his floor address, Madison admitted, "I have, since the subject was last before the House, examined the constitution with attention, and I acknowledge that it does not perfectly correspond with the ideas I entertained of it from the first glance." That is to say, Madison now reframed the question as "Is the power of displacing an executive power? I conceive that if any power whatsoever is in its nature executive, it is the power of appointing, overseeing, and controlling those who execute the laws." Furthermore: "Should we be authorized, in defiance of that clause in the constitution [vesting executive power in a president] . . . to unite the Senate with the President in the appointment to office? I conceive not. If it is admitted that we should not be authorized to do this, I think it may be disputed whether we have a right to associate them in removing persons from office, the one power being as much of an executive nature as the other" (*CP*, 150–52).

Once again Thach wants to correct misconceptions about Original Intent. Of the eighteen former members of the Convention now in Congress, "[t]he propriety of presidential superintendence and control, the right of the chief executive to act through the instrumentality of agents subject to his choice and direction was the basis of the position of all the twelve who voted for removal by the President alone." Partly for this reason, Thach feels that "enough is included to demonstrate the erroneousness of the commonly accepted explanation that the presidential control over administration is an accidental result of the possession of the power of removal. The exact reverse is the true explanation. The power of removal was rather derived from the general executive power of administrative control. The latter power has not been an extra-constitutional growth. It was the conscious creation of the men who made the Constitution" (*CP*, 158–59).

Turning specifically to foreign affairs, Thach recalls Madison's language that "the Senate is associated with the President by way of exception, and cannot, therefore, claim beyond the exception" to signify that its role was limited only to preventing bad appointments to diplomatic offices. Because the enabling legislation for the Treasury Department authorized the treasury secretary to report directly to Congress, a power not given to the secretary of state, this distinction indicates to Thach that, although the president had general control over his administration, "in the 'presidential' departments [state and partly war] he could determine what should be done, as well as . . . how it should be done." In so doing, Congress "recognized the difference" between Treasury, where "the duties of the secretary were completely defined by law," and State, where "Congress was extremely careful to see to it that their power of organizing the department did not take the form of [Congress] ordering the secretary what he should or should not do."[31]

Although Thach believes that only "few" members of the First Congress "desired that the President possess the unhampered power to make treaties," "it does not follow that these others desired to see the Senate transformed into an executive council." Thach offers this conjecture: "It is this, we believe, that determined the ready acquiescence given by the Senate to presidential negotiation without prior consultation. Had Washington chosen to make the issue sooner, there can be little doubt that he would have succeeded in maintaining his position" (CP, 164).

In his summary of what the removal debate portended for presidential leadership, Thach endorses the position "that the executive is not limited to the enumerated powers, and that the vesting clause is a grant of power." Nonetheless, "[e]xecutive power is under a definite restriction, even if the vesting clause be considered a grant, and one of a severe character. The national government is one of restricted powers. The President may do nothing that the national government may not do. But where, by the terms of the Constitution, the national government is vested with control over a certain sphere of action, that portion of the field is the President's which is executive in character" (CP, 165).

Conclusion

Does presidential power derive from the prerogatives of office or from the incumbent? To the degree that prerogative power may be conceptualized as constitutionally undefined authority, though sometimes implied by explicit constitutional language or the logic of separated powers, William Howard Taft held an expansive view: the veto was not limited to questions of constitutionality; the removal power, like the appointive power, is traced back to Original Intent; presidents can engage in warlike actions without a declaration; being the sole representative of the nation in foreign affairs affords the president wide discretion; and executive privilege has grounding in the separation-of-powers doctrine. Nothing here would dissociate Taft from Theodore Roosevelt, despite their unlike conceptualizations of prerogative power. What did distinguish Taft was his argument that TR was no Lincoln, despite Roosevelt's claims that he was. Lincoln never asserted the power to do anything—including the "unlawful" seizure of private property—on such fragile grounds as that nothing in statute law or in the Constitution prevented him from doing so. Taft counters that Lincoln traced all his actions to some constitutional mandate.

Coolidge seemingly agrees with Taft that presidential authority is pursuant to the Constitution and the law. As such, executive power is vested in his office; but with respect to its reach, Coolidge rejects both Taft and Roosevelt and aligns himself with President Jefferson's acquiring the Louisiana Purchase. To Taft and Roosevelt, Coolidge would say that constitutional questions are better tested when actual issues arise. However, Coolidge parts company with Jefferson over Jefferson's attempt to impeach the chief justice, which threatened judicial independence.

Thach argues that presidential power flowed from popular sovereignty, and again he ridicules any notion that Original Intent was transformed by modernity. "It is somewhat remarkable, indeed, that the electoral procedure set up by the Constitution should so soon have been regarded as the equivalent of popular election, that the position of the President as the one, great national representative should have been so readily accepted. But neither the one idea nor the other is a modern innovation. Both were inherent parts of [James] Wilson's concept" (*CP*, 167–68). If Thach had any normative purpose for writing his dissertation, it was to demonstrate that the separation-of-powers system was designed to liberate the executive from the legislature so that governing efficiency could be ensured. Thach completely debunks the notion that the Framers were guided by abstract theories in crafting Article 2. "The dogma of separation of powers and that of checks and balances . . . conditioned political thought, as did their interpretations, or rather misinterpretations, of the British constitutional system. But, it is submitted, they were not the determining influences. Otherwise, their teachings would not have meant one thing in 1776, another in 1787." "Indeed, the doctrine of separation fared far harder at the hands of the Convention than one would suppose from the continual appeals made to it." Thach continues, "The truth is that the Fathers used the theorists as sources from which to draw arguments rather than specific conclusions. The chief problem of distribution of functions and organization of government was to get a sufficiently strong executive" (*CP*, 169, 171).

Because the president was an independent agent, his power hinted of prerogative power. "As to the influence of the British prerogative powers on the American concept of the content of executive power . . . little objection can be made. The theoretical powers of the British Crown were, and remain, a very exhaustive catalogue. No executive power could well have been given that was not contained therein. We have seen that in the Senate debate on removal these powers were extolled as properly being executive, but, after all, it was the selective process which . . . was the important thing. The executive obtained those powers which the legislature was found unfit to possess" (*CP*, 173).

Does presidential influence depend upon the force of personality, rhetorical leadership, or partisanship? Political party is important to both ex-presidents. Taft and Coolidge visualize the president as the guardian of the public well-being. For Taft, this point related to reining in congressional budget extravagances; for Coolidge, Congress too often spoke for organized minority interests. Writing during a time of unified government—and the split between GOP conservatives and Progressives had eased considerably —Coolidge embraced party government, whereas Taft did so only after he left office. Coolidge sees the president as head of government and head of party, and he gave a sterling defense of responsible partyism as representative of popular mandates. Taft points to his successor—Wilson—to illustrate how, following an election, a party controlling the executive and legislative branches can govern effectively.

On the final page of his manuscript, Thach points out that the fullest potential of this unique American creation depends upon the force of personality. He takes note that "the history of the presidency reveals it as operating to a great degree as James Wilson envisaged it." True,

> [w]eak men have occupied the office without the ability to support its great responsibility. But there have always come into office at critical times men who would utilize its powers fearlessly, independently, and with a full acceptance of responsibility, striving each to be the 'man of the people,' to serve as a mouthpiece for the national will, to be the guardian of those great national interests intrusted to him, the conduct of war, maybe, the management of foreign affairs, the honest conduct of administrative business. These men have kept the original spirit of the Constitution alive. (CP, 177)

It takes no poetic license to understand that Thach believes that the "spirit" of the Constitution of 1787 was more than compatible with robust presidential leadership.

Does presidential leadership depend upon historical context, or is regime-building manifested through political, institutional, and constitutional developments? It goes without saying that the writings of Taft and Thach, if not those of Coolidge, were deeply influenced by their times. Taft was engaged explicitly in a debate with Theodore Roosevelt, the arch Progressive, and Thach was so engaged also, implicitly. Taft defended the separation of powers, saying the system was workable so long as cooperation colored the relationship of the two branches in their assigned areas. Where deadlock threatened, public opinion should intervene to bring about a spirit of teamwork.

Does presidential leadership vary between domestic and foreign affairs? Coolidge also believes that the separation of powers is adequate to safeguard the "welfare" of the country and, moreover, that the independent workings of the House and Senate caused most of his domestic program to become law without their "subserviency" to the president. The issue of presidential leadership focused on domestic policy more than foreign affairs; the latter caused no serious disagreement between Taft and Roosevelt.

Does the president actively or passively engage the legislative process and promote a policy agenda? Coolidge justified social lobbying of members of Congress at the White House and even resorted to popular appeals to spur congressional action. But he gives compelling reasons against making "going public" a routine strategy for presidential leadership of Congress. Taft sees no legal grounding for legislative leadership other than recommending action through presidential messages. However, he praises Wilson for delivering the Annual Address to Congress in person, explaining why that precedent-setting action would not have been well received had he done so himself. Taft also recommends a formal role for the cabinet in the legislative process, which, following the example of Alexander Hamilton, would allow those officials to discuss bills on the floor of Congress.

Similar thinking must have inspired Thach's assessment that "[e]ven with respect to the President's positive power to initiate legislation, there is no reason to believe that the same liberal interpretations were not held by many. Washington exercised, without objection, not only the right to recommend legislation in his annual message, but to recommend special measures, accompanying them with detailed reports." It is noteworthy that, at this point, Thach footnotes his opinion by saying that "[i]t is difficult to refrain from the conclusion that the influence of Washington on legislation was not greater than that of most subsequent presidents" (*CP*, 172). Taft also endorses the indirect Washington-Hamilton approach, to the point of endorsing cabinet access to the House and Senate floors in order to propose bills and engage in debate.

Does the organization of the executive branch service presidential leadership? Thach gives strong signals that the Framers wanted the chief executive to be the master of his administration, armed with explicit appointment and implicit removal powers and an expansive vesting clause. Administrative oversight is grounded in presidential prerogative, and administrative personnel are judged to be wholly subordinate to the chief executive. Moreover, the Revolutionary War taught the Framers that the executive should not be bound by any advisory council, excepting the Senate role in treaty-making. By the twentieth century, federal spending was sufficiently large that Taft recommends budgetary reforms, primarily to curb Congress and presumably to make government more efficient. Coolidge mentions how Jefferson opposed bureaucracy, but he says that we have come to quote Jefferson without following his philosophy of government. In other words, there is a hint in Taft and Coolidge that the big government may be becoming a problem for the chief executive, not simply a resource at his beck and call.

The most important lesson of this chapter is that Thach mounts a three-pronged attack on the modern criticism of the Founding by the Progressives (see chapter 4). First, and most important, the separation of powers was not designed to enfeeble government but to empower the executive. This point needs to be broadcast throughout political science. Second, and related, it is abundantly clear from the records of the Constitutional Convention, and from the arguments of those Framers who sat in the First Congress, including James Madison, that Congress was not supposed to meddle in administration: that was the sole responsibility of the chief executive. Third, the Framers intended that the president be involved in lawmaking, from setting the legislative agenda to acting in ways to secure the passage of the administration's program. The practice of George Washington was to exercise legislative leadership through the treasury secretary, so we do not presume that the sum totality of "modern" presidential leadership vis-à-vis Congress can be traced back to eighteenth-century practices. But the Jeffersonians surely got the message wrong when they repudiated the Washington-Hamilton precedents in favor of party-based leadership.

CHAPTER SIX

Sowing the Seeds of Progressivism
Liberalism and the Rise of the Heroic Presidency

The heroic or idealized presidency was a romanticized view promoted by liberal academics who were deeply inspired by the example of Franklin D. Roosevelt. Yet this interpretation was flawed from the beginning, because these scholars generally failed to distinguish between the domestic "crisis" that FDR faced and the relatively "normal" political times of his successors. Despite the political trauma of the Civil War and the presidential "dictatorship" spawned under Lincoln, scholars reflexively understand that Lincoln's rule was exceptional and not the norm for nineteenth-century presidents. No such nuance prevented the 1940s–60s generation of presidency watchers from idealizing each and every aspect of FDR's rule as the harbinger of modernity, the ideal by which all presidents should be judged. FDR cast a large spell over those academics, and we discuss their works, beginning with the British political scientist Harold Laski (1940), then the iconoclastic Herman Finer (1960), the highly regarded Clinton Rossiter (1956), James MacGregor Burns (1965), and Richard Neustadt, who made a truly seminal statement on presidential power (1960).

All these writers championed strong presidential leadership and discounted the potential of the constitutional regime, yet they veered in two directions with respect to one key point. Some emphasized party as the vehicle for presidential leadership and cabinet government along the British model, and others focused on the personal qualities needed for heroic leadership. Laski, Burns, and especially Finer exemplify the first approach; Neustadt and, to a lesser degree, Rossiter illustrate the second. The roots of this reinterpretation are found in Wilson's 1908 reassessment of presidential leadership (see chapter 4), but the intellectual community did not coalesce around this normative standard until they witnessed FDR in action.

Harold Laski and Class Politics

The first glimpse of things to come can be found in a 1940 book by Harold Laski of the London School of Economics and Political Science.[1] Laski acknowledges his intellectual debt to Charles Beard, the American historian, but surely Laski was more than a match for Beard's class interpretation of political life. Predictably, Laski is especially impressed with Roosevelt, who fought for the working classes and ended the legacy of weak executives who served to protect the "forces of privilege" in America: "America needs strong government; it needs strong leadership to attain strong government; only the president . . . can provide it with the leadership it requires. But against these needs must be set all the traditional impetus of the system. The Constitution makes against it partly by its separation of powers and partly by the way in which it has distributed functions between the states and the federation. It has now become of pivotal interest to the forces of privilege in the United States to maintain for their benefit both that separation and that distribution" (API, 243–44).

Also the weak U.S. party system had to be invigorated, because "the strong leadership America requires" will not be forthcoming "until the conflict between parties" is rationalized between the interests of labor and those of "giant capitalism" as manifested in "a realignment of parties into conservative and progressive" (API, 244, 245, 251). The New Deal is the "logical development" from Wilson's New Freedom, Progressivism, Populism, and, going further back, even Shay's Rebellion, since all "were rooted in the effort of the ordinary man to get more from the common stock of welfare than he conceived himself to be getting, in the strong belief that he was morally entitled to more" (API, 249–50). Reform is "inescapable," and reform "means the positive state" with its potent implications for the presidency. Beyond realigning party politics at the national level, the parties will have "to centralize their leadership"; "[c]entralization of leadership means, inevitably, a greater concentration of power in the president's hands," portending a presidential relationship to his party "far more like that of the British prime minister to his party than at any previous time" (API, 250–51).

Laski takes issue with Lord Bryce (see chapter 3), saying that eleven presidents "have been extraordinary men," however we may view their performance in office (API, 8). Yet there were many weak presidents following Lincoln and again after Wilson, for three reasons: (1) the president "is at no point the master of the legislature," and thus he "can initiate" but "cannot control" policy; (2) strong executives disturb business confidence, which is why "business men have always been alarmed" when the likes of a Jackson, a Wilson, or the two Roosevelts take office; and (3) "suspicion" of strong executives relates to their election as "a popular revolt . . . against the business man's dominating influence upon the exercise of political power"

(*API*, 12–15). Given the emergence of a vast American working class, Progressive "leadership can come from the president alone," since he is the "only person" charged with thinking "in terms of the whole Union," though there is no guarantee that he will have an accurate "conception of his duty" (*API*, 16, 20).

The solitary executive was a fatal flaw of the Founding. To combine the roles of ceremonial head, legislative leader, executive, and foreign policy leader in addition to his representation of the whole nation and of his own party calls "upon the energies of a single man unsurpassed by the exigencies of any other political office in the world" (*API*, 26). At base, the president's "real power is in the popular support he can rally," which means that somebody with a "common touch" should be recruited and, to establish the popular connection, the electoral college ought to be abolished in favor of election by direct popular vote and the tradition of two terms be abandoned (*API*, 35–36).

What our presidential candidates lack is not political experience per se but the "art" of handling Congress; in a familiar theme of parliamentarians, Laski observes that an English or French prime minister "will have served a long apprenticeship in the legislative assembly before obtaining the supreme office." One "decisive" test that the American system passes is its ability to recruit able presidents during the five crises that we faced (1789, 1800, 1861, 1914, and 1933). This is no accident, says Laski, but rather the consequence of a "national recognition that energy and direction are required, and the man chosen is the party response to that recognition" (*API*, 47, 53).

In sum, unlike the English prime minister, the president can never "be the master" of his legislative party, because he cannot threaten dissolution. The president is also obstructed by a Supreme Court that rarely departs from its "historic function" as "guardian of the rights of property," a judicial legacy that Laski traces to Federalist chief justice John Marshall (*API*, 61). Nor are the burdens of office eased by the cabinet, because "the American cabinet hardly corresponds to the classic idea of a cabinet to which representative government in Europe has accustomed us" (*API*, 70). Here Laski catalogs the usual list of political deficiencies: the cabinet lacks prestige, is not a ladder to high political office, has no collective responsibility, may have less advisory importance than an informal "kitchen cabinet" or congressional and party leaders, and lacks requisite expertise or experience in the affairs of state. The superiority of the British model leads Laski to ponder one reform then in vogue, namely that the cabinet be allowed to sit and speak on the floor of Congress. Laski harbors doubts about the wisdom of this idea, because cabinet officers may be overly "responsive to its [Congress's] will," and thus executive authority may ultimately reside "in the cabinet rather than in the president" (API, 109–10).

Turning to Congress, Laski says "the president . . . must envy the legislative position of a British prime minister," because, with the exception of an emergency, the president is "never the master" of Congress (API, 111–12). Laski's indictment of Congress has been heard again and again: that the Framers intended Congress not to be subservient to the executive, that its members are expected to serve their localities, and that Congress's prestige depends on its opposing presidential leadership. Both "incoherency and irresponsibility" result because legislation "is not unified" as would be the case when "derive[d] from a single mind" (API, 116), nor can voters allocate blame, given the diverse influences on the legislative process. The White House gains leverage over Congress "only when it would be fatal" for Congress to resist: during wartime or emergencies like 1933, or when "there may be a public opinion so widespread in favor of the presidential policy that the Congress finds it unwise to follow its own bent" (API, 121).

What political levers—other than crisis—may bring about unity of purpose between the executive and legislative branches? Laski's answer: majority party control, the "honeymoon period," political patronage, the veto (though its impact is problematic without an item veto), but mainly public opinion—the "real source" of presidential power (API, 138–47). What was lost on later scholars in the heroic tradition is Laski's critical distinction between "crisis" and "normal" conditions. The power that flows to a president during emergencies is dissipated by America's normal preference for weak government and the "negative state," which raises questions about whether fundamental economic reform can be achieved. The real test "by which the relationship between the president and Congress must be judged," says Laski, is "its ability to prevent the outbreak of emergency." "At the least, there are grounds for grave doubt" whether the American regime can "meet this test successfully" (API, 165).

Laski is more flattering about our handling of foreign relations, compared to England's way: "If no democratic people has yet satisfactorily solved the problem of its control of foreign relations, it can at least be said that nowhere has a more careful effort been made toward that end than in the United States." The Senate is unrivaled in the world "in its influence," by virtue of its ability to "scrutinize every step of the executive, and, in large degree, to control its outcome" (API, 166–67). The president is the "chief architect" of foreign affairs because of "the range of his initiative," which encompasses choosing (or dismissing) his "chief collaborators," including the secretary of state; unlimited discretion in the recognition of new governments; dispatching special agents abroad; "undefined" power to enter into compacts without Senate participation; treaty negotiations; policy formulation; and authority as commander in chief of the armed forces (*API*, 168–71).

In foreign affairs, the political system poses no obstacle. Says Laski: "In no other part of American political life has the separation of powers counted for so little as in the definition of this part." On treaty-making, however, Laski ponders the lessons of Wilson's failed Peace of Versailles (for which Wilson is ascribed much blame), but on balance, the Senate role in foreign affairs is more salutary than the "tragically subordinate position" of the House of Commons vis-à-vis "secret diplomacy" by the prime minister (*API*, 182, 191). Later Laski makes explicit reference to "the sacrifice of Czecho-Slovakia at Munich in 1938" as illustrating the "grave danger" that would befall the United States absent a Senate control on an "executive altogether" foreign policy (*API*, 200–201).

These early Laski themes became commonplace in the orthodoxy of Liberalism: a strong president at the helm of government, who holds power by leading the majority party, within a two-party system where liberals dominate over conservatives. Laski's affection for "responsible partyism" was endorsed a decade later (in 1950) by the Committee on Political Parties of the American Political Science Association.[2]

Herman Finer and Collective Government

Since the late nineteenth century, seemingly every generation has yielded some notable advocate of parliamentary government. Among the past devotees were Woodrow Wilson, Henry Clay Lockwood, Henry Jones Ford, and Harold Laski. In 1960 this intellectual love affair was manifested in the work of Herman Finer, a comparative politics professor at the University of Chicago. Finer argues that our political regime has to be redesigned as a necessary corrective to heroic presidents: "The transfixture of one man, one mortal, with the titanic authority and torturing responsibilities of the President constitutes the vital flaw in the government of the United States in the twentieth century."[3] After presenting his litany of domestic problems and international threats (notably the Russians) that confront the United States, Finer proceeds to "[a] serious, but *not* the most serious, fault of

American government . . . the separation of powers, and this, chiefly, between the legislature and the President." Beyond that, "Congress has many deficiencies to appall us . . . But the gravest problem of America's government is the inadequacy of the President, any President; all the more so because the office itself is not remedied and is not to be remedied by its auxiliary, Congress, which itself is debilitated and scarcely able to maintain a fumbling grasp on its own concerns."[4]

Finer's other basic indictment is that "[t]he vital interests of America are intrusted to the character of one man alone and made almost exclusively dependent on his intelligence, nerves, conscience, and beliefs." This causes Finer to part company with "the reformers" who, "[b]ereft of hope of congressional reform," thus "have concentrated on the Presidency. Their ideas in this respect have taken two directions—to add to the responsibilities of the President . . . and, second, to give him the assistance he needs—virtually, to overcome his solitary role, as established by the Constitution." In what must have been a moment of hyperbole, Finer asserts that the president "has a power on his own initiative to make decisions, to indulge choices, and to order action surpassing anything granted the British prime minister, a Stalin, or a Khrushchev," because an English prime minister has to consult a cabinet and parliament, and a Soviet premier needed support from a majority of the Soviet Presidium.[5]

Finer's "indispensable solution" spares little. He proposes a "President and a cabinet of eleven Vice-Presidents," all "elected on the same ticket every four years," without term limits and on a platform where "the President, House, and Senate would be more bound than now within their own political parties." To be eligible for nomination as president or any vice presidency, "the candidate must be presently a member of the House of Representatives or the Senate or must have served at least four years in either house." Finer intends to achieve a collective executive recruited from the legislative branch. Once in office, "[a]t the President's discretion, but only when supported by a majority of his cabinet, the presidential-cabinet may resign. Following this, elections for the House, the Senate, and the presidential-cabinet would take place, the term of office being four years." This was akin to a prime minister's getting a "vote of no confidence" in a parliamentary body, as Finer explains: "They [president and cabinet] cannot be forced to resign by a vote of no confidence from Congress, but, manifestly, a series of defeats of their measures, after all attempts to arrive at acceptable compromises . . . will make resignation the only course. They then make known their intention to resign. Certainly they will not do so early and often, having spent a lifetime to reach high office. And Congress will not be capricious, destructive, or malicious in refusing to support the President and his cabinet."[6]

Clinton Rossiter and Presidential Roles

In a complete change of pace from Herman Finer, Clinton Rossiter penned a work based on a series of six Walgreen Foundation lectures given at the University of Chicago. True to the heroic school, no superlatives were too excessive for Rossiter. He begins by calling the American presidency "one of the few truly successful institutions created by men in their endless quest for the blessings of free government." He admits his "own feeling of veneration, if not exactly reverence, for the authority and dignity of the Presidency" (*AP*, 15–16).[7] Best known for his analysis of presidential "roles," Rossiter discusses five as "strictly constitutional burden[s]" (chief of state, chief executive, commander in chief, chief diplomat, chief legislator) and five additional roles "piled on top of the original load" (chief of party, voice of the people, protector of the peace, manager of prosperity, world leader). Collectively the "burden of these ten functions is monstrous," as the presidency is "a one-man job in the Constitution and in the minds of the people," concludes Rossiter (*AP*, 30, 42–43).

However, Rossiter, unlike Laski and Finer, repudiates the English parliamentary model and defends the Framers, who preferred "imperfect safety to perfect efficiency," something that led later generations to suspect "that they wrought more shrewdly than they knew in separating the executive and legislative powers" (*AP*, 45). Here Rossiter also parts company with the Progressives, who bemoaned, and contemporary liberals like Burns, who criticized, separated powers. Rossiter has no fears that the presidential potential is "a matrix for dictatorship," because "the American system simply would not permit it." But he admits that a president can do "serious damage, if not irreparable injury, to the ideals and methods of American democracy" (*AP*, 46–47).

But that prospect is curbed by various "brakes" placed on presidential leadership, by Congress, arguably by the Supreme Court (though the Court has done more "to expand than to contract" presidential authority [*AP*, 58]), by a federal bureaucracy that can "hobble a crusading President," by the opposition party acting as a "roadblock" and his own party acting as "a drag," by federalism, by our free enterprise economy, by foreign leaders, and lastly (the "most effective check") by the "opinions of the people" as mobilized by pressure groups (AP, 61, 63, 68). But ultimately, the "checks that hold the President in line are internal rather than external." "His conscience and training, his sense of history and desire to be judged well by it, his awareness of the need to pace himself lest he collapse under the burden" curb his excesses (AP, 70). Rossiter concludes this discussion with perhaps the most grandiose (and myopic) statement of faith in the president, calling him "a kind of magnificent lion who can roam widely and do great deeds so long as he does not try to break loose from his broad reservation." The "final definition" of a "strong and successful" president is "one who knows just how far he can go in the direction he wants to go," and therefore, "[t]he power of the Presidency moves as a mighty host only *with* the grain of liberty and morality" (AP, 73).

Rossiter's vision was hardly tempered by his account of Lincoln during the early Civil War. Lincoln was, says Rossiter, "a democrat as well as a 'dictator,'" who "went to the well of power in behalf of humanity and rededicated the Presidency to the cause of liberty" (AP, 101).[8] In his final chapter Rossiter covers his political flank by reaffirming that he is not saying that "'strength' in the Presidency is to be equated with 'goodness' and 'greatness,'" because a "strong President is a bad President . . . unless his means are constitutional and his ends democratic, unless he acts in ways that are fair, dignified, and familiar, and pursues policies to which a 'persistent and undoubted' majority of the people has given support" (AP, 257).

In his prognosis, Rossiter takes note of "the gap between responsibility and authority, between promise and performance," which is most glaring in public administration but also appears in a legislative leader where a president's "tools of persuasion . . . are not one bit sharper than they were forty years ago." Thus he sees "a widening gap between what the people expect and what he can produce" (AP, 246, 249–50). This refinement is a minor caveat to Rossiter's firm commitment to presidential leadership.

One essential dimension puts Rossiter squarely within the heroic tradition—his devoting separate chapters to the "historical" and the "modern" presidents, beginning with FDR. The presidency today, observes Rossiter, has "much the same general outlines as it had in 1789" but "a hundred times magnified" (AP, 81). Why so? Because the president "cuts deeply into the powers of Congress," "is more heavily involved in making national policy," has been transformed "into a democratic office," and now has "a kind of prestige" unknown even under George Washington. In sum, Rossiter grandly concludes that "the outstanding feature of American constitutional development has been the growth of the power and prestige of the

Presidency." As to what precipitated this transformation, Rossiter cites five developments: the positive state, America's rise as a world power, domestic and foreign emergencies, the "long decline of Congress," and "the one giant force" (here he cites Henry Jones Ford; see chapter 4) of "the rise of American democracy" (AP, 82–83, 84–88).

But personality also matters. Rossiter considers eight presidents "major" figures (Washington, Jefferson, Jackson, Lincoln, Theodore and Franklin Roosevelt, Wilson, and Truman) and believes that six more had "credit-able" performances (Cleveland, Polk, Eisenhower, Hayes, John Adams, Andrew Johnson). Especially telling is Rossiter's assessment of Eisenhower, whom he ranks well below FDR and also below Truman, based on these eight criteria: "In what sort of times did he live?" "If the times were great, how bravely and imaginatively did he bear the burden of extraordinary responsibility?" "What was his philosophy of presidential power?" "What sort of technician was he?" "What men did he call on for help?" "What manner of man was he beneath the trappings of office?" "What was his influence on the Presidency?" "Finally, what was his influence on history?" By these standards FDR's impact was almost unprecedented, "fixed firmly in the hierarchy of great Presidents," slightly above Jackson and Wilson but below Washington and Lincoln, who "had his own rendezvous with his-tory, and history will be kind to him."[9] Truman was more uneven: there were, for example, his excellent appointments in foreign-military affairs but his partisan mediocrities in domestic affairs, though ultimately Rossiter judges that Truman "will eventually win a place as President along-side Jefferson and Theodore Roosevelt" (AP, 159).

On Eisenhower, Rossiter confesses "to a downward shift of opinion be-tween the first [1956] and second [1960] editions of this book." He now believes Eisenhower will be "left outside the magic circle of presidential greatness," for a number of reasons. His "times were certainly less exacting" than Roosevelt's or Truman's, and Eisenhower—as a self-proclaimed "mod-erate conservative"—was "an earth-smoother rather than an earth-shaker," who "never really put his heart in the attempt" (AP, 159–61). On the crisis of racial integration in the South, Eisenhower abdicated "moral and politi-cal leadership," was successful in foreign affairs "thanks largely" to his secretary of state, and "never did measure up to the lofty expectations" of the American people (AP, 163, 165). Nor was he "much more determined a leader of the administration"; and Eisenhower was singularly unsuccessful "in exchanging this [electoral] popularity for the hard currency of influ-ence" (AP, 165–66).

Moreover, his was a "modest conception of the authority" of the office, being "committed to the Whig theory" of executive-legislative relations. Managerially, Eisenhower "came much closer" than Roosevelt or Truman "to becoming a prisoner in his own overorganized house," one where Chief of Staff Sherman Adams "ruled" "as an autocrat" and "seemed to know the workings of the Presidency far better than" did Eisenhower (AP, 168–69). As to Eisenhower's cabinet, he "will not be especially remembered for the talents he assembled about him" (AP, 171). By 1957, Rossiter prophesies that "we had our fill of moderate conservatism" as the "times had begun to run ahead of our will and imagination, and they called for a leader who would rouse us from the lethargy of 'fat-dripping prosperity' and point out the hard road we would have to travel into a demanding future" (AP, 176).

In sum, Rossiter boldly "predict[s] that the historians of a century hence" will rank Eisenhower outside the first eight, even the first ten, presidents. "He was a good President, but far from a great one" (AP, 178). However, the historians chose not to wait that long before rushing to a historical judgment. In 1962 Arthur Schlesinger Sr. published his second poll on presidential greatness (the first was in 1948), and Eisenhower—having left office less than two years earlier—was tied (with Chester Arthur) for twenty-first and judged no better than "average" as compared to third-ranked FDR ("great") and eighth-ranked Truman (with Polk, a "near great").[10]

James MacGregor Burns's Typology

First published in 1965, Burns's view of "presidential government" fully develops his conception of executive leadership based on three models: Madisonian, Hamiltonian, and Jeffersonian.[11] Burns recollects that he came to understand that President Kennedy "was showing what could be done with the federal government without reforming it. As Chief Executive and Chief of State he was leading the executive branch with such vigor and style and imagination that in a sense he was 'tuning high' the whole national government, just as Alexander Hamilton had once done." That is, "in Kennedy's case it seemed to me a more directed and determined effort than it had been with most earlier Presidents, for as a student of American history and politics he well knew the alternatives." A very interesting perspective about a president who could point to few substantive accomplishments in domestic policy and a couple of blunders in foreign affairs. Yet Kennedy's "third model" (Hamiltonianism) gives Burns pause, because it poses "the great practical problem of the Presidency and the theoretical problem of this book." Here we show how Burns acknowledges Hamiltonianism, though he is disinclined to abandon Jeffersonianism as his ideal type.[12]

Going back to the Founding, Burns claims that "[p]erhaps the greatest concession the [constitutional] convention made to Hamilton in the final document was to leave executive power and organization rather undefined," which meant that "[c]learly the executive office would take its shape largely from the men who first manned it."[13] Burns mentions the "vital precedents" set by the Washington administration. "His [Hamilton's] legislative strategy was quite simple: to intervene in the framing of bills at the start and at the finish and all the way in between." Burns asserts that Hamilton, who wanted "the power to frame the great programs that would dominate legislative strategy in Congress," "unofficially filled" the role of floor leader and altered the "balance of legislative power between the President and Congress." Yet "there were more important precedents that he did set, for use by later Presidents if they so wished," primarily in foreign policy. Here Hamilton "was moving much more with the thrust of the Constitution" when he urged President Washington to exercise "sole discretion in the reception of envoys and hence in the recognition of nations," to refuse the House request "for papers relating to the negotiation of the Jay Treaty," to issue a proclamation of neutrality "on his own discretion." He endorsed Washington's having "never again collaborated directly with the Senate in the treaty-forming process" after the failed attempt on a proposed Indian treaty. As to war-making, Burns wrongly alleges that "there had never been much question of the clear primacy of the executive," and he points to the Whiskey Rebellion as giving "Hamilton the chance to laud the force and vigor that could be forthcoming only from the President."[14]

Burns approvingly invokes Edward Corwin, to whom he attributes the argument that "[t]he modern theory of presidential power . . . is the contribution primarily of Alexander Hamilton."[15] This ends Burns's accolades for Hamilton. "[T]he more one studies Hamilton's role, the more he appears the utter opportunist seeking any tolerable means of gaining the policies he favored," although Hamilton "failed to relate its means and its instrumental ends to broader, more ultimate goals—and this leads us straight to the great failing of the Hamiltonian model."[16]

In today's vernacular, Hamilton lacked vision or, more precisely, an egalitarian vision. Hamilton "did not have a central vision of ultimate goals; he did not have a single, universal, organizing principle in terms of which elitist politics and his developmental economics took on continuing meaning for the American people." He was not like Thomas Jefferson, who "had one supreme value, a monistic vision if you will . . . [of] a simple faith in the people—in all the people, in the living people, in the present generation, in the right of one generation to change the arrangements of a previous one, in the superior right of a majority over a minority simply because a majority embraced more people than a minority. Above all, he believed in liberty and equality."[17] In sum, Burns argues that Jeffersonianism is best for the nation:

> If the Hamiltonian model implied a federal government revolving around the Presidency, and depending on energy, resourcefulness, inventiveness, and a ruthless pragmatism in the executive office, and if the Madisonian model implied a prudent, less daring and active government, one that was balanced between the legislative and executive forces and powers, the Jeffersonian model was almost revolutionary, implying government by majority rule, under strong presidential leadership, with a highly competitive two-party system and with a more popular, democratic, and egalitarian impetus than the Madisonian. The Hamiltonian model was perhaps a more resourceful and flexible kind of government, the Madisonian more stable and prudent, and the Jeffersonian more democratic and potentially more powerful.[18]

Richard E. Neustadt and Presidential Influence

The publication of *Presidential Power* in 1960 made Richard E. Neustadt a household name—indeed an icon—among presidential scholars.[19] Virtually every work of scholarship on the presidency pays homage to his seminal view of presidential power as "influence" or persuasion. Clearly Neustadt rises above his peers as an authoritative figure, a living legend who also lived the opportunity to update his original treatise and address his critics. Less than one-half of his 1990 edition of 371 pages contains the 1960 original, at 163 pages. Our task, beyond offering a summary of his original, is to show where and why Neustadt felt obliged to make intellectual concessions to his critics.

Once an idealist, always an idealist; in 1990 Neustadt gave no ground with respect to his fundamental thesis. Neustadt "persist[s] in the belief expressed in earlier editions of this book—namely that pursuit of presidential power, rightly understood, constitutionally conditioned, looking ahead, serves purposes far broader than a President's satisfaction. It is good for the country as well as for him. The President who maximizes his prospective influence within the system helps to energize it in the process. He will enhance as well the prospect that the policies he chooses can be rendered viable: enactable, administrable, with staying power" (*PP*, xix).

Within a decade of its publication, Neustadt's thesis was characterized as the "statecraft" approach to presidential leadership.[20] Neustadt was well received because, apart from the novelty of his interpretation, his views were more compatible with (1) the ideological advocacy of presidential leadership by liberals and Democrats and (2) the unfolding behavioral revolution—itself a broadside attack on the historical, legalistic, and institutional framework of scholars like Corwin. By 1969 *Presidential Power* had "come to be regarded as one of the few truly significant statements about the American presidency" and was "well on its way toward becoming a classic of modern political science." These are the words of Peter W. Sperlich, whose critical essay was meant "to contribute to a critical understanding of Neustadt's propositions." Sperlich hoped also to "stimulate the long overdue serious examination and testing of a very important work."[21]

Neustadt, a political scientist at Columbia University, served as a White House aide under President Truman. His "statecraft" approach to White House politics was Machiavellian, because *Presidential Power* was essentially a "manual," "advising the President how best to employ those powers he already possesses," rather than a guidebook for policy action.[22] According to Paletz, four cornerstones of the Neustadt thesis are that (1) the president "has overwhelming responsibilities"; yet (2) "his powers are conspicuously limited"; (3) the "views and actions of the occupant are vital"; (4) thus, presidents like "Franklin D. Roosevelt with an activist conception of the office are infinitely preferable to passive occupants like Dwight D. Eisenhower."[23]

There is a beauty of simplicity in Neustadt's original thesis: the pillars of presidential power (or influence) are the president's "reputation" with the Washington establishment, his "prestige" (or popularity) with the American people, and the formal resources that give him leverage when bargaining with significant political others. Neustadt pointedly denies that formal status—authority—alone can transform a president from his traditional "clerkship" duties to robust leadership, because *"the probabilities of power do not derive from the literary theory of the Constitution"* (*PP*, 37). Because decisions are not self-executing, a president needs the cooperation of other political actors to achieve his ends.

To prove that direct commands do not work, Neustadt uses three case studies: Truman's firing of General Douglas MacArthur, his seizure of the steel mills during the Korean War, and Eisenhower's deploying troops to desegregate Little Rock High School. Only under five exceptional circumstances might commands produce compliance: (1) the president directly issues an order, (2) his meaning is clear, (3) the order is highly publicized, (4) the president has the ability to execute his order, and (5) "what he wants is his by right," meaning that it is buttressed by simple legitimacy or, better yet, by "some specific grant of constitutional authority." Yet Neustadt's three episodes "stand out precisely" not only because "[w]hat they represent is relatively rare" but, more to the point, because each of the three orders "was a painful last resort, a forced response to the exhaustion of all other remedies, suggestive less of mastery than failure—the failure of attempts to gain an end by softer means."[24]

Command is inadequate because of the structure of American government. The Constitutional Convention was "supposed to have created a government of 'separated powers.' It did nothing of the sort." After this comment Neustadt states what arguably has become his most quotable quote: "Rather, it created a government of separated institutions *sharing* powers" (PP, 29). As such, the political system necessitates bargaining, and the president must cope with the separated system on its terms. The task for presidential governing is nicely encapsulated in one brief paragraph:

> The power to persuade is the power to bargain. Status and authority yield bargaining advantages. But in a government of "separated institutions sharing powers," they yield them to all sides. With the array of vantage points at his disposal, a President may be far more persuasive than his logic or his charm could make him. But outcomes are not guaranteed by his advantages. There remain the counter pressures those whom he would influence can bring to bear on him from vantage points at their disposal. Command has limited utility; persuasion becomes give-and-take. It is well that the White House holds the vantage points it does. In such a business any President may need them all—and more. (PP, 32)

In other words, his formal position gives the president a supreme "vantage point" because other political actors need his authority, and thus he is empowered to engage in bargaining with them. "The essence of a President's persuasive task, with congressmen and everybody else, is to induce them to believe that what he wants of them is what their own appraisal of their own responsibilities requires them to do in their interest, not his" (PP, 40).

Neustadt has in mind primarily the Washington establishment, which raises a tactical question about whether any president needs to deal with the legislature solely on bargaining terms. No quid-pro-quo is necessary where shared values are involved, says Sperlich, who countered "that many presidential requests are acted upon without bargaining and without commanding." Attempts at presidential influence "based on appeals to duty, pride, role-conception, ideology, conscience, interpersonal identification," and the like "are notoriously non-reciprocal," because the "influence attempt appeals to internalized values" of other political actors.[25]

Yet Sperlich caused Neustadt to add this caveat in his revision. As a positive force within the separated system, loyalty cannot replace bargaining; but "if loyalty cannot manage to move mountains it certainly can produce catastrophic side effects," as Watergate showed. Thus Neustadt says his "critics were right for the wrong reasons." Because Chief of Staff H. R. Haldeman had been so loyal to Nixon, Nixon "felt he should reciprocate loyalty received," and so he remained supportive for too long, at his own peril (*PP*, 191). However, Sperlich was less concerned about moving mountains than motivating Congress, whereas Neustadt—then and now—chose not to discuss executive-legislative dynamics, "lest I alter this book's character," since it "never was and is not now a comprehensive commentary on the literature" (*PP*, xxvii). For this reason, Sperlich's criticism that bargaining is "instrumental persuasion," whereas appealing to "internalized values" is "symbolic persuasion," identifies a critical, missing link in Neustadt's argument.[26]

There is only one reference to Corwin in the 1960 original, but it is especially telling. After prognosticating about the 1960s and four policy "areas of controversy," Neustadt suggests "an evident necessity for government more energetic, policies more viable, than we have been enjoying in the fifties." All this calls for White House expertise. An expert "does not guarantee effective policy, but lacking such an expert every hope is placed in doubt." "The responses of our system remain markedly dependent on the person of the President. 'As matters have stood,' Edward Corwin writes, '. . . presidential power has been at times dangerously *personalized*,' and with unerring instinct for an expertise in influence he distrusts Franklin Roosevelt almost as much as Abraham Lincoln. But if one wants effective policy from the American system, danger does not lie in our dependence on a man; it lies in our capacity to make ourselves depend upon a man who is inexpert" (*PP*, 161–62).

The backlash against Johnson and Nixon influenced Neustadt. In his subsequent edition, Neustadt identifies various developments that affect the presidency, two of which are directly related to Vietnam.[27] One involves the breakdown of bipartisan consultation during times of emergency. So impressed was Neustadt with earlier advisory networks "that I took it for a time to be the sign of a new check" on presidential war-making. "In 1970, however, Nixon proved me wrong, as Arthur Schlesinger [his *Imperial Presidency*; see chapter 7] noted more tactfully than I deserve." The second involves "the continuation of hostilities once forces are engaged without a declaration of war," where both Johnson and Nixon can be faulted. Yet Neustadt seems incapable of openly admitting to a war-making prerogative even though he discounts the War Powers Resolution, because "[w]hat the resolution puts beyond dispute is that he [the president] does possess precisely the initiative asserted by Truman and Nixon" (*PP*, 195–97).

Given Corwin's preference for Eisenhower, Neustadt's view of Eisenhower is implicitly directed to Corwin as well. If only one person—the president—can be attuned to his own "power stakes" in every matter of "choice," such personalized politics cannot be delegated to anybody, his cabinet and closest advisers included. That is why human qualities loom so large for Neustadt. In a retrospective nearly two decades after his original appeared, Neustadt recalls "two widely quoted, singularly unhelpful generalizations: 'The Presidency is no place for amateurs' and needs 'experienced politicians of extraordinary temperament.'" Therefore he had urged recruiting presidents with "a sense of purpose, a feel for power, and a source of confidence," but "[a]fter Johnson and Nixon, experienced both and beyond doubt extraordinary, I no longer can leave it at that!" (*PP*, 203). Whereupon Neustadt acknowledges the insights of George Reedy and James David Barber (see chapter 8) and concurs with them to this extent: "The simple lesson, then, is to beware the insecure." As a remedy to presidential paranoia, Neustadt adds two qualifications: first that "enjoyment of the job, and on it, and an ease in it, together with enjoyment of one's self, seem of the essence" and, second, that we look to the president's "previous employment" and episodes that are most analogous to the presidential experience, because "the nearer the comparisons the more suggestive" they will be about his temperament for the highest office (*PP*, 207–8).

If fundamental personality flaws afflicted Johnson and Nixon, how does Neustadt go about explaining the ill-fated presidency of Jimmy Carter? He applies four criteria in judging the thirty-ninth president. It was not a "physical" burden that Carter faced, nor was the "moral and emotional" burden of "mutual nuclear risks" much different than it had been since Eisenhower. Intellectually, the 1970s were arguably more confusing than the 1960s, but hardly more so than the travail of the 1930s. The fourth presidential burden is "operational," more "mundane" but perhaps more revealing than the others insofar as it invites Neustadt to ask if Carter had the "capacity to cope." Neustadt's guarded judgment was "Yes . . . maybe" (*PP*, 230–32).

Most basic to evaluating Carter, says Neustadt, were the escalating standards being applied to him by press commentators and congressional critics. Here we get a taste of what would become a major theme of contemporary scholarship (see chapter 10)—the expectations gap. "Washingtonians, like less attentive publics, tend to project onto the Presidency expectations far exceeding anyone's assured capacity to carry through" (*PP*, 234). In what would become a mainstay of Carter revisionism (see chapter 8), Neustadt identifies "four trends that seem to complicate the job of being President and [which] give Carter's defenders sorely needed ammunition." First, there are decentralizing forces within Congress, such as weaker parties and stronger subcommittees. Second, there are more fragmentation and less coherence within the executive branch, despite the growth of federal responsibilities. Third, there is a proliferation of organized interests and notably single-issue groups. Fourth, there is a "rise of professional staff" in Washington and in states and localities which engage the policy process through issue networks (*PP*, 234–37).

President Carter "suffered from the very scale, diversity, complexity of his initial legislative program," which, in many respects, "required implementation by executives outside the government, in places where the President's authority was weakest," namely the private sector and foreign leaders. Also Carter "ran afoul" of "transition hazards" associated with "newness *in* office" and "newness *to* it," unlike what had befallen other newly elected administrations. This consideration prompts Neustadt to compare two earlier post-inaugural glitches: Kennedy's ill-fated Bay of Pigs invasion of Cuba and the Bert Lance affair (a banker-friend whom Carter appointed OMB director despite conflicts of interest). It is not just that Kennedy quickly learned to cut his political losses, unlike Carter, but the expansion of television coverage assured that Carter's mistakes would be "subject[ed] to the swiftest public punishment in reputation or prestige or both. Presumably these same conditions will confront Carter's successors" (*PP*, 238–39, 254). At base, Neustadt's assessment of Carter is a precursor to the revisionist studies published later that decade (see chapter 8).

Two years after Neustadt published his 1980 update, Fred Greenstein authored a widely praised book of Eisenhower revisionism, which later caused Neustadt to partially reassess his original view of Ike (see chapter

10). At one level, Eisenhower had to gain ground in light of the liberal assault on Johnson and Nixon. In terms of personality, Neustadt puts Eisenhower in the company of FDR, Truman, JFK, and even Ford, because none of them were so "driven, so surrounded, or so self-indulgent in the small as LBJ and RMN" (*PP*, 204). But FDR remains Neustadt's preferred model, despite a few lapses (e.g., the court-packing debacle, which, Neustadt said, fueled the "conservative coalition" in Congress), with JFK ranked second (despite the Bay of Pigs and, as Neustadt notes, the devastating potential risk to his power from Kennedy's sexual escapades in the White House). As late as 1980, Neustadt still criticized the first-term Eisenhower for his staffing and managerial style, "[y]et by the time of the 'new Eisenhower,' late in his second term—personalities smoothed down, or out, Adams and Dulles departed, the survivors grown accustomed to each other and to him—Eisenhower's White House, although differing in form and size, became in substance much more personal, more nearly like a Democrat's. It fitted him more closely than before. By then, of course, his time was running out" (*PP*, 223). So Ike learned the error of his ways, but too slowly.

It is curious that Neustadt in 1960 chose not to evaluate Eisenhower as commander in chief, given that military prowess was Ike's unique forte. By 1990 Neustadt does shift gears. In his final chapter ("Two Cases of Self-Help"), he favorably compares Eisenhower's wise decision not to send U.S. troops to rescue the French at Diem Bien Phu with Kennedy's magnificent performance during the Cuban Missile Crisis. For Eisenhower, "[i]t casts a somewhat different light on his Presidency than does the characterization" given in the 1960 original. Neustadt's defense was ignorance, that this 1954 episode "would have been another perfect illustration for me had I known enough about it then," but he did not, and now does, and "happily redress[es] the lack" (*PP*, 295).

The details of Diem Bien Phu show that Eisenhower did so much right that Neustadt wonders "who advised him to be so self-protective?" No advisers can make that claim, and most likely it was Eisenhower who "drew those considerations out of his own head." Neustadt exclaims: "Is this the 'stranger still to politics and power' I described . . . as of 1959? Hardly! Not in 1954, not fifteen months before his heart attack; not on issues so directly linked to his accustomed interests and experience." In other words, we now learn that Eisenhower was a master of military strategy who knew firsthand the world leaders involved in this quagmire in French Indochina. Yet Eisenhower "still puzzles me on these scores," and Neustadt speculates that "[p]erhaps the illnesses of 1955 and 1957 cost him crucial margins of time and strength." So Neustadt is not wholly convinced by Greenstein, although "in 1954, no sickness yet in sight, Eisenhower offered us a model of how present choices could be turned to the account of future influence by somebody equipped to serve as his own expert on the subject" (*PP*, 300–302).

On Ronald Reagan, Neustadt may be prophetic about revisionist trends. The cases of Diem Bien Phu and the Cuban Missile Crisis illustrate "modern Presidents who thought hard and effectively about prospective power stakes in present acts of choice—especially the stakes of congressional and public standing." Based on those positive lessons, Neustadt asks "[w]hat distinguishes these two from Reagan in the Iran-Contra case?" (*PP*, 308–9). Admittedly, Iran-Contra was not Reagan's finest hour, yet Neustadt does not view that sorry episode as the standard for judgment. Here Neustadt makes several telling points that draw parallels between Ronald Reagan and Franklin D. Roosevelt as being exceptional among the "modern" presidents.

In four respects Reagan's "conduct of office was a compelling commentary on the argument" that Neustadt puts forward. First, if FDR begins the modern presidency, then "Reagan was the last Roosevelt Democrat we shall see as President." Reagan "restored the public image of the office to a fair . . . approximation of its Rooseveltian mold: a place of popularity, influence, and initiative, a source of programmatic and symbolic leadership, both pacesetter and tonesetter, the nation's voice to both the world and us, and—like or hate the policies—a presence many of us loved to see as Chief of State." Second, as the "first President to have been professionally trained as an actor and a televised spokesman," Reagan "opens an era, as well as closing one. This is to be underscored and watched." Third, Reagan "seems to have combined less intellectual curiosity, less interest in detail, than any President at least since Calvin Coolidge . . . with more initial and sustained commitments, more convictions independent of events or evidence, than any President at least since Woodrow Wilson championed the League." This combination Neustadt finds "unique," and it "framed Reagan's operating style and seemingly accounted for his impacts on the course of public policy," which. "[i]n anybody's reckoning" were "substantial." Fourth, the downside is that "this peculiar combination exaggerated every risk to which a President is heir by virtue of imperfect information," meaning of course Iran-Contra. "Save for that, our business schools and others now might be extolling Reagan's clean-desk management, and its mythology might have bedeviled presidential studies for years to come." For Neustadt, Iran-Contra "is indeed a classic case" of what *Presidential Power* argued throughout, that a president "has nothing he himself . . . can bring to bear on his prospects for effective future influence save present choices. And there is no one he can count on but himself to help him gauge the prospects, choice by choice" (*PP*, 269–71).

Neustadt much prefers presidents who are "more skeptical than trustful, more curious than committed, more nearly Roosevelts than Reagans." He also decries "Reagan's tone" ("heard by all too many as 'enrich your-selves'"), but in the end he gives Reagan his due (*PP*, 316–17). Says Neu-stadt, Iran-Contra "dominates this chapter in a way it will not dominate his history. For Reagan recovered from it. Indeed, the recovery is a success story, which I regret I lack the space to tell. The prior story gets the space instead because it illustrates so neatly my whole argument, from first to last. Whatever else he did, Reagan offered up a perfect illustration, and I mean to make the most of it. But let no one believe I think it tantamount to the entire record of his Presidency; it wasn't" (*PP*, 279).

Conclusion

Of these five authors, Finer seems the outlier by being less well known and more rarely quoted than Neustadt, Rossiter, Burns, or Laski. Perhaps it was his outlandish call for eleven vice presidents or his full embrace of parlia-mentary government that made him a minority of one among presidency scholars. Yet something else may have contributed to his smaller stature: his calling into question one hallmark quality of heroic leadership. Finer argued that the burdens are too great for any one man—thus the need for collective government. Collective government was essentially a repudia-tion of what those committed to the Rooseveltian model believed.

Does presidential power derive from the prerogatives of office or from the incumbent? The fundamental purpose of *Presidential Power* was to dis-parage command-and-control. Neustadt argued that prerogative powers are inadequate even in national security policy. His position on this issue is extreme, since Burns, Laski, Rossiter, and especially Finer tie presidential authority to foreign affairs. On prerogative, Burns seems closest to Neu-stadt, since even foreign affairs involve constraints that require political ingenuity. Says Burns: "The seeming paradox of the President's sweeping formal powers over foreign policy and the actual restrictions on him can be resolved in part if we distinguish once again between his powers of management and his capacity for innovation and leadership."[28] A more decisive answer comes from Laski, who argued that in foreign affairs presidential prerogative overcomes the separation of powers, but not in domestic policymaking, where the president must resort to an array of political resources.

Rossiter mimics Corwin in his understanding of executive "primacy" in foreign affairs: "Yet the growth of presidential authority in this area seems to have been almost inevitable . . . Constitution, laws, custom, the practice of other nations, and the logic of history have combined to place the President in a dominant position. Secrecy, dispatch, unity, continuity, and access to information—the ingredients of successful diplomacy—are properties of his office, and Congress . . . possesses none of them" (*AP*, 26). Command is one of the twelve "qualities of political leadership" listed by Finer, and—apart from being "an order"—command "might function more effectively . . . through persuasion and argument," insofar as "behind presidential persuasion looms his [the president's] vested authority—he plays his role with the influence of his constitutional status bearing down on the minds of other men." The coming of nuclear deterrents so strengthened presidential prerogative that Finer is fearful that "Congress cannot assert control even if, in the age of the H-bomb, he commit the nation to perdition!"[29]

Does presidential influence depend upon the force of personality, rhetorical leadership, or partisanship? Burns acknowledges Hamiltonianism in *Presidential Government* but persists in arguing that Jeffersonianism is the ideal model for presidential leadership, because responsible party is more reliable than executive energy. For Laski, since the working class holds the moral high ground and because separated powers serve to defend business interests, he regards leadership of public opinion to be the most important source of presidential power. Personalized power through persuasion is the linchpin of presidential power, argues Neustadt, whereas Rossiter inventories the range of political resources.

Does presidential leadership depend upon historical context, or is regime-building manifested through political, institutional, and constitutional developments? It goes without saying that Franklin D. Roosevelt enjoys heroic stature in the eyes of these scholars. FDR is the standard by which Eisenhower's stature is reduced. In a larger sense, however, this literature is a rejection of gradual constitutional development, because, politically speaking, something new is afoot: class upheaval for Laski, party politics for Burns, nuclear holocaust for Finer, role multiplication for Rossiter, the institutionalized presidency for all. Fred Greenstein may have written the intellectual rationale for labeling FDR the first "modern" president (see chapter 10), but that viewpoint was implicit in all these books.

Does presidential leadership vary between domestic and foreign affairs? Both domestic policy and foreign affairs influenced these authors, but in varying proportions. For Herman Finer, a comparative government expert, internationalism and the horrors of the nuclear age colored his analysis of the presidential office. Although Rossiter also mentioned the moral burden accompanying the threat of nuclear warfare, and Neustadt did so in his later revisions, the cold war and its ominous potentialities did not hit home as forcefully with them as with Finer. Burns was mainly concerned with domestic politics and legislative-executive relations, and Laski focused on the class-driven politics of the Depression era.

Does the president actively or passively engage the legislative process and promote a policy agenda? If legislative leadership was a hallmark of the New Deal (and modernity), it is odd that Richard Neustadt gave it so little coverage. Burns, Rossiter, Laski, and even Finer all give attention to the chief legislator. This omission by Neustadt makes it difficult to fully test his hypothesis—power as influence—with respect to the 535 members of Congress, as the critic Peter Sperlich implied. Legislative-executive relations are important to Burns's understanding of the Madisonian, Hamiltonian, and Jeffersonian models of presidential leadership.

Does the organization of the executive branch service presidential leadership? This question on the administrative presidency is now highly relevant, since FDR established the Executive Office of the President (EOP) in 1939. Writing in 1940, Laski could not comment on the actual operations of the EOP, though he was aware of the Brownlow Committee. Although Laski celebrated the collective responsibility of the British cabinet, he said little about administration other than to recommend a "secretariat"—but not along the lines of Brownlow's opinion that White House staffers have a "passion for anonymity." Says Laski, a dictatorship can afford "the *eminence grise,*" but in a democracy "the more we know of the men who actually assist in the shaping of policy, the more honest that policy is likely to be." His secretariat would consist of a body of personal secretaries to the president. It would lighten the presidential load by "act[ing] as a liaison between the president and the departments, between the president and the legislature, and, to some extent at least, between the president, the press, and the public" (*API*, 261, 263).

Two decades later Rossiter claims that the "most notable development" in the presidency was the "change in structure rather than a growth of power," namely the EOP. He says the institutionalized presidency "is here to stay" and has "momentous administrative significance" by converting the presidency "into an instrument of twentieth-century government" (*AP*, 127, 134). Looking to the future, Rossiter sees a problem. "The real problem of the Executive Office is potential rather than actual: the danger that the President might be buried under his own machinery. The institutionalization of the Presidency could be carried so far that the man who occupies it would become a prisoner in his own house, a victim of too much and too rigid organization." To prevent that, there is "an outer limit beyond which it would be unwise to expand" the EOP. It "must be big enough to make it possible for the President to supervise the administration, but not so big that he has trouble supervising it" (*AP*, 243–44).

James MacGregor Burns discounts both Edward Corwin and C. Perry Patterson (see chapter 7), saying they were biased against big government. But he took more seriously the concerns voiced by Finer, Rexford Tugwell (see chapter 8), and Charles S. Hyneman that one man faced excessive burdens. Hyneman had recommended a central council of administrators and legislators to formulate and implement the presidential program.[30] For Burns, the administrative process involved the president, his staffers, the EOP, and certain administrators as "central decision makers." It included other "policy makers throughout the executive branch somewhat less dependent on the President and more responsive to congressional, clientele, ideological and other forces," whom Burns calls "exterior decision makers," and finally the "bureaucratic decision makers" responsible for "directing the more routine, settled, and specialized operations" of government. All these relationships are dynamic, although decision-makers further removed from the Oval Office will enjoy more administrative discretion. In other words, Burns does not presume any presidential chain of command. Moreover, he also "conclude[d] that more centralized control has not meant more 'one-man' control of the executive branch. The real danger . . . is just the reverse—whether we have created such an institutionalized Presidency that the President will be smothered by the machinery, whether he will lose the vitality, independence and inventiveness necessary for creative leadership."[31]

Neustadt, according to Burns, had "taken a far more confident view of the effectiveness and responsibility of the President" than other presidency scholars, including Rossiter.[32] We agree, in the sense that Neustadt seemingly believed that persuasion would enable a president to influence bureaucratic subordinates, like anybody else, and that persuasion was essential because command-and-control usually was inadequate (even for Commander-in-Chief Truman). Institutionalization helps the clerkship president, but "[h]elping a President perform his chores is a far cry from helping him see personal stakes in his own acts of choice" (*PP*, 128). In the vital matter of personalized power, relying on staff is counterproductive, because "[e]xposure to details of operation and of policy provides the frame of reference for details of information. To be effective as his own director of intelligence, a President need be his own executive assistant" (*PP*, 130).

Roosevelt was the master of his own political fate because his "technique for information-gathering was competition" (here Neustadt references Schlesinger), which was "literally the opposite" of how Eisenhower operated. Eisenhower personified the burdensome side of organization, and political science had to wait until 1982 for Greenstein to set the record straight (see chapter 10). According to Neustadt, "Eisenhower often was reported . . . to have transformed the White House into an Army Headquarters. That he did not do—nobody could—but he did manage to impart more superficial symmetry and order to his flow of information and of choices than was ever done before. Thereby, he became typically the last man in his office to know tangible details and the last to come to grips with acts of choice" (*PP*, 133). Without belaboring this myth, with a political amateur like Eisenhower at the helm of government, the administrative presidency hurts more than it helps leadership.

Going beyond the Brownlow Committee's declaration that the chief executive "needs help," Finer says he "needs rescue" but dissents from Brownlow by arguing that "[i]nstitutionalization has proved, overwhelmingly, to be an impasse—or worse, an added avalanche under which to bury the President." On this score Finer is a close second to Neustadt in his Eisenhower-bashing, a major complaint being that authority lodged in unelected White House staffers (namely Chief of Staff Sherman Adams) means that the nation "has a right to ask, Who is governing us? Who is responsible?"[33] Finer, like Laski, gives the common litany of reasons why the president's cabinet is much inferior to the English cabinet, which has collective responsibility; Finer additionally favors a British-style "permanent body of senior civil servants," as recommended by the 1955 Hoover Commission. But Finer has doubts about institutional reforms, because "[w]ith the constitutional authority vested in one man alone, the government remains and must remain a mere assemblage of virtually separate policy-making bodies and policy-executing agencies."[34]

In other words, Finer offers a full-fledged criticism of the institutionalized presidency as disabling accountability without enabling policy coordination. Perhaps the liberal Herman Finer, had he enjoyed more intellectual currency at the time, could have breached the divide with constitutionalists like Edward Corwin and cultivated more respect for collective governance. Corwin also favored institutional reform to harmonize executive-legislative relations, as will be shown in chapter 7 on the anti-aggrandizement scholars.

CHAPTER SEVEN

Anti-Aggrandizement Scholars
Attacking Liberal Government and Liberal Presidents

Three decades ago an essay by David Paletz categorized the writings of Edward S. Corwin, C. Perry Patterson, and Alfred de Grazia as representing the "anti-aggrandizement" viewpoint of "[c]onstitutionalists who put their faith in the balance and separation of powers" and thus "look with dismay at the increased powers and importance of the presidency. They might agree that the United States faces many difficult problems, but they scarcely consider this sufficient reason sanguinely to increase the number and nature of presidential roles, or to enhance presidential power—particularly at the expense of Congress."[1] The best way to refute Paletz's judgment of Edward Corwin, which is also Neustadt's (see chapter 6), is to begin this discussion with the strident views of Patterson and de Grazia as points of contrast to Corwin.

C. Perry Patterson

The grand indictment of presidential government by C. Perry Patterson was published seven years after the first edition (1940) of Corwin. Patterson's thesis is that "we have changed our constitutional democracy into a political democracy. By this is meant that we have converted a limited into an unlimited democracy and, thereby, substituted an unwritten for a written constitution and a government of laws for a government of men. This means that the principles of the American Revolution, as the foundation of our constitutional system, have been destroyed and that we have returned to the principles of the British system."[2] Because the "effects of the party system" resulted in "the establishment of the political hegemony of the President," the political corrective requires that American parties be made accountable through a modified form of responsible cabinet government: "If the party system has secured control of the Constitution, then the party system should be responsible to the American people through their representatives in the Congress. If party control has superceded constitutional control of the government and unless the American people control the

132

party system, they will have both an unlimited and irresponsible government. Our problem now is to make an unlimited government responsible." Thus, argues Patterson, "responsible cabinet government is the best possible means in the absence of constitutional restraint to prevent the permanent establishment of irresponsible executive government in this country in the hands of one man."[3]

The essentials of his indictment can be easily summarized. Patterson believes "the literary theory of the Constitution" has been overthrown by the Supreme Court, whose rulings have allowed "a fairly consistent nationalistic interpretation of the powers of the national government."[4] Although those powers originally flowed to Congress, ultimately they came to reside in the executive branch. "*Congressional supremacy, therefore, is only the means of presidential supremacy.* As head of the nation, head of his party, mouthpiece of the American people, and political executive of the Government of the Day, he [the president] is in position to govern the nation. Whether he does or not is not a fault of the system but a matter of the personal capacity of the President." Patterson reminds us that "[t]he history of tyranny is primarily a record of executive despotism which has generally taken place at the expense of legislative and judicial agencies either by their coercion or by their abolition."[5] His following chapters assess the president as "constitutional executive" and the "royal character" of his powers, his roles as party leader, political executive, and chief administrator, and his domination "over the judiciary."

Patterson observes that, beginning with Wilson, recommending messages to Congress now "includes the power to recommend drafted bills and to insist that they be enacted immediately into law without change," just as the status of the veto "has changed from that of merely a constitutional check upon Congress to a positive and controlling agency of legislation." Treaty-making he considers to have been "pre-eminently a legislative power" until Washington paved the way for presidential domination of the negotiating process. And because the war powers are "most extensive and absolute and may be used in times of either peace or war," Patterson ominously concludes: "Is it comforting to say that it is true that the President is a dictator, but thanks to the Supreme Court, he is a 'constitutional dictator'?"[6]

The "royal character" of presidential powers is tied to presidential supremacy, which resulted from national unity, congressional supremacy, growth of government, shifting "from *laissez faire* to a planned economy" and "a negative state into a positive state," and the rise "of a few major [world] powers." All of this leads Patterson to believe that the United States in 1947 was "about where the English were in 1688" in terms of the relationship of the executive to the legislature. Take note that here Patterson recalls that "[t]his problem and its solution" have been "graphically and powerfully impressed though conservatively stated" by Edwin Corwin.[7]

The evolution of party government transformed Original Intent, because "[t]he unity of the constitutional and political executive . . . was not . . . even anticipated by its framers. The President envisaged by the Constitution is an exclusively constitutional agent, a nonpartisan adviser of the Congress. He was expected to be a Whig king, and in no sense was he to be the product of the instrument of politics." But party government evolved as an "extraconstitutional system of government" insofar as (1) "an unwritten constitution of a strictly national character" has converted (2) "the personnel of all units of our government system into partisans" who control "the constitutional machinery of our system," such that (3) the president is "its political executive," with new powers adding "additional force to his own constitutional powers and giving him a large measure of control" over Congress and the judiciary.[8]

To show how incumbents have acted as political executives, Patterson focuses on Hamiltonianism—a president possesses "all executive power inherent in the nation subject only to the limitations of the Constitution"— as being "the theory of presidential powers" held by both Roosevelts and Wilson and "sustained by the Supreme Court" in its ruling that the removal power is inherently presidential (*Myers v. United States*, 1926). At base, "A highly regulated and socialistic type of society forces centralization and requires an executive type of government for its administration. It cannot be operated on any other basis. Under present arrangements the President must be not merely the constitutional but the political head of the government."[9]

One point where Corwin is decidedly "conservative" compared with Patterson involves the presidential reach "over the judiciary" (his choice of words). FDR's attempt to "pack" the Supreme Court was only a difference in degree from the way his predecessors, since Washington, tried to shape jurisprudence through their appointments. Says Patterson, "My thesis is that while the court is over the Constitution, the President is over the court. I am not trying to justify either the court or the President. I am giving only such a running account of the decisions of the court as is necessary to show that the constitutional theory of the Presidents who appointed the majority of the court is, in the main, upheld by the court." Patterson minces no words, submitting "that our new constitutionalism dangerously concentrates too much power in the hands of one man, regardless of who the man may be. It is dangerous because no man can exercise this power in person. The most of it must be delegated to subordinates whom he is unable to supervise. This power finally gets so far away from the President that it becomes irresponsible."[10]

To achieve a "readjustment" of executive-legislative relations, Patterson recommends his cabinet-style government. Unlike our situation, "in Great Britain the executive is plural and collectively responsible to Parliament while in the United States the executive is singular and irresponsible."[11] Not only have we "made a political executive out of a single individual and have failed to make him responsible to the representatives of the people either as legislators or partisans," but "[b]y virtue of his fixed term of office and his independence of Congress he can never be made a responsible executive."[12] Thus a responsible presidential government requires accountability to the legislative branch, and congressional leaders must guide responsible partyism, not the president. Unlike those Progressives-Liberals who yearned for parliamentary government to empower our president vis-à-vis Congress, Patterson is the only constitutionalist we will encounter who looks abroad for guidance on how to restrain presidential power.

Toward that grand objective, Patterson urges the adoption of an elaborate new kind of extraconstitutional parliamentary-style cabinet. A "prime minister" would be selected by a caucus of the majority party of both houses, being most likely a member of the House, and he in turn would choose the other members of the cabinet with approval by the party caucus. Both House and Senate would be under the leadership of the cabinet, whose members would initiate legislation on both floors of Congress that relates to their own departmental jurisdiction (the legislative cabinet would have two members for each department, one per chamber, though formally the departments still would be managed by a presidential appointee subject to Senate confirmation). Since the party majority is responsive to the cabinet, which interacts with the president in formulating a legislative program, in fact the White House would have to accommodate the cabinet, since it is accountable to the rank and file of the majority party. It makes no sense for the president ever to veto legislation, and should the majority either of the House or the Senate refuse to enact a program recommended by the legislative cabinet (this would be extremely rare), then the cabinet leaders from that chamber would have to step down and allow the opposition party to install its own leaders within the cabinet. The

House-Senate cabinet, therefore, might be comprised of one party or both parties—a coalition—depending upon which party holds the majority support in each of the two chambers.

All of this can be implemented by Congress internally, but unlike the existing cabinet, this new agency "would be responsible to the Congress for its advice in that it would fall if its policies were not approved." It ultimately would achieve Patterson's goal: "By this connecting link between the President and the Congress, by means of a political executive responsible to the Congress, the best efforts of the President and the Congress, in both legislation and administration, can be obtained by thoroughly democratic and responsible processes. An able and strong cabinet is provided with collective responsibility subject to the advice of the President and the control of the Congress in both legislation and administration."[13]

Alfred de Grazia

The thesis developed by Alfred de Grazia, coming in 1965 at the high-water mark of the Great Society, is that "the executive of the national government represents and leads the national movement towards a society of order. Congress . . . expresses the national urge to liberty. The Executive Force is winning and . . . [t]he congressional or Republican Force . . . is weakening."[14] What he calls the "dogmas of the responsible political party" have "sparked the movement of the Executive Force in this century," dating back to Wilson. De Grazia is a dissenter, because he "considers the great danger that the [responsible] political party will be the means by which the government is converted from a republic into an executive bureaucracy."[15]

The "myth" of the president as "a single heroic leader" defies the "collectivity of his behavior" (meaning the institutionalized presidency), insofar as the Constitution provided for a president, not "explicitly for the presidency" and surely not "for an all-seeing all-doing executive." The "President is 'liberal' by the nature of his office and the character of his constituency" and "is alleged to have a pipeline to the great people that he in fact does not have." Challenging the liberalism of academia, de Grazia doubts that the president can be the tribune of the people, and to call him the "custodian of the public interest or of the national interest is presumptuous," because he "is custodian of a public interest, his own, and that may be popular or not, shared by Congress or not."[16] When de Grazia speaks of the "problem of dictatorship," he is citing the growth of the executive apparatus. That is to say, "there is a dictator only because the bureaucratic state must have a face."[17]

The civil service is viewed by de Grazia as "the great engine of the Executive Force," not Congress, because "Congress . . . is an institution deeply imbedded in federalism, the free enterprise system, and decentralization of society and politics. It represents basically these values." Congress becomes an accomplice, however, to the degree that, when "the Executive Force does triumph" and presidential partisans take control, eventually "the Republican Force in Congress will wither away and be replaced by a weak but 'satisfactory' representation of the Executive Force."[18]

Concerning both the "ends" and the "means" of government, Alfred de Grazia is a conservative. His values concerning what government should and should not be doing are explicit, and he much prefers congressional to executive policymaking. He is not troubled (as was James MacGregor Burns; see chapter 1) about "oligarchy and seniority" wielding disproportionate influence within the legislative process, because *"Congress operates principally through the decision system of successive majorities."* By that, de Grazia means that different majorities rule in subcommittees, committees, and the floors of each house of Congress. And here de Grazia echoes Wilmoore Kendall (though he does not cite Kendall; see chapter 1): "A rich variety of representational forces filters through the system of successive majorities. Neither the presidency, nor the civil service, nor the pressure groups, nor the courts, nor the political party, nor the press could individually or all together duplicate the process and provide the same 'product mix.' "[19]

Edward S. Corwin

Corwin wrote his seminal work on the presidency in 1940 (the fourth edition was published in 1957) as "a study in American public law," focusing on the "development and contemporary status of presidential power and of the presidential office under the Constitution" (*POP*, vii).[20] The Constitution and legal developments lie at the heart of Corwin's analysis of presidential power. He scrupulously details the constitutional language and interpretations of presidents and courts over time. It was this emphasis on constitutionalism that caused Richard Neustadt to author his *Presidential Power* as essentially a rebuttal to Corwin (see chapter 6).

Corwin organizes his volume in terms of presidential "roles" and, within each, analyzes the legal foundations of the president's power as administrative chief, chief executive, organ of foreign relations, commander in chief, and legislative leader. According to Corwin, "the history of the presidency is a history of aggrandizement, but the story is a highly discontinuous one. Of the thirty-three individuals who have filled the office not more than one in three has contributed to the development of its powers; under other incumbents things have either stood still or gone backward." So the force of personality matters in shaping the presidency: "Precedents established by a forceful or politically successful personality in the office are available to less gifted successors, and permanently so because of the difficulty with which the Constitution is amended" (*POP*, 29–30).

Corwin regularly argues that the Constitution endows the president with prerogative powers—which often are validated by Supreme Court rulings. Because he is the administrative chief, the *"duty to 'take care that the laws be faithfully executed' thus becomes the equivalent of the duty and power to execute them himself according to his own construction of them."* President Jackson's removal of Treasury Secretary Duane was "constitutionally ordained," based on *"his power and duty to control all his subordinates in all their official actions of public consequence"* (*POP*, 84). Similarly, Corwin conceptualizes a far-reaching doctrine of executive privilege that can withstand congressional investigation (*POP*, 116). These examples, but especially the war-making prerogative, led historian Arthur Schlesinger Jr. to label Corwin an advocate of "high prerogative" in *The Imperial Presidency* (see chapter 8).

In law enforcement, Corwin argues that the Lockean maxim that "the legislature may not delegate its power" means, in actuality, "that the legislature may not *abdicate* its powers." That line is preserved by use of the legislative veto, opines Corwin, with which Congress can render "the delegated powers recoverable without the consent" of the president (*POP*, 122, 130). After reviewing the use of military power in domestic law enforcement, martial law during insurrection, and emergency powers, Corwin gives a broad reading of Lockean prerogative. Locke saw prerogative "as limited to wartime, or even to situations of great urgency." For Corwin, "[i]t was sufficient if the 'public good' might be advanced by its exercise" (labeled *stewardship theory* by Theodore Roosevelt). Therefore Corwin takes issue with William Howard Taft, who denied Roosevelt's claim (see chapter 5), and he retorts that "the 'Stewardship Theory' has been proved by events to have been prophetic of developments" in the field of industrial relations, beginning with TR's intervention in the anthracite coal strike of 1902 (*POP*, 147–48, 153).

In foreign affairs, the constitutional grants of power to both popular branches constitute, in words Corwin made famous, "an invitation to struggle for the privilege of directing American foreign policy," although the president holds "certain great advantages" in terms of unity, secrecy, dispatch, and information. The precedents established by George Washington with respect to the president as the "sole organ" for conducting diplomacy, his recognition of foreign governments, the denial of any "advice" along with "consent" by the Senate in treaty-making, and his use of "personal" diplomatic agents led Corwin to conclude that Hamiltonianism has prevailed. Says Corwin: "The President today is not only the organ of communication of the United States with foreign governments—he is the *only* organ thereof; as such he is entitled to shape the foreign policies of the United States so far as he is actually able to do so within the conditions imposed by the acts of Congress; and more often than not Congress chooses to follow the leadership that his conspicuous advantages of position serve to confer on him" (*POP*, 225–26).

On war-making, Corwin sounds a cautionary note. The commander in chief is discussed in the context of "total" war—Civil War, World War I, World War II—which affects domestic life as much as military strategy and thus requires the president to rally the entire resources of the nation behind the war effort. Corwin agrees that the Framers viewed this clause as bestowing "nothing more than the supreme command and direction of the military and naval forces, as first General and Admiral of the Confederacy." The monumental change he attributes to Lincoln: "The sudden emergence of the 'Commander-in-Chief' clause as one of the most highly charged provisions of the Constitution occurred almost overnight in consequence of Lincoln's wedding it to the clause that makes it the duty of the President 'to take care that the laws be faithfully executed.' From these two clauses thus united Lincoln proceeded to derive what he termed the 'war power,' to justify the series of extraordinary measures that he took in the interval between the fall of Fort Sumter and the convening of Congress in special session on July 4, 1861" (*POP*, 228–29).

Neither President Wilson nor President Franklin Roosevelt ignored his prerogative powers, and Corwin refers to "stewardship theory in total war" with respect to their imposition of wartime controls on the private economy. Here Roosevelt's crisis presidency harked back to Lincoln (*POP*, 250–52). In sum, Corwin believes that the war power has been transformed in three ways. First, "its constitutional basis has been shifted from the doctrine of delegated powers to the doctrine of inherent powers"; second, presidential power "as Commander-in-Chief has been transformed from a simple power of military command to a vast reservoir of indeterminate powers in time of emergency"; and third, "the indefinite legislative powers claimable by Congress" (because of the first development) "may today be delegated by Congress to the President to any extent; that is to say, may be merged to any extent with the indefinite powers of the Commander-in-Chief" (POP, 261–62, 265).

As indicated, the bulk of Corwin's analysis was constitutionally grounded, with scant reference to parties, presidential popularity, or bargaining. Those levers of power surfaced with legislative leadership, a development of the twentieth century: "The present-day role of the President as policy deter-miner in the legislative field is largely the creation of the two Roosevelts and Woodrow Wilson" and thus was not mandated by Original Intent. Here Corwin chronicles the leadership tools utilized by these presidents: the "bully pulpit," drafting bills for Congress, personal appearances before Congress, personal delivery of the State of the Union address, use of the congressional party caucus to guide legislation, well-timed special messages to Congress, exploiting the "honeymoon" period, forging interest group coalition, and veto threats.

All of these techniques are highly personal, so much so that Corwin wonders "whether the presidency is a potential matrix of dictatorship," that is, "domination." Corwin's remedy, like Patterson's, is a new type of cabi-net. Corwin demurs to those critics who view presidential domination "as solely a *menace* to democratic institutions," since "it is the [popular] de-mand that government assume an *active* role in matters of general concern, and especially in matters affecting the material welfare of the great masses of the people." Thus, says Corwin, we cannot blame presidential leader-ship "as such" for intruding on *"liberty"* as "present expanded theories of governmental function entail." What one can ask, however, is whether presidential leadership is a reliable instrument to service that demand (POP, 291, 294).

Critics specifically point out that presidential leadership is "discon-tinuous" and "too dependent on the personality" of the incumbent, that presidents are "insufficiently informed" on various matters but especially about "administrative feasibility," and that the executive-legislative rela-tionship operates "at the mercy of either's whim." This governing dilemma has two interrelated problems: "first, that of bringing presidential power in *all* its reaches under some kind of institutional control; secondly, that of relieving presidential leadership in the legislative field of its excessive dependence on the accident of personality and the unevenness of performance that this involves" (*POP*, 294–95).

His was a modest reform (although Corwin termed it "a more radical proposal"): "*simply that the President should construct his Cabinet from a joint Legislative Council to be created by the two houses of Congress and to contain its leading members.* Then to this central core of advisers could be added at times such heads of departments and chairmen of independent agencies as the business forward at the moment naturally indicated" (*POP*, 297). This kind of cabinet would "be a body of *advisors.*" Corwin reasons that collective decision-making within the executive would "be [by] a body both capable of *controlling* the President and of *supporting* him; of guaranteeing that the things needing to be done would be done on time, but that, on the other hand, the judgment that they needed to be done represented a wide consensus, a vastly wider consensus than the President can by himself supply" (*POP*, 298).

Corwin is skeptical that "the problem of the 'Personalized Presidency'" was solved by the coming of the "Institutionalized Presidency." If there is any model presidency for Corwin, it is the first Eisenhower administration, but he doubts that Eisenhower's organizational style would survive the 1950s. Why? Because "there is a long-term trend at work in the world that consolidates power in the executive departments of all governments, first in the person of one individual, then in an 'administration.' The era of Roosevelt, Churchill, Stalin, Hitler, Mussolini—each a cornerstone of the national 'cult of personality'—has been followed by collegial rule, collective responsibility, and *ad hoc* policies flowing out of completed staff work" (*POP*, 299–300, 304).

In his conclusion, Corwin attributes the "great accession to presidential power in recent decades" to "the breakdown of the two great structural principles" of constitutionalism—namely federalism and separation of powers—as well as to "the replacement of the *laissez-faire* theory of government with the idea that government should make itself an *active, reforming* force" in the private economy. To gain accomplishments, presidents "have made themselves spokesmen of the altered outlook," "have converted their parties to it," and "with the popular support thus obtained, have asserted a powerful legislative initiative." Yet Congress also "aggrandize[d] his [the president's] executive role enormously" by authorizing him to subdelegate power through "administrative regulations" in ways unknown to the Framers (*POP*, 310–11).

The "first exponent of the new presidency was Theodore Roosevelt," but it was FDR "who beyond all twentieth-century Presidents put the stamp both of *personality* and *crisis* on the presidency." In dealing with "a crisis greater than war," Roosevelt claimed for the federal government and the presidency "powers hitherto exercised only on the justification of war." Thus Corwin ends on this ominous note: "Does the presidency, then, in the light of these facts, constitute a standing menace to popular government and to those conceptions of personal liberty to which popular government is, in part, traceable?" Maybe, unless his recommendation about new institutional forms is taken to heart:

> [P]residential power has been at times dangerously *personalized*, and this in two senses: first, that the leadership it affords was dependent altogether on the accident of personality, against which our haphazard method of selecting Presidents offers no guarantee; and, secondly, that there is no governmental body that could be relied on to give the President independent advice and that he was nevertheless bound to consult. As a remedy calculated to meet both phases of the problem I have suggested a new type of Cabinet. At least, if a solution is to be sought in *institutional* terms, it must consist in *stabilizing* in some way or other the relationship between President and Congress. (*POP*, 311–12)

That phrase—"presidential power has been at times dangerously *personalized*"—is the only one quoted by Richard Neustadt (see chapter 6) to illustrate Corwin's fear of personalized power, a quality that Neustadt thoroughly embraced in his treatise on presidential power.

Conclusion

Does presidential leadership vary between domestic and foreign affairs? The anti-aggrandizement school was so named by Paletz because these scholars were alarmed about the growth of presidential powers and the diminution of Congress in our system of separated powers. Clearly there was an ideological underpinning to these works, because concern about domestic policy—the welfare state—is the subtext for the political grievances voiced by Patterson and de Grazia (also Willmoore Kendall; see chapter 1), not foreign policy. Although Patterson discusses presidential dominance of foreign affairs since Washington, his substantive concern is that Congress lost ground rather than taking issue with the content of U.S. foreign policy. The New Deal and the Fair Deal riled Patterson and Kendall just as the Great Society troubled de Grazia. Thus, for Patterson, de Grazia, and Kendall, the term *conservative* may be equated with this concept of the "anti-aggrandizement" presidency. They oppose the growth of executive power not only because it threatens separation of powers but also because they do not subscribe to the liberal policy thrusts of FDR and LBJ.

However, there are quite profound differences among these authors in their pessimism. Even if some actions by FDR were grounds for concern, Corwin surely does not mount a wholesale attack on the New Deal. Patterson and de Grazia make explicit their worries about the welfare state, but Corwin merely takes note of those trends in our political economy. Because Corwin displays virtually no bias in terms of his own policy preferences, his concern about "personalized" power is not fueled by some obsession about dictatorship but rather by a healthy assessment that the nation cannot put its faith in one human being unabated by institutions for collective decision-making. This theme is not exceptional in the presidency literature; it also has been advanced by some scholars in the Liberal tradition (see Herman Finer in chapter 6).

Does presidential leadership depend upon historical context, or is regime-building manifested through political, institutional, and constitutional developments? In his discussion of constitutional development, Corwin chronicles how presidential prerogative, judicial rulings, statutory delegations, and customary practice have built upon—and changed—Original Intent. Not so with Patterson and de Grazia, who, like Kendall, seem trapped in the eighteenth century. Their view of Article 2 seems to allow for no growth. Unlike Corwin, moreover, Patterson and de Grazia see a fundamental divide in the "political culture" of the American regime. Patterson flatly claims that the principles of the Founding have been displaced by British principles, though he agrees with Corwin that changing from the negative to the positive state played a role. De Grazia conceptualizes his Executive Force and Republican Force as embodying divergent "political cultures"—order versus liberty. And the president, says de Grazia, has a liberal mind-set that endears him to academia but does not resonate with the American people (shades of the "two majorities" thesis argued by Willmoore Kendall; see chapter 1).

Does presidential power derive from the prerogatives of office or from the incumbent? Corwin argues that the Framers anticipated an expansive presidential prerogative, and he further asserts that prerogative power is not limited to wartime or times of "great urgency" but can be employed to advance the "public good," as was illustrated by the "stewardship" theory of Theodore Roosevelt. On that, Corwin takes issue with Taft's misgivings about TR. However, Corwin takes umbrage with FDR's 1942 threat to repeal, if Congress did not, parts of the Emergency Price Control Act because his action would be diametrically opposed to what the Framers had intended when they authored the "take care that laws be faithfully executed" clause. No doubt it was this comment by Corwin—that "Roosevelt's crisis presidency harkened back to Lincoln"—that prompted Neustadt's solitary observation that Corwin feared personalized power! On this score, Corwin seems more realistic than Neustadt in *not* rationalizing the "crisis" presidencies of Lincoln and Franklin Roosevelt as a "normal" state of executive-legislative affairs.

Prerogative power is not the mainstay of presidential leadership for Patterson or de Grazia. Indeed, Patterson appears to debunk Hamiltonianism as being incompatible with Original Intent, a position very much at odds with the 1980s movement conservatives who followed in Reagan's wake and who embraced Hamilton's energetic executive (see chapter 9). Patterson is appalled by Hamilton's theory that presidents possess "all executive power inherent in the nation," subject only to constitutional limitations (an implicit rejection of Taft's counterargument). That, says Patterson, was the guiding principle for both Roosevelts and Wilson.

Does presidential influence depend upon the force of personality, rhetorical leadership, or partisanship? What matters to Patterson is the "personal capacity" of the incumbent to bring about a "nationalization" of the presidency through his varied roles as head of the nation, party leader, mouthpiece of public opinion, and political executive. Because Alfred de Grazia views bureaucratization as being at the heart of Executive Force, he sees the president as an "all-seeing all-doing" executive, but he does not emphasize any one president. Patterson and de Grazia both de-emphasize incumbency, because they believe that party government is key to transforming presidential leadership in this political system.

Let us cut to the heart of Neustadt's criticism of Corwin. Corwin alleges that "the history of the presidency is a history of aggrandizement." "Precedents established by a forceful or politically successful personality in the office are available to less gifted successors, and permanently so because of the difficulty with which the Constitution is amended." That is regime-building, or the accumulation of precedents supporting presidential leadership today. On this point Corwin is simply reporting the facts, neither praising them nor bemoaning them in ways that bespeak Patterson or de Grazia. Because the office has become so grand, the republic needs some guarantee that the presidency will not depend wholly on the "accident" of personality. Corwin advocates an institutional arrangement (his cabinet proposal), not only to offer restraint but also to improve the prospects for cooperation between the branches. Whereas Neustadt gambles that we can regularly recruit an FDR-type president, Corwin observes that only one in three presidents have had any singular impact on the office. This is why Corwin assumes that most presidents would need help in governing.

Does the president actively or passively engage the legislative process and promote a policy agenda? Given Patterson's and de Grazia's defense of the separation of powers as traditionally understood, coupled with their transparent ideological preferences, both seemingly would be more comfortable with a Whig in the White House. Corwin believes that the Founders did not mandate legislative leadership, but he explains how that role was inaugurated by Theodore Roosevelt, Wilson, and Franklin D. Roosevelt. The presidential arsenal, to promote effectiveness in this role, involves some prerogative powers (the State of the Union message and special messages, plus the veto) but mainly "political" weapons: rallying the people, use of the party caucus to guide legislation, the "honeymoon" period following inauguration, and developing coalitions of interest groups to support presidential priorities.

Does the organization of the executive branch service presidential leadership? What early insights did these authors have about the post–New Deal administrative state and the advent of the "institutionalized presidency" after FDR established the Executive Office of the President? Patterson argues that a "regulated and socialistic" society requires the executive to head a centralized administration, though his parliamentary-style cabinet allowed for each department to be managed by a presidential appointee, subject to Senate confirmation. Given Patterson's diagnosis of presidential hegemony, he presumes that the "political head" has effective control over every aspect of governance. At least there is no hint that the permanent government is anything other than subservient to the president's wishes. For de Grazia the Leviathan is the bureaucracy, and the federal civil service is "the great engine" of the Executive Force. De Grazia seems to conceptualize the entire federal government working in lockstep with the White House.

Any dispassionate reader would conclude that the ideological prism by which Patterson and de Grazia conceptualize presidential dominance does not allow for a nuanced understanding of bureaucracy as an autonomous political force. Given his legalistic frame, Corwin discusses the "executive" and "take care" and removal powers in terms of prerogative. But big government requires that Congress delegate authority to the chief executive, who, in turn, subdelegates that authority to his administrative subordinates. To gain some accountability, Corwin urges the "legislative veto" as a way for Congress to retain ultimate authority—without the need for presidential consent. Sometimes Congress lodges administrative responsibility in "independent" regulatory commissions and thus determines "what degree of freedom from presidential control such bodies as the ICC, the FTC . . . shall enjoy." Although the Brownlow Committee proposed integrating the headless "fourth branch" of government into the regular departments, Corwin is skeptical about its report, which he terms "thoroughgoingly Jacksonian," since "a considerable part of the administrative tasks of government will always have to be performed by the functionaries *immediately* charged with them, without any opportunity for 'over-all management' to be consulted or, in fact, intelligently applied." The "world of administration is a *pluralistic* rather than a *monistic* world and reposes in great measure on the loyalty and competence of individual bureaucrats." "[T]o conceive of the President as a potential 'boss of the works' save in situations raising broad issues of policy would be both absurd and calamitous" (*POP,* 95–96, 98).

Corwin is not hopeful that the "problem" of the personalized presidency would be solved by institutionalization. Although he believes that Eisenhower's military experience helped to perfect the "institutionalizing process" beyond what FDR or Truman achieved, he doubts that the Eisenhower experience would tame the "long-term trend" that personalizes power in the president. Corwin also suggests "[t]hat Congress in setting up the principal constituent elements of the Executive Office of the President may have been motivated in part by the idea of aggrandizing its own power at the expense of the presidency, rather than by that of assisting him in his task of leading the nation and managing the government, may be conceded" (*POP,* 301, 304). Thus Corwin gives clues to being more realistic in his understanding of public administration and the real limits of a president's managerial span of control.

From Imperialism to Impotency
Liberal Malaise with Liberal Presidents

To characterize the 1960s and 1970s as an era, even a period, in the intellectual development of the presidency is somewhat oxymoronic. Perhaps *reflex action* is a better phrase, given that two different and diametrically opposing viewpoints surfaced so quickly during that time. One commonality is that both were championed by academics who were liberals and Democrats, some of whom had been architects of the "heroic" presidency thesis. President Johnson's tragic blunder in Vietnam, coupled with the Watergate scandals and President Nixon's abuse of executive authority, provoked a strong negative reaction within the scholarly community. This literature gave birth to a "revisionist" interpretation of presidential power, which was popularized in books by historian Arthur Schlesinger Jr., political scientist James David Barber, and George Reedy, former press secretary to President Johnson.

A second literature focused on the failings of Gerald R. Ford and James Earl Carter, and the Democrat bore the brunt of scholarly criticism, because pundits had expected so much more from Carter's administration after eight years of Republican rule. Not only did Carter fail in his own right, but he also failed in the minds of academics and journalists, who drew unflattering comparisons with Franklin D. Roosevelt. When former Carter speechwriter James Fallows referred to his ex-boss's tenure as "the passionless presidency," that characterization stuck.[1] Books about the Carter and Ford administrations with titles like *The Tethered Presidency* and *The Illusion of Presidential Government* were telling indications of how scholars viewed the office. So discredited was Carter that efforts by two highly regarded presidency scholars, Erwin Hargrove and Charles O. Jones, to offer a "revisionist" defense of Carter proved ineffectual.

Lyndon B. Johnson and Richard M. Nixon

The intellectual fallout from Vietnam and Watergate was a collective mea culpa throughout liberal academia. Presidency scholar Dorothy Buckton

James in 1969 took note of the "assumption in this [scholarly] writing [by Richard Neustadt and Clinton Rossiter] that the President will be liberal. He should be powerful because it is assumed that he will work for the interest of the country. The deep frustration that liberals have felt with President Johnson's Vietnamese War policy has exposed the flaw in that assumption."[2] Philippa Strum was one reawakened liberal who similarly observed that "[e]ver since the New Deal . . . the majority of political scientists have assumed that presidents are good and Congress is bad." Because, as she elaborated,

> political scientists have recognized the great need for change . . . to enable it [the United States] to meet the challenges of the twentieth century, they have tended to view congressmen as a bunch of stick-in-the-muds whose function has been to overrepresent the worst tendencies of their constituents and to prevent dynamic presidents from getting anything accomplished. It will be surprising if this trend is not superseded in the next few years by a countertendency to view the president as the bad guy and congressmen as potential heroes. The new trend is resulting from liberal dissatisfaction with the foreign policies of Presidents Johnson and Nixon, and with their Vietnam policies in particular.[3]

Later Strum focuses on Southeast Asia and issues a congressional call to arms. Saying "the American presence in Vietnam and Cambodia should lead even the most diehard proponents of increased presidential power to question their assumption that expansion of power is always a good thing," Strum tells us that Congress, for all its imperfections, "is the only institution that can possibly keep presidential power within bounds on a day-to-day basis. It is not necessary for Congress to increase its power, but the time has come for Congress to exercise some of the powers which it has always formally possessed but which have been permitted to all but wither away."[4] These voices of protesting liberals were joined by a few conservatives, one being the highly regarded constitutional scholar Raoul Berger. He argued that Nixon's claim of "executive privilege" was a constitutional "myth," since such presidential authority was not mentioned—explicitly or implicitly—in the Constitution. More recent scholarship by Mark Rozell doubts the accuracy of Berger's claim.[5]

George E. Reedy

One of the most influential books of this genre is George E. Reedy's devastating critique of how the White House can lose touch with political reality.

Reedy, a former press secretary to President Johnson, summarizes his thesis aptly at the outset: "The life of the White House is the life of a court. It is a structure designed for one purpose only—to serve the material needs and the desires of a single man. It is felt that this man is grappling with problems of such tremendous consequence that every effort must be made to relieve him of the irritations that vex the average citizen. His mind, it is held, must be absolutely free of petty annoyances so that he can concentrate his faculties upon the 'great issues' of the day."[6]

The king's court and the president's staff are literally one and the same. "Among the fundamental characteristics of monarchy is untouchability"; moreover, "[b]y the twentieth century, the presidency had taken on all the regalia of monarchy except the robes, a scepter, and a crown." That special status encourages presidents to think they have all the answers: "The environment of deference, approaching sycophancy, helps to foster another insidious factor. It is a belief that the president and a few of his most trusted advisers are possessed of a special knowledge which must be closely held within a small group lest plans and the designs of the United States be anticipated and frustrated by enemies." Ultimately, then, dysfunction occurs when political deference coupled with self-proclaimed expertise isolates the White House from political reality. Reedy recalls a controversial proposal by LBJ to merge the Departments of Labor and of Commerce: "The truly baffling question, however, is how a man with the political sensitivity of Lyndon B. Johnson would ever embark on such a futile enterprise," given his political acumen while Senate majority leader.[7] Reedy cites other examples: Wilson and the League of Nations, Roosevelt's court-packing plan, and Truman's inept handling of the Communist spy scare. Then he draws the "inescapable" inference "that the White House is an institution which dulls the sensitivity of political men and ultimately reduces them to bungling amateurs in their basic craft—the art of politics."[8]

The cause of presidential isolation lies within. Reedy argues "that the office neither elevates nor degrades a man. What it does is to provide a stage upon which all of his personality traits are magnified and accentuated. The aspects of his character which were not noted previously are not really new. They were merely hidden from view in lesser positions, where he was only one of many politicians competing for public attention." Being a president gives rise to special psychological dynamics. "In Congress he is only one of a large group of advocates, and the end product of his activities will be tempered by his need for arriving at an accommodation with the others." But presidential performance is an entirely different matter, because "[r]estraint must come from within the presidential soul and prudence from within the presidential mind. The adversary forces which temper the actions of others do not come into play until it is too late to change course."[9]

It is here that Reedy offers a caveat to Neustadt. Neustadt, says Reedy, wrote that expertise in presidential power "seems to be the province not of politicians as a class but of extraordinary politicians." But Reedy would modify the last phrase to "extraordinary *men* who have become politicians," to suggest "the crucial importance of personality to the success of a president."[10] In point of fact, the president is the master of his fate in ways that most people are not. Reedy asserts that "a president makes his decisions as he wishes to make them, under conditions which he himself has established, and at times of his own determination." Although presidents may be confronted by forces and circumstances foisted upon them, "how they deal with them is up to the presidents themselves. A president, in a peculiar sense that does not apply to other people, is the master of his own fate and the captain of his own soul."[11]

The "isolation" of the White House, paradoxically, affects "strong" presidents more than "weak" presidents, because "[t]he strong man has a propensity to create an environment to his liking and to weed out ruthlessly those assistants who might persist in presenting him with irritating thoughts," whereas a weak president "is more susceptible to conflicting currents and less ready to eliminate strong-minded people from his immediate vicinity." To those who would argue that presidents need to assemble "mature men" to be their advisers, Reedy answers that this option "is only a possibility— rarely, if ever, consummated. The White House is a court. Inevitably, in a battle between courtiers and advisers, the courtiers will win out. This represents the greatest of all barriers to presidential access to reality and raises a problem which will plague the White House so long as the president is a reigning monarch rather than an elected administrator."[12]

Reedy admits that he is no psychiatrist but warns us that "[a] highly irrational personality, who under other circumstances might be medically certifiable for treatment, could take over the White House and the event never be known with any degree of assurance." Citizens are tolerant, too tolerant, of aberrant presidential behavior, because "[a]t bottom, it is a reflection of the ultimate nature of the presidential office—an environment in which for all practical purposes the standards of normal conduct are set by the president himself. To those immediately around him, he is the one who determines what is rational and what is irrational, and the public reaction to whatever he does is not immediate unless it brings on catastrophe."[13]

"Politics and neurosis are inextricably intermingled because the neurotic personality is usually more articulate and more logical in expressing stands on the great issues of the day. Politics probably would not exist at all without neurotic drives that compel men to exert leadership and extend their personalities to dominance over others." What keeps "most political leaders from rushing headlong into catastrophe is the fact that their own neurotic drives must clash with the neurotic drives of others." But such is not the case with the presidential office, which exists "in an environment which is free of many of the restraints with which all other political leaders must contend."[14] Reedy offers no panacea for paranoia in the presidency, but academia moved in that direction with the publication of James David Barber's classic psychobiographical study in 1972.[15]

James David Barber

For years presidency scholars had differentiated between "active" and "passive" presidents.[16] One of them was Erwin C. Hargrove, who authored a personality-based theory six years before James David Barber published his work. Hargrove contrasted "Presidents of Action" (TR, Wilson, FDR, Truman, JFK, and LBJ) with "Presidents of Restraint" (Taft and Hoover), with each president in the first group viewed as "a political artist whose deepest needs and talents were served by a political career"; the latter group "did not put a high value on personal or presidential power, and in the course of their careers they did not develop political skills."[17]

Barber's counterthesis that personal insecurity is linked to aberrant presidential behavior during crises forced Hargrove to reassess his earlier position: "In the heyday of Lyndon Johnson [I] developed the thesis that personal insecurity and political skill were linked. The creative politician was depicted as the man who required attention and needed to dominate and therefore had developed skills of self-dramatization and persuasion that would serve those needs." In an especially candid admission of his own willingness to excuse the misuse of power by our strong presidents, Hargrove acknowledged that such rationalizations were based on the misguided assumption that "[p]residents were guided by moral purpose and it was frankly biased in the direction of the liberal, power-maximizing Presidents . . . the argument was made that such power-striving, if rooted in personal needs, could lead to self-defeating eruptions of personality such as Theodore Roosevelt's in 1912, Wilson's rigidity in the League [of Nations] fight, and FDR's plan to pack the Supreme Court. However, it was assumed that institutional checks and balances were sufficient to control such behavior. The price was worth paying because strong political leadership was required."[18] Now, in 1974, the challenge according to Hargrove is to fashion a psychological profile of men who have the appropriate "democratic character" to be president.[19]

Although presidency scholars may not all accept the psychological theory that Barber formulated, standard textbooks now virtually always give attention to the problem of an aberrant personality in the White House. In 1975 Louis Koenig drew a distinction between "high-democracy" presidents and "low-democracy" presidents, the former reflecting the values of the "heroic" president and the latter representing presidents like Nixon. Aaron Wildavsky in 1978 also devised four presidential models to explain the noble and ignoble sides of presidential behavior.[20]

James David Barber made his reputation when the first edition of *The Presidential Character* was published in 1972. In its preface, Barber announced his intention to "produce psychological interpretations of political behavior" and thus "move through theory to prediction."[21] What made his fame was his prediction that Richard Nixon would self-destruct; with Watergate, his forecast paid off handsomely. But Barber's psychological profiles have been anything but clairvoyant, since, with four exceptions (Eisenhower, Johnson, Nixon, and Reagan), he considered every president beginning with Franklin D. Roosevelt to be well-adjusted.

Barber argues that the president is "a human being like the rest of us, a person trying to cope with a difficult environment. To that task he brings his own character, his own view of the world, his own political style."[22] Barber's advice to us, as citizens, is that we should evaluate a presidential campaign not in terms of the candidates' issue positions, regional connections, or ideology, because "the connection between his character and his Presidential actions emerges as paramount." Character gives clues to future behavior: "The lives of Presidents past and of the one still with us show, I think, how a start from character makes possible a realistic estimate of what will endure into a man's White House years." In sum, "[t]he issues will change, the character of the President will last."[23]

The three crucial psychological elements are character (which Barber thinks is developed during childhood), worldview (which comes later, during adolescence), and style (developed during adulthood). But "character" is key, and the "most important thing to know about a President or candidate is where he fits among these four types, defined according to (a) how active he is [active or passive] and (b) whether or not he gives the impression he enjoys his political life [positive or negative]."[24] From those two dimensions Barber constructed a fourfold typology by which he classifies various (but not all) presidents. Much preferred is the active-positive character exhibited by Jefferson, Franklin D. Roosevelt, Truman, and Kennedy (later he added Ford, Carter, Bush, and Clinton).[25] These presidents exhibit "a consistency, between much activity and the enjoyment of it, indicating relatively high self-esteem and relative success in relating to the environment." They are flexible and adaptive and there is an "emphasis on rational mastery, on using the brain to move the feet."[26]

His passive-positives included Madison, Taft, Harding, and (his later addition) Reagan; the passive-negatives are Washington, Coolidge, and Eisenhower (a "mixed" case, says Barber). The passive-positive president is "the receptive, compliant, other-directed character whose life is a search for affection as a reward for being agreeable and cooperative rather than personally assertive"; such presidents "help soften the harsh edges of politics," although "their dependence and the fragility of their hopes and enjoyments make disappointment in politics likely." The positive-negative president is basically drawn into politics as a public duty. Barber questions, "Why is someone who does little in politics and enjoys it less there at all?" and the answer is "rooted orientation toward doing dutiful service," which "compensates for low self-esteem based on a sense of uselessness." These presidents are in politics "because they think they ought to be" but "lack the experience and flexibility to perform effectively as political leaders."[27] Which leaves us with the active-negatives: John Adams, Wilson, Hoover, Lyndon Johnson, and Nixon. An active-negative president is problematic if not dangerous, according to Barber: "The contradiction here is between relatively intense effort and relatively low emotional reward for that effort. The activity has a compulsive quality, as if the man were trying to make up for something or to escape from anxiety into hard work. He seems ambitious, striving upward, power-seeking . . . Life is a hard struggle to achieve and hold power, hampered by the condemnations of a perfectionist conscience. Active-negative types pour energy into the political system, but it is an energy distorted from within."[28]

Putting Johnson and Nixon side by side certainly satisfied the "political" problem that Barber would have faced had he tried to glorify LBJ based on domestic legislation. No liberal academic would have challenged his characterization of Hoover or Nixon, but what about Woodrow Wilson, considered to be "great" by many presidency observers? Happily for Barber, he was not the first to throw unsavory psychological darts at Wilson; years earlier the celebrated Sigmund Freud did so.[29] The glaring failure of

Barber's paradigm is Abraham Lincoln, who most likely would be considered an active-negative personality.[30]

Arthur M. Schlesinger Jr.

No book personified the liberal malaise with presidential power more than Schlesinger's The Imperial Presidency. It was published in 1973, one year before Nixon's forced retirement.[31] A comparison of Schlesinger's views of presidential power between late 1966, when he debated Alfred de Grazia (see chapter 7) and 1973 (also in his 1989 epilogue to the second edition of The Imperial Presidency) is an intellectual time capsule of his thinking during and after Vietnam. De Grazia offers a fixed ideological point from which to judge Schlesinger, because de Grazia consistently preferred a Congress-dominated government.

In their debate, Schlesinger begins with the oft-quoted remark of Richard Neustadt that our government is "a government of separated institutions *sharing* powers," to make the point that the "calculated ambiguities" of the Constitution foster "permanent guerrilla warfare" between the two branches of government.[32] The problem of "drawing the line remains a major preoccupation of American history," but Schlesinger believes that opportunism and ideology explain one's preference for the executive or the legislative branch. Taking the example of Jefferson's flip-flop on presidential prerogatives (regarding the Louisiana Purchase), Schlesinger says, "from the start, views of the proper distribution of powers . . . depended a good deal less on considerations of high principle than on preferences about the uses to which the power was put."[33]

There are two presidential schools of thought, argued Schlesinger in 1966. One was the Jackson-Lincoln view held by FDR, Truman, Kennedy, and Johnson; the other was the Buchanan-Taft view of Harding, Coolidge, Hoover, and Eisenhower. Schlesinger claims that Jackson "invented the modern presidency," just as FDR "must be credited with inventing the contemporary presidency," based on the expansion in the functions of the national government and the "indispensable enlargement in the instrumentalities of presidential management and control."[34] In this light, Schlesinger agrees that "the presidency is a good deal stronger today than it was, say, 75 years ago" but "not notably stronger than the presidency imagined in the Federalist Papers." Yet in the same breath he claims that the president also "in significant respects . . . has lost power" to the executive bureaucracy (by virtue of its resistance to change), the Supreme Court (here citing the Steel Seizure Case), and Congress (given its oversight powers).[35] On Vietnam, Schlesinger emphasizes that the division of powers in foreign affairs, as in domestic affairs, "is a matter not of right or wrong but of practical results. Thus some of us in the past who have been all-out supporters of the presidential prerogative have been forced to think again as a consequence of the present involvement in Vietnam." According to Schlesinger:

> Since activist Presidents want to change things, since domestic policy has been the main field of presidential action through our history, and since Congress, partly for its own institutional reasons, tends in due course to oppose presidential activism, liberals, in general, have argued for the presidency and conservatives for the Congress. But this has been the result of circumstance, not of principle—as suggested by the fact that today, for perhaps the first time in our history, a strong President proposes to use presidential powers (in Vietnam) for purposes which liberals, in general, question and conservatives, in general, approve. Conceivably this, if protracted here and applied to other issues, could result in an exchange of positions comparable to that between the Federalists and the Jeffersonians from 1800 to 1814.[36]

This admission begs the question of whether Lyndon Johnson represented as fundamental an ideological departure for conservatives as he apparently did for liberals, since Schlesinger assumes that conservatives since the Founding have looked to Congress for both domestic and foreign policy. Schlesinger's "own feeling" is that Congress should give the president more administrative discretion, and in turn, "something must be done to assure the Congress a more authoritative and continuing voice in fundamental decisions in foreign policy," because we cannot allow the president such "wide tactical flexibility" that "he can impose by himself the decisions which may make the difference between peace and war in the nuclear age."[37] This spongy advice on Vietnam provoked some questions, including one on "how the hand of Congress" could be strengthened in foreign affairs. Schlesinger did not rise to the challenge but simply repeated his opposition to "any structural changes that will work miracles" and persisted in the belief that Congress may "play a more effective role through political means—either through attempts at private communication, persuasion of the executive branch, or . . . through the development of political pressures outside," as demonstrated by the senatorial hearings on Vietnam.[38]

In his final exchange with de Grazia, Schlesinger was forced to respond to a suggestion by de Grazia that Congress be allowed to select one member who would share with the president the power to retaliate against foreign aggression. Schlesinger thought that plan was totally impractical and violated the tenets of the *Federalist* for "unity, dispatch, and secrecy in the discharge of foreign affairs," but then he proceeded with a statement that wonderfully recalls his roots within the "idealized" school of presidential scholarship (see chapter 6): "I think one of the great myths of the presidency is that the President is the most lonely man in the world . . . no one sees more people or is exposed to a wider range of opinion . . . He is not the loneliest man in the world. He knows more, he is aware of more and he is aware of more possibilities and more probable reactions and objections than anyone else. And the President knows that he has to incorporate in himself a sense of all this if what he does is going to be accepted."[39]

The Schlesinger of 1966 may have been upset about Vietnam, but he was not so distressed as to retreat fully from his hero-worship of strong presidents. When he revisited this issue in 1973, was Schlesinger merely formulating a partisan attack on Nixon? Since he argues that taking sides in the executive-legislative rivalry is largely opportunistic, was he simply another opportunist?[40]

His foreword alleges that the "constitutional Presidency—as events so apparently disparate as the Indochina War and the Watergate affair showed —has become the imperial Presidency and threatens to be the revolutionary Presidency," given the "shift in the *constitutional* balance" that has resulted from "the appropriation" by the contemporary presidency "of powers reserved by the Constitution and by long historical practice to Congress" (*IP*, viii). His purpose for writing this book is twofold: first, his "concern" that the presidency "has gotten out of control and badly needs new definition and restraint," and second, "[t]he answer to the runaway presidency is not the messenger-boy Presidency" but rather "a strong Presidency *within the Constitution*" (*IP*, x).

Why did this shift in the constitutional balance of power unfold? Here Schlesinger "doubted that a messianic foreign policy, America as world savior, was reconcilable with the American Constitution," because "[w]hen an American President conceives himself the appointed guardian of a world in which an eternal foreign threat requires a rapid and incessant deployment of men, weapons and decisions behind a wall of secrecy, the result can only be a radical disruption of the balance of the American Constitution. It is hard to reconcile the separation of powers with a foreign policy driven by an indignant ideology and disposed to intervene unilaterally and secretly everywhere around the planet" (*IP*, 497–98).

What precisely are the attributes of presidential imperialism? The "critical tests," says Schlesinger, are three: "the war-making power; the secrecy system; and the employment against the American people of emergency authority acquired for use against foreign enemies" (*IP*, 441). All three characterized the Nixon administration, and in his 1989 epilogue, Schlesinger mentions Reagan as "a portent of the revival of the imperial Presidency," since Reagan "used them all to fend off Congress and the press and to strengthen executive domination of foreign policy." Unlike Nixon, though, he did not stigmatize his opponents as traitors (*IP*, 457). Monarchical Nixon is the president Schlesinger had in mind when he entitled this book, and whatever sins he attributes to LBJ, Nixon was worse.

On impoundment, presidents going back to Jefferson were "within the legitimate powers of the Commander in Chief," whereas Nixon used the "'policy impoundment' . . . to set aside or nullify the expressed will of Congress." "Nor did Nixon, like Johnson, consult with congressional leaders on impoundment questions" (*IP*, 236, 238). On executive privilege, which Johnson never formally invoked, Nixon made "executive privilege a far more effective instrument of presidential domination than ever before"; were his interpretation to survive, "it would . . . deprive Congress of information necessary for its own survival as a partner in the constitutional order" (*IP*, 247, 251–52). On war-making, the historic transformation involves "what Presidents believed they have the inherent right to do." In the late twentieth century, "Presidents made sweeping claims of inherent power, neglected the collection of consent, withheld information *ad libitum* and went to war against sovereign states." Nineteenth-century presidents acted militarily, "typically against brigands, pirates, revolutionaries and other stateless and lawless groups," not "against sovereign states" (*IP*, 443).

For Johnson's decision to Americanize the Vietnam War "[t]here were no serious precedents"; "[u]nlike Roosevelt's Atlantic policy in 1941, Johnson was ordering American troops into immediate and calculated combat. Unlike Truman's decision in Korea, there were no UN resolutions to confer international legality, nor had there been [a] clear-cut invasion across frontiers. Unlike the Cuban missile crisis, there was no emergency threat to the United States itself to compel secret and unilateral presidential decision" (*IP*, 179). In sum, there were striking parallels that set Johnson and Nixon apart from other presidents. "Johnson and Nixon had surpassed all their predecessors in claiming that inherent and exclusive presidential authority, unaccompanied by emergencies threatening the life of the nation, unaccompanied by the authorization of Congress or the blessing of an international organization, permitted a President to order troops into battle at his unilateral pleasure" (*IP*, 193).

Proceeding to White House operations, although admittedly "[e]very President reconstructs the Presidency to meet his own psychological needs," it is Nixon who "displayed more monarchical yearnings than any of his predecessors": "the expression of a regal state of mind" led "Nixon, far more even than Johnson, to banish challenge from the presidential environment" (*IP*, 218–19). Here Schlesinger reframes Reedy's court-courtier interpretation of the Johnson White House, because "[t]hat was not one's experience in the Kennedy years nor particularly one's reading of the Roosevelt, or Jackson, years." Reedy's law was "penetrating but not absolute," says Schlesinger, because "[i]ronically his thesis applied more precisely to Johnson's successor than to Johnson himself." Ultimately Schlesinger argues that "[p]ower isolates Presidents only to the extent they wish to be isolated" and that "[m]ediocre Presidents passively accept information percolating up through official channels," but "[g]reat Presidents reach out for information not contaminated by self-serving bureaucratic processes." Thus we are reminded that a "quantum leap in the White House staff took place under Nixon," who "interposed his swollen White House staff" between himself and most cabinet members as well as Congress and eventually "interposed an inner circle of palace guards" between himself and most other White House staffers (*IP*, 494–95).

Finally, consider personality. If the "fit" between Johnson's personality and imperialism "was by no means perfect," with Nixon came "a singular confluence of the job with the man," whose "inner mix of vulnerability and ambition impelled him to push the historical logic to its extremity." Schlesinger concludes that for Nixon, "a man so constituted, the imperial Presidency was the perfect shield and refuge" (*IP*, 216).

Schlesinger is disinclined to recommend procedural reform in order to strengthen Congress vis-à-vis the executive branch. The War Powers Resolution, "the most publicized shackle, turned out to be a toy handcuff," he argues, given that it was "yielding the President what he had heretofore lacked: statutory authority to begin wars without congressional consent" (*IP*, 433–34).[41] With respect to the use of emergency powers, Schlesinger declares that "[t]he perennial question is how to distinguish real crises threatening the life of the republic from nightmares troubling the minds of paranoid Presidents"—that is, "[h]ow to distinguish the actions of Lincoln during the Civil War and the second Roosevelt immediately before the

Second World War from Jefferson's actions in face of the Burr conspiracy, Truman's seizure of the steel mills, Nixon's lawlessness in 1972–1973 and the Reagan administration's covert policies toward Iran and the contras." Curiously, he does not include FDR's forced Japanese relocation (*IP*, 458–59).[42]

In his epilogue to the 1989 edition, Schlesinger gives attention to presidential imperialism under Ronald Reagan, but he also uses the opportunity to assess the criticisms of the political pundits who bemoaned the nadir of presidential leadership under Ford and Carter. Schlesinger debunks all the faddish theories about presidential decline, arguing that such excuses were ahistorical because "the political irritations allegedly imperiling" the 1970s presidency were all "old hat in American history." He also alleges that the presidency "has been a personalized office from the start" and, from this perspective, rebuts the "[m]ost far-fetched of recent explanations" (by Theodore J. Lowi; see chapter 10) that "the Presidency did itself in when recent Presidents started personalizing the office, appealing over the heads of Congress to the people and arousing expectations beyond hope of fulfillment." Schlesinger essentially denies that plebiscitary politics began with FDR or JFK (*IP*, 423–25, 428).

Historical context matters, but what matters more is presidential leadership. Although the 1970s commentators pointed to "unprecedentedly intractable problems, excessive personalization of the office, excessive expectations in the country, the constitutional separation of powers, the post-Watergate resurgence of Congress, [and] the rise of single-issue movements," they "got their order wrong," because, on closer examination, personal presidential failings accounted for those conditions. The presidency is in trouble "because President Nixon . . . acted in a manner contrary to his trust as President and subversive of constitutional government, and because of the feebleness of the leadership Presidents Ford and Carter provided and of the remedies they proposed" (*IP*, 431, 437).

All this allows for Schlesinger's (partial) vindication of Reagan, who "quickly showed that the reports of the death of the Presidency were greatly exaggerated," since Reagan understood "that an effective President must meet two indispensable requirements." The first is "to point the republic in one or another direction," which means that "the man in the White House possesses . . . a vision of the ideal America." The second is "to explain to the electorate why the direction the President proposes is right for the nation" (*IP*, 438, 441) What is ironic is that these factors, identified by liberal Schlesinger to validate President Reagan, also are mentioned by conservatives who believed that Reagan failed to redirect the American nation (see chapter 9).

How can the United States undo the imperial presidency? Schlesinger recalls the Framers, who "devised a pretty good engine of government in 1787" that "has chugged along fairly well for two hundred years" by proving "equal to most contingencies." But the Constitution is nothing without the political resolve to make it work, meaning that it "requires Presidents, Congresses and citizens who are responsive to constitutional standards. The hope lies in a campaign of national consciousness-raising," for presidents "so that they will honor the system of accountability," for Congresses "so that they will discharge their constitutional responsibilities," and for citizens "so that, as they enter the voting booth, they will think about a candidate's openness, integrity and commitment to constitutional values as well as about his program and his charm" (IP, 491–92). Shades of James David Barber! Presumably, voters made those judgments about Johnson and Nixon when they elected them. All of this seems a bit naive, given the raw abuse of presidential power that Schlesinger chronicles in his 588-page tome.

Gerald R. Ford and James Earl Carter

Gerald Ford and Jimmy Carter represented a repudiation of the "imperial" presidency thesis, since they were largely portrayed as ineffective. *Society* magazine published six essays under the title "Post-Imperial Presidency." In one, Thomas Cronin observed that "[a] mere seven years after Watergate there is again an intensified call for vigorous presidential leadership."[43] Gerald Ford was not elected, having succeeded from vice president to president when Nixon resigned, and he faced the daunting prospect of trying to resurrect the stature of the White House, put the national nightmare of Watergate behind us, and cope with a Congress solidly controlled by the Democrats. President Carter bears more responsibility for the way intellectuals characterized the presidency during the late 1970s. Neither Ford nor Carter enjoyed much of a "honeymoon" period, because they immediately faced a barrage of negative press. Journalists frequently contrasted Carter, Rozell demonstrates, "against idealized recollections of the leadership approaches of such previous Democratic presidents as Franklin D. Roosevelt and Lyndon B. Johnson."[44]

With the advent of unified government, Carter was expected to deliver on his campaign promises, but that was not to be. Thus Crabb and Mulcahy conclude, regarding his foreign policy record, that "Carter (whether fairly or not) came to exemplify the 'impotent presidency'—a chief executive who apparently lacked the power or the will (or both) to respond to events decisively and in ways that effectively protected America's vital interests abroad."[45] There were two edited volumes in this genre—one by Thomas M. Franck and the other coedited by Hugh Heclo and Lester M. Salamon.[46] Both focused on statutory delegations, judicial precedents, institutional arrangements, and organizational processes to ground their argument that an enfeebled presidency was a more-or-less permanent feature of the political landscape. Bringing the rhetoric about presidential leadership to terms with the realities of presidential power was an avowed purpose of Heclo and Salamon, and the same theme implicitly drove Franck.

The Tethered Presidency

The essays in the Franck volume share a concern about whether congressional involvement in foreign affairs is compatible with the requirements of modern diplomacy. Says Franck: "As we enter the century's dangerous eighth decade, the nation's leaders cannot afford to dissipate our strained capacity to endure stress. Reflexive, unproductive confrontations between Congress and the president will leave us a benighted land, with a cynical population of diminished resolve. The tethered presidency is no remedy for past sins of *imperium*."[47] The critical perspective of these essays, authored by scholars and political leaders who attended a conference at the New York University Law School in 1979, is indicated by the kind of topics covered: legislative veto in foreign affairs; congressional changes in treaty obligations; congressional micromanagement of U.S. "human rights" policy abroad; and legislative oversight of intelligence activities.

The lead essay, by Theodore C. Sorensen (adviser to President Kennedy), lays out their collective assumptions. Vietnam and Watergate had "created a wholly different atmosphere in Washington" as "[t]he evils of the 'imperial presidency' were exposed and attacked." As a consequence, "[t]he fracture of the national consensus and the failure of presidential credibility were mutually reinforcing. Neither Jimmy Carter nor his predecessor nor his successor could be expected any longer to monopolize the center stage of U.S. foreign policy with a solo performance bringing nothing but cheers from the public, press, and Congress seated respectfully in the audience. Now there were many voices and many actors, often speaking at the same time."[48] The president "should not demur; he cannot dominate; he must, therefore, try to lead." By leadership Sorensen means "not so much in the presidential *powers* granted by Constitution and stat-ute but in the *opportunities* afforded by his high office." Sorensen names three: to persuade, to initiate, and to build his own foreign policy team.[49]

The concluding observations by Dean Redlich of the NYU Law School offer a curious interpretation that "[i]f it appears difficult precisely to de-fine, or limit, the powers of the president and Congress in the shaping and implementing of foreign policy, it is because neither the text of the Consti-tution nor almost two centuries of interpretation have provided answers to some of the most difficult questions involving the role of the respective branches."[50] His ultimate prognosis speaks not to constitutionalism or do-mestic politics or personalities but rather to world politics. A "polarized world, relying on one-to-one personal diplomacy, shifts power to the presi-dent," whereas "[a] less polarized world will probably see a continuation of the turn toward Congress."[51]

The Illusion of Presidential Government

The Heclo and Salamon volume resulted from a conference panel spon-sored by the National Academy of Public Administration. The opening lines by Hugh Heclo establish the normative agenda, and clearly he has Richard Neustadt in mind. "Presidential government is an illusion—an illusion that misleads presidents no less than the media and the American public, an illusion that often brings about the destruction of the very men who hold the office." Each contributor, he says, "probes a different facet of the image of presidential government, but the conclusions are the same. Far from being in charge or running the government, the president must struggle even to comprehend what is going on." In our constitutional sys-tem, the presidential role "is not to lead a followership; it is to elicit leader-ship from the other institutions of self-government and help make that leadership effective."[52]

Heclo identifies two highly complex forces supporting the "illusion" of presidential government. First, the sheer magnitude of government, the variety of federal functions, and the cumulative impact of government on society lead him to conclude that "[t]he inherent structural need for the president in our modern policy system means that we cannot give up on the presidency when it seems to be working poorly." Second, the presiden-tial need for the mass media is symptomatic of "a more general phenome-non," which Heclo calls "the need to build what might be called a presi-dential party." Why? Because of "recent trends in American politics: a more politically volatile, less party-oriented public; a less manageable, more individualistic Congress; disappearing party hierarchies; and pro-liferating groups of single-minded policy activists," all of which "add[s] up to a sandy, shifting political base of support for presidents."[53] Given the herculean task of governing, presidents try to convey the image that they are in charge.

Other essays provide ammunition for that grand thesis. Allen Schick discusses a budget process out of control; Louis Fisher shows how executive-legislative relationship affects administration; G. Calvin Mackenzie demonstrates that the executive and legislative branches (also academia) did not agree on what values should embody federal administration. Essays on domestic, economic, and national security policy show that each was afflicted by bureaucratic infighting, ad hoc arrangements, failed coordination, and threats to the ideal of neutral competence in public service. I. M. Destler observes that the inclination of presidents for personal, loyal, and strong advisers undermined those executive agencies which provided continuity to government.

In the concluding essay, Lester Salamon asks that we move beyond presidential illusion toward a "constitutional" presidency. He believes "[t]he 1970s marked the end of the presidential era in American politics," though, to be sure, presidential government "was always largely an illusion," because "[p]ower was too dispersed, the presidency too ill equipped, and the range of federal involvement too limited to make the concept a reality." The ultimate irony of the 1960s and 1970s, however, is that the "illusory quality of presidential government ceased being a cause for concern and became instead something to be applauded." "[F]or a brief period, the illusion of presidential government came close to being translated into reality," and the results turned out to be "far more frightening, than its champions had expected."[54]

Arguments to strengthen the presidency, says Salamon, seem reasonable "to deal effectively with these other natural centers of political power"— Congress, localistic political parties, interest groups, and the mass media— but "these other potential centers of power have undergone changes in the opposite direction"—toward weakness. This gave rise to the contemporary situation of "presidents [with] increased incentives to mobilize their own political coalitions while undermining the positions of those who can share with them the responsibility for governing." This situation, more to the point, made the country "ripe either for stultifying paralysis or gross abuse of power." Since we need presidential leadership, and cannot downsize the office, the question Salamon poses is "how to sustain the illusion while avoiding the reality." For the answer, he turns to the Framers: we need "what might be termed a modern 'constitutional presidency,' a presidency equipped to act effectively but also required to act cooperatively."[55]

Salamon proposes three institutional changes. We need to redefine the president "not as the ultimate decision maker but as the preeminent 'national highlighter,'" who identifies "a handful of issues of truly national importance." Moreover, since "it is impossible for a president to resolve all these issues personally or to wish them away," presidents need to "pay more attention to the establishment and maintenance of reliable processes through which these issues can be handled." Finally, and most important, he says, "in the last analysis, it is not presidential self-restraint and forbearance, but the effective exercise of power elsewhere in the political system that is the ultimate safeguard of constitutional government."[56]

Salamon is not entirely sanguine about the efficacy of institutional changes aimed at strengthening Congress (budget reforms, the War Powers Act, the legislative veto) because, though they "may provide some assurance against the reemergence of an imperial presidency," they "do not yet supply, and may even subvert, the peculiar twist that the historic concept of balance of powers needs to make it applicable to the governance problem that is likely to confront the nation over the foreseeable future."[57]

Carter Revisionism

Two attempts at Carter "revisionism" by presidency scholars Erwin Hargrove and Charles Jones argue that events undermined his presidency and that Congress reexerted its authority in the aftermath of Vietnam and Watergate. Jones's book on the "trusteeship" presidency was the first volume in the Carter Oral History Project of the White Burkett Miller Center of Public Affairs at the University of Virginia. Based on interviews with Carter and his senior White House aides, Jones's analysis is limited to the policy arena where this president got his lowest marks: legislative leadership. The title—*The Trusteeship Presidency*—reveals the thrust of Jones's revisionism: a trustee president focuses on national issues, acts independently, and seeks comprehensive policy solutions. In "doing what's right, not what's political," the Carter administration collided with the contrary dictum of Harold Lasswell that politics is the "art of the possible."[58] President Carter is given a sympathetic hearing by Jones, but any reader would get the distinct impression that America repudiated Carter's leadership just as surely as the English electorate rejected Burkean trusteeship.

Jones tries to salvage Carter's reputation by linking the development of trusteeship leadership to his personality, unique political conditions, and the policy issues that he confronted. Jimmy Carter defined his lack of Washington experience and his "outsider" status as advantages in the post-Watergate era, and he was able to cultivate a positive image with the public during a lengthy nomination process in which he faced relatively weak competitors. By being elected without making deals with the power brokers, however, his route to the White House reinforced Carter's preoccupation about how politics ought to be practiced.

At the same time, the legislative branch was being reshaped by membership turnover and institutional reforms to produce a Congress with more individualism, energy, and participatory spirit. It is within this context that Jones evaluates Carter as legislative leader, and Carter comes up short. Legislative liaison requires legislative skills, and Carter is compared unfavorably with every president since Eisenhower based on legislative experience, policy objectives, personal involvement, partisan support in Congress, electoral mandate, and public approval. Jones then elaborates upon —and points out the obvious deficiencies of—how President Carter developed his congressional policy agenda and his White House legislative liaison system.

Carter's disastrous 1977 leads Jones to conclude that "[n]o modern president had experienced as difficult a first year with Congress as did Jimmy Carter."[59] It provoked soul-searching at the White House, but the president, says Jones, would not back down from his determination to tackle the difficult issues. By Carter's last year in office, the political situation had badly deteriorated as a result of foreign policy crises—the Soviet invasion of Afghanistan and the Iran hostage stalemate—as well as the economic stagflation that forced Carter to embrace budgetary retrenchment, thereby provoking a backlash from liberal Democrats led by Senator Ted Kennedy (D-MA). Thus, at the end of his presidency, Jimmy Carter remained as much a political outsider as he was at the start of his term. But, Jones argues, "Carter probably would not have wished it to be otherwise. He was unwilling to become a part of the Washington establishment. Indeed, as he read his mandate, to have accepted the dominant norms would violate his trusteeship."[60]

Erwin C. Hargrove took up the intellectual cudgels to advance an interpretation analogous to Jones's—that Carter personified the "politics of the public good." Also relying on the Carter Oral History Project, Hargrove fully appreciates that his effort to redeem Jimmy Carter faced heavy odds: "The final irony was that he [Carter] became the scapegoat for all unresolved national and international problems. Everybody—politicians, the public, interest groups and media—piled on him. This may explain his great unpopularity in the years after his presidency. His memory left a bad taste."[61] Hargrove begins with a brief psychological profile of Carter. Explains Hargrove: "The keystone of Carter's understanding of himself as a political leader was his belief that the essential responsibility of leadership was to articulate the good of the entire community rather than any part of it . . . He presented himself to the public as a political leader who represented the public interest."[62]

Whereas Jones focused exclusively on executive-legislative relations, Hargrove covers myriad aspects of White House operations. In dealing with domestic policy formation, Hargrove offers the most (perhaps the only!) plausible rationale with which future generations might look more favorably on the Carter administration. He uses mini case studies to argue that domestic policymaking "was played out against a political background of tension between a centrist Democratic president and a Democratic party and its constituent groups that wished him to be more 'liberal' than he wished to be. Carter's search for comprehensive policies that would combine liberal goals with tight financial limits often fell between liberal and conservative poles, too cautious for the first and too radical for the second."[63]

Hargrove's insights on the Carter managerial style, in contrast, appear to confirm our worst suspicions: the economic policymaking apparatus degenerated into "ad-hocracy" as key advisers disagreed about the economic problem. Moreover, Carter's "economic advisers had to . . . establish routines for doing their business with one another without any guidance from the president."[64] Yet again, Hargrove sees a logic to economic policy insofar as "[w]hat appeared to be a policy of zigzag . . . was actually a coherent strategy of balancing opposites." But once double-digit inflation hit, Carter could not be a Reagan: "Ronald Reagan addressed the same problems differently in 1981 but he was not a Democratic president who had, by the logic of his political coalition, to combat inflation without inducing recession."[65] In other words, context rules.

Nor was Carter like Reagan in foreign affairs. His representation of "an idealistic, 'Wilsonian' world view which valued peace and human rights" is the key to understanding Carter's role in such decisions as the Camp David Accord and the Panama Canal Treaty. But again, President Carter failed to impose order on his national security team, so he had to cope with another balancing act: the rivalries between his secretary of state (Cyrus Vance) and his national security adviser (Zbigniew Brzezinski). Hargrove does not attempt a full-blown revisionist account of Carter's foreign policy, which did not emerge from the Carter Oral History Project until a decade later.[66]

Hargrove reframes the critical question of whether Carter was an effective leader as one involving a trade-off between presidential political skills and historical conditions. Without doubt, many commentators place the blame squarely on Carter's shoulders, but Hargrove retorts that by "[u]sing considerable skill the president struggled in unfavorable conditions with weak political resources and achieved some notable successes and some failures." And when observers come to depreciate Jimmy Carter in comparison with Ronald Reagan, Hargrove counters that Carter ought to be contrasted with his predecessor and not his successor: "Jimmy Carter was president at a time of transition, after a Democratic period of reform and achievement and before a Republican resurgence. The Ford and Carter presidencies belong together in this respect, both providing few possibilities for heroic leadership."[67] Simply put, Jimmy Carter was the wrong president of the wrong party at the wrong time.

To argue that President Carter should be judged on his own terms bespeaks a kind of post hoc rationalization. Essentially Jones and Hargrove say that Carter ought to be understood as a high-minded technocrat who faced intractable problems that were not amenable to standard liberal Democratic solutions. That is the justification underlying their "public good" and "trusteeship" characterizations of Carter. Because the Jones and Hargrove projects aim to salvage Carter *from* the legacy of the "heroic" presidency, Phillip Henderson chides all Carter revisionists for failing to "build a convincing case that concepts like bargaining, accommodation and persuasion are any less meaningful norms of analysis for understanding presidential politics during and after Carter's presidency than they were before he assumed office."[68]

Back to Parliamentarianism

Arthur Schlesinger Jr. claims that "constitutional reformers" who advocate the parliamentary model hold contradictory motivations: "the post-Watergate reformers because they believed it would assure legislative supremacy; and the post-Carter reformers because they believed it would assure executive supremacy." The second have the better of the argument, Schlesinger believes, because "[w]hile the parliamentary model formally assumes legislative omnipotence, in practice it produces an almost unassailable dominance of the executive over the legislature" (*IP*, 465). Schlesinger referred to Charles M. Hardin and James Sundquist, but a detailed look indicates that Schlesinger may have overstated his case.

Charles M. Hardin

Charles M. Hardin offers a full-blown parliamentary-style reform package to rescue the United States. In 1973 he declared, "America was gripped by its gravest political crisis since the Civil War" because the "president all too often was out of control," although this crisis "had been foreshadowed. Presidential abuse of power . . . had been visible for decades"; for that reason, corrective action would require "constitutional surgery at least as severe as that of 1787" in order to secure presidential power and accountability or, to put it another way, "presidential leadership and party government."[69] Schlesinger feels that Hardin's argument lay "in the domain of political fantasy," though he admits that Hardin had "shrewd insights" into American politics (*IP*, 463 n).

Although Hardin's ultimate political goal is to institutionalize a loyal opposition as much as to elevate Congress, we agree with Schlesinger that his proposals were so radical as to be utopian: the defeated presidential candidate would get a seat in the House of Representatives and become the opposition leader; both branches would be elected simultaneously to four-year terms; the office of vice president would be abolished; congressional candidates of each party would be the de facto nominating convention for presidential candidates; the size of the House of Representatives would be increased by another 150 at-large candidates to assure the winning presidential candidate a majority of seats; the Senate would be deprived of its power to approve treaties and presidential nominations; any legislation rejected by the Senate could be reapproved by the House and forwarded to the president; finally, presidential vetoes could be overridden only by the House of Representatives. These reforms would not "in themselves provide a vote of confidence," but they would "create the setting in which such votes should naturally evolve," because "an essential assumption would be that a president needs a majority in the House of Representatives to govern. If he loses the majority he will be incapacitated and it would be logical for him to resign." An adverse "vote of confidence" effectively should "make way for another evolutionary step, namely, dissolving government and holding new elections. Once this step is taken, it is hoped, it will become the normal way that one government ends and another is chosen," which would transform "the endless nominating and electoral campaigns" into a procedure lasting a few weeks.[70]

Hardin believes that "[a] dangerous initiative has been vested in the president . . . by the Constitution and by Supreme Court decisions and enlarged by his predecessors [which] enable[s] him to take the first crucial steps in foreign affairs." Nor is the public any obstacle, given the "national blindness to the dangers of presidential initiative."[71] The only durable solution to the dual problems—"maintenance of presidential leadership *and* its control—lies in party government." This "will give the citizen his due share in both political power *and* responsibility" by "giving him a recognizable, understandable role in the awesome task of creating a government—or an opposition" and thus "end the present malaise of public opinion that results from the fiction that each citizen is the sovereign arbiter" of issues but frustrated by the "political labyrinth" of our government.[72]

The president, says Hardin, "stands on an incomparable political pinnacle," and although he is "[s]urrounded as he is by able men, they are still *his* men" and "compete for his favor and are subject to the relentless appeal of loyalty" (Hardin cites George Reedy). No staff system and no fountain of wisdom can "satisfy the need for *political* confrontation," which a healthy president requires.[73] Hardin finds James David Barber's diagnosis of presidential character "faults" to be "persuasive" and "illuminating" but, nonetheless, believes that Reedy's thesis of presidential isolation is more relevant. Historical cases of decision-making indicate to Hardin that "the president's associates are the weakest of all recourses to correct his tendencies toward malevolent actions—even before his mind is fully made up, let alone afterward."[74]

The corrective is party government. As Hardin emphatically puts it: "*Along with the people . . . the president is responsible for the general welfare or the public interest. People and president share an obligation from which the interests are excused: a responsibility to the political community as a whole.*" We conclude with Hardin's summary judgment on why the political system must be changed: "To maintain and control a vigorous president; to reestablish the writ of the general government over the bureaucracy; to invest public policy with greater internal coherence and more preeminence over the importunities of pressure groups—all these justify major constitutional adjustments. So does the need to resolve the social and psychological tensions that arise when a limited and divided—indeed, a splintered—government confronts the problems of a collectivist age."[75]

James L. Sundquist

With the country heading toward the bicentennial celebration of the Constitution, some prominent Americans collected their thoughts on the "crisis" gripping the American republic. Late in 1983 the Committee on the Constitutional System was incorporated, with former Treasury Secretary (to Kennedy) Douglas Dillon, former White House counsel (to Carter) Lloyd M. Cutler, and Senator Nancy Landon Kassebaum (R-KS) as cochairs. James MacGregor Burns was also a "founder" of the Committee on the Constitutional System.[76] Dillon echoes Burns's decades-old fascination with the "deadlock" thesis (see chapter 1) by writing that "our governmental problems do not lie with the quality or character of our elected representatives," but rather "with a system which promotes divisiveness and makes it difficult, if not impossible, to develop truly national policies." Struggles between the executive and legislative branches make "stalemate" inevitable, and "no one can place the blame," since "[t]he president blames the Congress, the Congress blames the president, and the public remains confused and disgusted with government in Washington."[77] In the last year of the Carter presidency, Lloyd N. Cutler authored an essay, arguing that "under the U.S. Constitution it is not now feasible to 'form a Government'" that is "able to carry out an overall program, and is held accountable for its success or failure."[78]

Another academic activist in this grand constitutional undertaking is James L. Sundquist, a political scientist long enamored with strong parties. Sundquist packages "an ideal series of [eight] amendments to the American Constitution" as his reform agenda. First, a "team ticket" vote would combine each party's candidates for president, vice president, Senate, and House into one huge slate. Second, the midterm election would be abolished and terms increased to four years for the House and likely eight years for the Senate. Third, "special elections to reconstitute a failed government" could be called by the president or a simple majority of the House or Senate, necessitating new elections for the executive and the legislature. Fourth, the constitutional ban on "dual officeholding" would be abolished so that a member of Congress could serve in the cabinet. Fifth and sixth, an "item veto" would be allowed, subject to override by absolute majorities of the House and Senate, and Congress would gain a two-house "legislative veto" on administrative regulations and executive decrees. Seventh, the 1973 War Powers Resolution would be incorporated into the Constitution. And last, a national "referendum"—submitted to the voters by both houses of Congress or by the president acting with either House or Senate—would be designed to break any policy deadlocks between the elected branches of government. What motivates Sundquist are two "paramount" dangers: that the separation of powers makes it impossible to achieve "fiscal sanity" without "economic calamity" and that "paralysis in foreign policy" is manifested when no president conducts foreign relations with congressional support.[79]

What really troubles Sundquist, just as it concerned James MacGregor Burns two decades earlier (see chapter 1), is "the central problem of executive-legislative stalemate" with regard to domestic policy. In laying out his argument that "[a] government too inefficient to embark on adventurous efforts to change society will also be, by necessity, too inefficient to meet its inescapable, imperative responsibilities," Sundquist states that U.S. "history abounds with illustrations of governmental failures that, if they did not destroy 'freedom, stability, and prosperity,' at least threatened and sometimes impaired them." Sundquist believes that "the country clearly approves of social security, unemployment compensation, medicare, civil rights, and federal efforts to raise the standards of education, housing, and nutrition and to alleviate poverty," yet he bemoans the fact that "the welfare state came late to the United States" compared to Europe, just as "[c]ivil rights legislation was stalled for years, even decades." One final point in his litany is Watergate, including the fact that "the country witnessed the collapse of an administration mired in crime but lacked the means to place a new leader in the White House" until Nixon was forced to resign after the tapes were uncovered. The American people wrongly blame their elected leaders, mainly the president, for policy failures, but "the American constitutional system places extraordinary obstacles in the path of any leader," since the "president is expected to lead the Congress, but its two houses are independent institutions and . . . one or both are controlled by his political opposition."[80]

Given the nature of Sundquist's indictment, a structural fix is required, but any effort at constitutional reform will involve the "debate between liberals and conservatives, the former seeing the separation of powers as a barrier to, and the latter as a protection against, government activism." Sundquist believes this debate is "essentially unresolvable," but there is a "second impulse toward constitutional reform" emanating "from those who have helped to conduct the nation's foreign affairs." Here Sundquist points to the blocked SALT II treaty under Carter and to how "conservatives Richard Nixon, Gerald Ford, and Ronald Reagan found their foreign policies undercut by congressional liberals, leaving the country often with no clear foreign policy at all." Perhaps, he speculates, "conservatives and liberals may some day find constitutional reform, for the first time, a common cause." But then again "perhaps not," since he conjectures that liberals may "find new merit in the obstacles that similarly blocked the path of Ronald Reagan."[81] In other words, Sundquist apparently hopes that conservatives would not, any more than liberals, hold a "principled" position against constitutional reform. The ideological debate simply revolves around the winners and losers in the policy debate. In his penultimate paragraph, Sundquist acknowledges that his prognosis for reform is "pessimistic," because "[n]othing is likely to happen short of crisis"—which is typically "the case with all fundamental constitutional reform, in every country of the world and throughout history."[82]

Rexford G. Tugwell

The most radical transformation of American constitutionalism was advocated by the famous Rexford G. Tugwell, formerly on the faculty of Columbia University and the University of Chicago but best known as a member of President Roosevelt's original Brains Trust of advisers. An architect of the New Deal presidency, Tugwell experienced an intellectual metamorphosis. Unlike Hardin and Sundquist, whose reforms are targeted to strengthening presidential leadership and accountability, Tugwell argues for a wholesale scrapping of the Constitution. Politically that is a hopeless task, but what concerns us is the rationale that Tugwell develops for his grand scheme for the presidential role in his new regime.

Tugwell published his magnum opus on "the emerging Constitution" in 1974, the same year he coedited with political scientist Thomas E. Cronin a volume specific to the presidency.[83] The "central theme" for Tugwell and Cronin is "the ability of the Presidency . . . to furnish needed leadership while remaining, at the same time, responsive to the will of the people." Tugwell and Cronin explain that the presidency "is now deep in controversy" because "[t]here is no doubt that it has been ignoring the rule of self-restraint implicit in the Constitution. The silences of the Constitution present ambiguities and wide opportunities for aggrandizement by all the branches," but "Presidents have been notable offenders," insofar as "the checks and balances of the Constitution have operated more effectively on the legislative and judicial branches than they have on the Presidency."[84] Tugwell summarizes his own position in the final essay, alluding to "the near approach to dictatorship clearly developing in recent years" and the need for "drastic" changes, including "changes in a basic law that has been essentially unchanged for nearly two centuries," in order that "[t]hat law might regain its credibility and usefulness by such a reconstitution."[85] That is Tugwell's grand objective.

After more than two hundred years, our "emergent constitution has become something its framers would not recognize." Tugwell argues that, because formal amendments are next to impossible to approve, the Constitution had to evolve as a "living" document through the process by which the executive, legislative, and judicial branches *all* took advantage of those silences and ambiguities in its text. "None of these—States, Presidency, Congress, or Judiciary—is recognizably the original constitutional prescription; even the resemblance is clouded."[86] However, Tugwell views the legislature as reactive and the executive as proactive and, more precisely, subscribes to the notion that the Framers "built stalemate into the Constitution," since political "[i]nitiative could not come from a legislature with several hundred members" or even "the most renowned senators [who] have been more notable for resistance than for inventiveness." Inevitably "[i]t had to come from the single national representative, the president; yet he lacked many of the requisites of leadership; and such as he did have were extraconstitutional. They emerged from a political system the framers had meant to avoid [that is, from parties]." But party government never unfolded, since members of Congress often disagreed partially or entirely with their party's platform. As a consequence, "Congress has for the most part become an obstructive body, made so by the framers' structuring."[87] So discredited is Congress in Tugwell's mind that "no American can regard [it] with pride": "There is a minimum of attention to national problems; there is a well-developed system of trading for local improvements; there is interference in matters members are not competent to handle; there is no possibility of creative leadership and an incessant resistance to that of the president. Worst of all, there is a sickeningly supine posture before the swarming lobbyists."[88]

The president did not escape harsh criticism from Tugwell. Tugwell believes that we expect more from the president than any single incumbent can deliver, which is why he advocates a massive restructuring of the national government. To the existing three branches, Tugwell proposes adding three more—"political, planning, regulatory"—with the ostensible purpose of freeing the president from burdensome administrative matters so that he can devote his energies to the more important roles of "director of foreign relations, the chief legislator, the political leader, and, in an immensely extended sense, commander in chief."[89]

According to Tugwell's thesis, "the growth in scope and responsibility of the presidential office was altogether extraconstitutional, a development not anticipated by the framers, and so not provided for." As a consequence (here Tugwell parts company with other presidency scholars), he thinks the "enlargements [of the modern presidency] are not legitimized," that "vast areas of presidential activity are in constant controversy," and furthermore, because such developments have been allowed "to proceed without the constriction of rigid definition," what can happen "is easily illustrated from historical incidents, sometimes very costly indeed and with sinister implications for the future." In sum, Tugwell offers "a dismal assessment of the emergent president," because "[t]he interpretation of the original Constitution has been so unrestrained that the contemplated figure is no longer recognizable except as chief of state."[90]

Tugwell points to Lincoln (his suspension of the writ of habeas corpus and his freeing the slaves), FDR (the forced relocation of the Japanese), and "other presidents [who] have carried on virtual wars abroad without asking for a declaration" (including Johnson and Nixon). This situation arose, explains Tugwell, because "[a]mong the baffling characteristics of their [the Framers'] document none is more difficult to understand than the failure to make provision for inevitable circumstances. Emergency was one of these." "What presidents have considered imperative in time of national peril they have done; they have confronted foreign powers, sent armies abroad, deployed the navy in international waters, sent spy planes aloft, suspended civil rights, repressed rebellions, and used unappropriated funds; no one knows the extent of the intelligence activities directed by them, or the undercover activities of their operatives. All of these have taken on frightening dimensions under modern circumstances, but that the precedents reach far into the past cannot be denied."[91]

But there is a difference between past and present. The Doctrine of Necessity used by Washington, Jefferson, Jackson, and Lincoln was subjected to an unwritten Rule of Self-restraint. "Later presidents . . . have not had uniform success when they have not conformed to the *rule* their predecessors understood so well. It was the cause of Truman's [Korean] failure, and of Johnson's [in Vietnam] as well. Neither made sure of popular support; neither seemed willing to apply the art of conciliation."[92] So it seems that Korea and Vietnam are the limiting cases for Tugwell: "It was when interventions were not for the purpose of restoring order but in pursuit of global strategy that the emergency powers strained their customary bounds and began to be widely criticized": "[e]xpeditions of such massive size as those to Korea and Vietnam could not be sustained as mere exercises for temporary effect. They were given an arbitrary cast, they went on too long, and they were too distant for the threat to be credible."[93]

What is his constitutional remedy? Tugwell proposes giving the president one nine-year term, subject to recall by 60 percent of the voters after three years. The president would be supported by two vice presidents, one for "internal affairs" and the other for "general affairs." The operational use of military forces would be under a chancellor of military affairs, and any presidential proposal for military action would be subject to denial by a special national security committee of the Senate or ultimately by the entire Senate. In lieu of the Doctrine of Necessity, Tugwell would provide that the Senate "may declare a national emergency and may authorize the President to take appropriate action."[94]

Conclusion

Does presidential power derive from the prerogatives of office or from the incumbent? These two presidency literatures have a different perspective on prerogative power. The imperial presidency thesis argues that the modern presidents have an unstoppable quantity of prerogative power, which prompted these scholars to urge Congress to curb presidential war-making. But those scholars concerned about presidential impotency, like Sundquist, talk more about the failures of political leadership, especially in Carter's case.

Does presidential influence depend upon the force of personality, rhetorical leadership, or partisanship? Who is elected to the White House primarily concerns Hargrove, Barber, Reedy, Koenig, and Wildavsky, among others. Of course we recruited psychologically "healthy" but (to listen to the critics) totally ineffectual presidents in Gerald Ford and Jimmy Carter. Thus, presidents have either too much prerogative power or too few political skills, and in either case, a partial corrective is finding the "right" personality to fill the president's shoes. The boundaries of presidential imperialism or impotency, however, are not circumscribed by partisanship or rhetorical ability: nobody was terrified that, through force of personality, LBJ, Nixon, Ford, or Carter would mobilize public opinion to undermine our Constitution or the separation of powers. Any threat to the political regime from Nixon resulted because of prerogative power coupled with the abdication of congressional responsibility, most would agree.

Does presidential leadership vary between domestic and foreign affairs?

The answer is implicit in these two literatures. Presidential imperialism was grounded in war-making (nobody called President Johnson imperious when he micromanaged congressional enactment of his Great Society!). Presidential impotence over domestic policy motivates those political scientists who bemoan deadlock, gridlock, and stalemate.

Does the president actively or passively engage the legislative process and promote a policy agenda? The issue of war-making complicates our answer to this question. One corrective to the war prerogative is the restoration of Congress within the separation-of-powers system (so argues Schlesinger), if not legislative supremacy within a reconfigured parliamentary-style regime as urged by Hardin, Tugwell, and Sundquist. A strengthened Congress posed no problem for Hardin, Tugwell, and Sundquist because—beyond holding the president politically accountable—the coupling of the legislature with the executive through concurrent elections and other devices is designed to assure their cooperation. The problem of executive-legislative relations is answered in two words: divided government.

What forced Gerald Ford to pursue a veto strategy was the determined opposition of Democrats in the House and Senate. In the long term, Sundquist sees many missed opportunities for enacting far-reaching domestic programs because of the separation of powers. Presidential impotence thus is linked to partisanship, sharpening the legislative-executive divide. Decades earlier liberal reformers naively believed that "responsible" parties would overcome the separation of powers, but divided government forced Sundquist, Hardin, and Tugwell to embrace even more utopian reforms of our constitutional system. For Carter, though unified government existed during his tenure, Charles Jones and Erwin Hargrove argue that his policies were technically correct—but politically doomed—given the ideological mind-set of liberal Democrats in Congress. In addition, revisionists Jones and Hargrove, as well as Heclo and Salamon, argue that changes in the political system (weakened parties, single-issue groups) and the institutional system (democratization within Congress) were largely responsible for the legislative failures of Carter and Ford. Even Neustadt, we pointed out (see chapter 6), cites the same litany of structural problems befalling President Carter.

Does presidential leadership depend upon historical context, or is regime-building manifested through political, institutional, and constitutional developments? Obviously Vietnam and Watergate had everything to do with the reactions of these scholars to Johnson and Nixon. Even the troubles faced by Ford and Carter were largely "contextual" in nature, if we accept the revisionism of Jones and Hargrove. Looking back—and ahead—the themes of imperialism and impotence that surfaced during the 1960s and 1970s seem so time-bound as to comprise footnotes in this intellectual history. Listen to Schlesinger, and Johnson and Nixon are constitutional deviants; read Tugwell, Hardin, or Sundquist, and Woodrow Wilson comes to mind (see chapter 4), except that Wilson later embraced a strong president, not parliamentary government; believe Jones or Hargrove, and Carter was so uniquely placed in history that we need new criteria to judge him.

Does the organization of the executive branch service presidential leadership? The administrative presidency also implicates divided government, because Nixon's attempt to circumvent the normal political process and centralize power in the White House reflected his view of congressional Democrats as the political enemy. Also many of the articles in *The Tethered Presidency* by Franck and *The Illusion of Presidential Government* by Heclo and Salamon (which, we noted, began at a conference sponsored by the National Academy of Public Administration) give strong suggestions that the post-Watergate Congress was imperious vis-à-vis the White House and the executive branch (a theme pursued by conservative scholars in the 1980s; see chapter 9). The picture that emerges is that the permanent government is no monolithic force under presidential control; rather there are congressional meddling, bureaucratic infighting, failed administrative coordination, and violations of neutral competence. Within the White House, those early warnings by Rossiter, Finer, and Burns (see chapter 6) that the Executive Office of the President may not be an absolute blessing were understated, given the analogies to monarchy by George Reedy. Schlesinger adds to Reedy's regal picture of the Johnson White House by adding a large dose of Nixon paranoia to the mix. So powerful is this indictment of the presidential inner circle that even Richard Neustadt admits that Nixon, and Schlesinger, proved him wrong. The general impression is that the bureaucratic processes are beyond the White House span of control and that White House staffers are politically too intimate with the president to serve as a check on his blind ambitions. This is a government in disarray, the scholarly analog to the polls that show mounting public distrust of governing institutions.

CHAPTER NINE

Return to Hamiltonianism
Ronald Reagan and the
Movement Conservatives

Just as the liberal malaise with liberal presidents was personified in the overreaching of Lyndon Johnson and the underachieving of Jimmy Carter, it stands to reason that scholars on the political right would rally behind the presidential leadership of Ronald Reagan. However, since conservatives take pride in their commitment to constitutionalism, an interesting question is whether this generation of "movement" conservatives has much in common with the previous generations of conservative critics of Progressive and Liberal presidential government. The Reagan-Bush era spawned three well-known critiques of presidential leadership by people associated with conservative and neoconservatives causes, including members of those Republican administrations. Two are anthologies: *The Fettered Presidency*, by L. Gordon Crovitz and Jeremy A. Rabkin, and *The Imperial Congress*, by Gordon S. Jones and John A. Marini. The third volume, *Energy in the Executive*, was authored by Terry Eastland, an official in the Reagan Department of Justice.[1]

Robert Spitzer characterizes the argument in the anthologies as a 1980s conservative retake on what liberals complained about forty years earlier: "From the 1940s to the 1960s this complaint emanated primarily from liberals who objected to the efforts of congressional conservatives to resist the advance of progressive presidential agendas." Similarly, he says that "[i]n the 1980s this theme was picked up with renewed vigor primarily by conservatives who rankled at congressional moves toward reassertion in the 1970s and 1980s and who felt frustrated when Democratic Congresses succeeded in amending or thwarting many of Ronald Reagan's initiatives."[2] Because Spitzer believes that this argument is deeply influenced by "ideology and partisanship," his position is a good beginning point to assess whether the 1980s conservatives have any commonalities with their 1940s–60s counterparts. If we can show some continuity, then Spitzer's argument —that this new conservative position is simply an ideological weapon— does damage to the constitutionalists' devotion to our regime. As Spitzer put it, "[l]iberal-conservative clashes over politics and policy are the legitimate stuff of American politics, but when that debate is cast in abstract, institutional terms involving the possibility of structural shifts between the branches of government, partisan motives must be identified and reconciled with the consequences of proposed changes."[3]

Spitzer's observations are not groundless when one considers the policy agenda of the Jones and Marini as well as the Crovitz and Rabkin editions. Various contributors express opposition to the War Powers Resolution and the Boland Amendment (limiting aid to the Nicaraguan Contras) as eroding presidential prerogatives; the independent counsel as usurping executive law enforcement functions; and the use of "omnibus" (budget) continuing resolutions as undercutting the veto power. These three developments also are explicitly attacked by Terry Eastland. The Jones and Marini volume seems to promote presidential power based largely on legal authority and prerogative, trying to bolster inherent presidential powers against a Congress that seems determined to rein in executive discretion with precise statutory language. The Crovitz and Rabkin anthology leans toward presidential leadership grounded mostly in legal authority but also based on politics. Eastland similarly urges conservative presidents to go public.

There are several references in all three books to Hamiltonian justifications of executive energy. Hamilton is employed to rationalize *both* styles of presidential leadership: authority-plus-prerogative and authority-plus-politics. If the conservatives of an earlier era were concerned about excessive spending, socialism, or a planned economy, generally these volumes focus less on any substantive agenda (though Eastland does raise the cry against racial quotas) as compared to the institutional and legal relationships that impinge upon national security policy and fiscal policy. Finally, the political reality underlying these volumes is stated repeatedly: a realization that tensions between the executive and legislative branches are fueled by the partisan and ideological conflicts of divided government.

The Fettered Presidency

In his foreword, conservative appellate judge (and defeated Supreme Court nominee) Robert H. Bork explains that the book's essays "demonstrate that the office of the president of the United States has been significantly weakened in recent years and that Congress is largely, but not entirely, responsible." Bork joins the chorus of critics who believe the legislature has usurped executive prerogative:

The War Powers Act is merely the most dramatic example of a congressional attempt to weaken the presidency. Recent years have produced as well intrusive and debilitating congressional oversight of intelligence activities, the combination of budgets and substantive lawmaking in vetoproof continuing resolutions, the removal of part of the president's law enforcement responsibility through the creation of independent counsel in the Ethics in Government Act, vacillating incursions into foreign policy as with the five different Boland amendments that crippled policy toward the hostile Marxist regime in Nicaragua, and much more.[4]

The papers and commentary in the Jones and Marini anthology were previously presented at an American Enterprise Institute conference in April of 1988. In their introduction, L. Gordon Crovitz, editor with the *Wall Street Journal*, and political scientist Jeremy A. Rabkin tell us that their book "addresses the proliferation of legal constraints on policy making in the executive branch of the federal government and highlights the risks and dangers this poses for public policy." Thus they "concentrate particularly on what seemed to us a disturbing trend toward excessive reliance on legal standards in the formulation and control of public policy," insofar as "more and more aspects of public policy making have come under judicial control."[5]

This "institutional power battle" masks an "underlying reality" that for nearly two decades the president and Congress have been controlled by opposing political parties. Say Crovitz and Rabkin, much frustration by their contributors "might be interpreted as the cries of one set of partisans against the institutional leverage of their partisan opponents."[6] Especially in foreign affairs, many voice the sentiment that "[t]he liberal majority in the Democratic party was generally skeptical if not out-right hostile toward the exercise of U.S. strength in world affairs." Yet domestic affairs, notably fiscal policy, were hardly immune to criticism, because "[t]he opposing objectives" of Republican presidents meant that Democratic Congresses "had every incentive to resist presidential strength: hence the maneuvers in Congress to circumvent the presidential veto power with new budgeting techniques, including vetoproof, last-minute, and all-in-one continuing resolutions."[7]

What should be done? Crovitz and Rabkin ultimately advocate what may be termed the authority-plus-politics style of presidential leadership. "[T]he best solution is to build up the political strength of the presidency, not to litigate the constitutional rights of the office." This means that "[t]he issue immediately becomes a direct confrontation between rival parties and competing partisan interests," with appeals "made to the cause of the president's followers, not to the prerogatives of the office." This strategy is attractive if the president and his partisans can "rally the most popular support" but looks less promising "to those who fear that the president will lose in such confrontations and carry to defeat not just his own policies but also the institutional preconditions for any president successfully implementing his policies: that is, both the president and the presidency will lose."[8]

That caveat notwithstanding, the editors ultimately come down on the side of politics, rather than prerogative, because,

[l]ike it or not, the president must be a politician as well as a manager. The framers intended a president who would manage the government; yet they understood the inherent difficulties in managing a nation that is not naturally a single community with entirely harmonious interests. Inevitably, only a president who is an able politician will enjoy the freedom and discretion necessary to carry out his administrative responsibilities. The executive has many inherent powers at his disposal to protect against the legal constraints that cripple effective policy making. The lesson of the past eight years is that these powers must be used with greater vigor and resolve if the presidency is to fulfill its intended role.[9]

One essay on national security, by Gary Schmitt and Abram Shulsky, calls upon Lockean prerogative and argues that "[b]y culling out executive from legislative power and housing it in a largely independent and unitary office, the framers were signaling their intent to move decisively away from the incompetence of congressionally dominated government, particularly in the areas of war and foreign affairs."[10] Furthermore, any requirement of prior notification to Congress about covert operations is likely an unconstitutional intrusion on the commander in chief. Caspar Weinberger, who was defense secretary under Reagan, echoes that sentiment in alleging that the War Powers Act was wrongheaded and that Presidents Nixon, Ford, Carter, and Reagan were all justified in viewing that law as being unconstitutional.[11]

In discussing the budget "breakdown" and the "vitiation" of the veto, political scientist Judith Best says she believes presidents "must be willing to cry foul *publicly* when they are constrained by congressional strategies to sign bills containing provisions they deem unconstitutional."[12] Framers Gouverneur Morris and James Madison, she says, "repudiate[d] the Whig theory of the president as a mere clerk who faithfully executes the will of the legislature." Moreover, to read the proceedings of the Constitutional Convention "as an argument for Whiggism is to read it backward."[13]

The "highly formalistic model" of the executive-legislative relationship adopted by the Supreme Court to nullify the legislative veto (*Immigration and Naturalization Service v. Chadha*, 1983, and the Gramm-Rudman deficit-reduction law [*Bowsher v. Synar*, 1986]) is criticized by Louis Fisher of the Congressional Research Service: "The Constitution contemplates an overlapping, not a separation, of powers."[14] C. Boyden Gray, counselor to Vice President Bush, argued that because "today's Congress is the champion of the entrenched special interest and the executive branch is the advocate for opportunity and innovation," the ability of the United States "to compete internationally" will depend partly on the "executive's ability to reassert its constitutional role to represent all the people and to induce Congress to engage in internal reform of its own to reduce the fragmenting and paralyzing influence of special interests."[15]

Michael Malbin, a GOP congressional staffer, looks at legal changes to tighten the requirement of advanced legislative notification of covert activities, which he believes raise enough "constitutional difficulties" that "the president should let it be known . . . that he intends to defend his own institutional power whenever that power is challenged by Congress."[16] An essay by former attorney general William French Smith takes aim at the independent counsel law, viewing it as a clear-cut usurpation of the executive law enforcement function.[17] Suzanne Garment observes that "[t]here has been increasing comment in the past few years over the fact that Congress has legislated harsh ethics rules for the executive branch but more or less left itself out of the movement for reform and moral purity."[18]

In the final discussion roundtable, it is Irving Kristol, neoconservative coeditor of the *Public Interest*, who most forcefully advocates that the president join this battle publicly. The fundamental problem, worse than divided government, is that "what has radically transformed the whole situation is the ideological polarization of the political parties"; they have become "more intensely ideological, more intensely combative, more unprincipled in their combativeness," even though "the people have not become more ideological." As a consequence, voters split their ballots between Republicans and Democrats as "the only way they can figure out to cope with ideological parties that they do not really want, at least not when they are intensely ideological parties." Kristol believes "[t]he president is a victim not just of Congress but of *this* Congress with *these* particular ideas, a Congress that wants to weaken the presidency to establish the supremacy of these ideas, in foreign policy and in domestic policy." He chides Republicans for being "timid" and urges that "the president can learn from the example of Franklin D. Roosevelt," who, when faced with congressional resistance, "got his program through by defining the presidency not as one branch of the government but as the tribune of the people." Roosevelt succeeded "by going to the people and using popular pressure on Congress to achieve his ends. That is the only way an executive under current circumstances can intimidate Congress." Especially in military and foreign policy, Kristol wants the president to "tap the vein not only of patriotism but of nationalism," because "[i]f the president goes to the American people and wraps himself in the American flag and lets Congress wrap itself in the white flag of surrender, the president will win."[19]

The Imperial Congress

Taking a similar perspective, Gordon S. Jones and John A. Marini invited Congressman Newt Gingrich (R-GA), who would become the Speaker of the 104th Congress, to write their foreword. According to Gingrich, "Madison, Jefferson and Hamilton tried to insure against the rise of an imperial Congress," but "as the separation of powers continues to erode, the present-day Congress has become the most unrepresentative and corrupt of the modern era," lusting for power but evading its responsibility, "[i]ncreasingly dominated by a corrupt machine that deceives the American public," and exempting "itself from the standards of conduct it imposes on the executive branch and the American people."[20]

Gordon Jones of the Heritage Foundation and political scientist John Marini argue that "America faces a constitutional crisis stemming from two causes: the congressional failure to observe traditional limits on its power, and the acquiescence of the other two branches of government in the resulting arrogation of power." More to the point, Congress "is increasingly engaged in the executive function of administering laws as it delegates more and more of its traditional law-making responsibilities to the federal courts and to 'independent agencies.' "[21] Jones and Marini's collection of essays details the origins of the bureaucratic state and the displacement of the governing function by administration, as well as how congressional behavior "encroaches on the prerogatives of the executive branch." It then offers corrective steps "largely by the executive branch reasserting its prerogatives, and through electoral politics."[22]

Marini argues that members of Congress are "good at representing organized interests and constituencies, but Congress as an institution has become almost incapable of pursuing a public interest." Furthermore, the heightened congressional role in administration threatens "to undermine the energy of the executive." Thus "[i]t is difficult to retain a Constitution with a genuine separation of powers when the principal branches no longer perform their constitutional functions."[23] Much testimony from the contributors supports his intellectual indictment. Political scientist Charles R. Kesler points to the thousand-page Continuing Resolution and 1988 Budget Reconciliation Act as "a sign that the Congress is losing the capacity, or the desire, to legislate responsibly, and that the presidency . . . is resigned to the legislature's abdication of constitutional authority."[24]

Douglas A. Jeffrey is critical of the War Powers Act not simply for its provisions but also for "its implicit (and gloriously unconstitutional) assumption that Congress, as opposed to the Constitution itself, is the fount of presidential power." He also notes the "[u]nprecedented use of the power of the purse to control foreign policy," which suggests that the bipartisanship of the Truman era in foreign affairs has collapsed.[25] Professor John Adams Wettergreen, also a political scientist, observes that Congress has come to regard "the independent agencies not as truly independent, but only as independent of the executive branch, and perhaps as arms of the Congress," since Congress, "especially the House, has a natural sympathy with administration because of its closer ties to narrower interests." Because the Democrats created most federal agencies, they act as "the representatives of private and parochial interests; the more bureaucratized those interests are the more strongly they support the Democratic party."[26]

An anonymous Department of Defense official voices his complaint that Congress micromanages national defense, and another unidentified legislative and executive staffer focuses on congressional micromanagement of domestic policy. Other essayists target the budget mess, committee assignments, and legislative rules.[27] What Gordon Crovitz calls the "criminalization" of politics means that "policy differences by a liberal-dominated Congress against a conservative Reagan Administration took the separation of powers battle into a new and politically dangerous dimension." Congress has "perfected the art of transforming political differences into potentially indictable offenses."[28] The legislative culprit is the Ethics in Government Act and the use of independent counsels against various officials in the Reagan administration. That law is constitutionally suspect, because "the clear sole authority under the Constitution" is for "the executive branch to execute the laws, including prosecuting offenders." Iran-Contra was "the low point" of the Reagan administration, but "perhaps the greater sin will have been the complete failure of the executive branch to protect its privileges or its officials against a Congress driven by blood-lust headed by an extraordinarily aggressive prosecutor."[29]

Three final essays search for antidotes to congressional imperialism. The first, by Gordon S. Jones, reminds conservatives that their viewpoint needs to change. "It may seem strange that conservatives . . . should bemoan the weakness of the executive," because "[i]t has been an article of faith for conservatives that the Constitution really does give an edge to Congress in the battle with the executive for supremacy." Conservatives distrust concentrations of power. "Beginning in the 1940s and continuing through the 1950s and 1960s, conservatives saw power flowing to the executive, and they instinctively sought a check on that power, first in the courts, and when that avenue failed, in Congress." However, Jones believes that the conservative preference for Congress was less "a general preference than a situational one," meaning that "it was a preference for the branch that was striving to counter the dominant branch." What conservatives really want, says Jones, is "divided power and limits on the scope of government. The problem is always a concentration of power in one branch to the extent that the liberties of Americans are threatened. A generation ago, the threat came from the executive. Today, it comes from Congress. Perhaps another day will come when it will be the executive again."[30]

Jones traces the transformation in conservative outlook to Ronald Reagan. "When Reagan was elected in 1980, he shattered the myth that the president was, should, and would be the repository of institutionalized liberalism in the United States."[31] Echoing other contributors, however, Jones says "the fact that the policy views of the center-right majority of Americans have not been translated into policy itself reflects a failure of conception and execution by the president." Reagan will leave the presidency "weaker than he found it," because he dropped the conservative ball.[32] Looking ahead, "a popular president will have to reach beyond the existing elites, to ordinary Americans, grass-roots members of America's social and religious organizations, and communicate directly with them."[33]

Political theorist Thomas G. West argues that congressional "[p]ower . . . is exercised primarily by an aggregation of individual committee and subcommittee chairmen" but that "Congress as a body deliberates infrequently over policy."[34] Boldly advocating an assertive presidential leadership, West advises the chief executive to back up his subordinates who defy rather than defer to congressmen, force Congress to stop exempting itself from ethics laws, and refuse to sign Continuing [budget] Resolutions, since they meddle with administration. But he mostly argues that "[f]or Congress to change, public opinion about Congress has to change." To shape mass attitudes, the president must take the lead, because "only the president has the public visibility and prestige to articulate authoritatively the reasons for dismantling congressional imperialism. The president should address the opinions of the public directly, by his own words and deeds, not just indirectly through private authorities."[35] Ultimately, argues West, constitutionalism through partisanship is good, because "[t]he purpose of decent partisanship is not victory for its own sake but for the common good. When the Constitution is at risk, citizens must organize against those who are already organized to benefit at the expense of the liberty and property of the majority."[36]

The last essay, by another anonymous executive and legislative staffer, differentiates between the culture of the nation and the culture of opinion elites. Calling attention to Reagan's 1989 State of the Union message, it argues that "the Reagan Administration should have used them [speeches] more often, but more to the point of rallying the people against its congressional foes. Grandstanding is not bad, so long as it facilitates, rather than substitutes for, fundamental changes in the power equation between the White House and Capitol." This essayist concludes that the president "must become the tribune of the people. This is the only role that will allow him to effectively counter the enormous institutional clout of Congress. It was the role Andrew Jackson, correctly or not, assumed for himself, thereby drawing such vilification and outrage as would frighten most modern presidents. He did survive it, however, and his place in the history of the presidency might tempt a future chief executive to be as daring."[37] The subtext, of course, is that Ronald Reagan was no Andrew Jackson!

Energy in the Executive

Terry Eastland appears to mimic that position by urging conservatives to adopt Neustadtian leadership techniques. Eastland faults Reagan, and Bush as well, for not appealing to the court of public opinion in holding Congress at bay. Thus he counsels the use of heroic means to achieve the ends of smaller government and chides those conservatives who look backward, saying that "Reagan demonstrated that the strong presidency is necessary to effect ends sought by most conservatives," such as tax reform, cuts in the marginal tax rates, and an arms race that hastened the end of the cold war. To the charge that conservatives are becoming no less opportunistic than liberals were, Eastland asserts that conservatives can mount a principled defense of executive energy. On this score, it is worth quoting Eastland at length:

> Cynics will be forgiven for thinking that conservatives have been attracted to a strong executive on purely instrumental grounds, for there have been few efforts on the part of conservatives to discuss the strong presidency in terms other than political self-interest. But if the only explanation conservatives have for their new faith in the presidency is pragmatic, they will find themselves bereft of principle and thus in sync with those many liberals, journalists, and academics who are impatient with governing forms and procedures.
>
> Conservatives definitely should embrace a strong executive, but for the best of reasons: the Constitution. For what the Constitution proposes to establish is limited government that can maintain the conditions of freedom against internal and external threat, administer the nation's laws, and encourage rational deliberation and choice on the part of a self-governing people. And the presidency it regards as necessary for achieving this government, which the framers saw as *good* government, is a strong one. Or, as Alexander Hamilton preferred to say in the vocabulary of his time, an energetic one. As Hamilton succinctly stated the matter in the *Federalist Papers*, "energy in the executive is the leading character[istic] of good government."[38]

With that in mind, Eastland proceeds with a highly ambitious leadership agenda. Eastland approves of presidents "going public" as a constitutionally grounded strategy for legislative success. "In recommending legislation to Congress, the strong President will speak publicly in its behalf. Today he has no choice but to do that if he is to meet his constitutional duty—he cannot be silent in the manner of nineteenth century Presidents." However, partly in deference to Jeffrey Tulis (on his critique of the "rhetorical" president, see chapter 10), Eastland agrees that guidance "is not found in the Wilsonian notion that presidential leadership depends not upon the President's place within the constitutional order but upon his contingent personal traits, especially his ability to read the thoughts of the American people and stir them to action through rhetoric." Rhetoric can be ill-used or underused, but properly employed, "as Reagan used it in behalf of tax reform," presidential rhetoric has the purpose of "arguing, not merely asserting, or sound-biting, the President's legislative case." Eastland's disagreement with Neustadt is seen in his criticism of President Bush. "Reagan generally understood, as Bush in his budget summitry performance did not, that a modern President cannot 'bargain' his way to consensus with legislators from both parties." He feels that Bush's approach—"the style of leadership endorsed by Richard E. Neustadt in 1960—assumed a consensus in the electorate itself that was missing." Because the "electorate [is] conflicted over major domestic policy questions," the "President must make a public legislative case."[39]

Eastland further believes that the presidential oath of office is a "unique source of energy in government" and that beyond the "self-defense veto" foreseen by Hamilton, "in an era of divided government . . . the policy veto is a compelling tool of governance." Saying that a president "should not rely on the [Supreme] Court to protect the office he holds," Eastland adds that "Jackson prevailed in his fight with Congress; the idea of a national bank died. And, thus, by the way, did a strong presidency defeat bigger government."[40]

Along with veto statements, Eastland advocates so-called presidential "signing statements" (which many scholars believe are constitutionally suspect) to influence law enforcement, if not lawmaking. "When approving legislation, the strong President will append statements to the most important bills, and in this way speak to Congress (although it is under no obligation to listen) and the executive branch (which is). Laws must be interpreted before they can be enforced. Signing statements thus become for the President vehicles . . . for communicating to his 'instruments of execution' how a new law should be implemented."[41]

Eastland envisions a sweeping prerogative power in war-making. Although he believes that President Bush "probably did need a law before he could have acted militarily against Iraq"[42] (since that was not a defensive action), Eastland argues that Bush had tremendous latitude to impose military force without a declaration of war. He says that "Bush would not have needed a law of Congress to maintain troops for purely defensive reasons in Saudi Arabia, nor to turn them loose in an offensive manner had they been attacked . . . Nor would Bush have needed a law had he decided only to strike the chemical, nuclear, and biological warfare facilities inside Iraq. But the sheer magnitude of the offensive operation" led President Bush to believe that a "law was necessary as the nation went to *this* war, and the Iraq Resolution, in effect, declared war."[43]

The prerogative power is tied to Lincoln, not Nixon, whom Eastland believes laid "claim to the Lincoln tradition of acting in the national interest as a defense for actions that may be deemed illegal. Suffice to say, Nixon did not face a clearly discernible crisis, as Lincoln manifestly had." Adds

Eastland: "Only a Constitution large enough to allow actions against the law for the public good is, ironically, law adequate to democratic government; as Lincoln understood, the Constitution 'is different *in its application* in cases of Rebellion or Invasion, involving the Public Safety, from what it is in times of profound peace and public security.'"[44]

Eastland also endorses an "administrative presidency" strategy, though he understands that bureaucratic politics, being normally liberal, poses difficulties for conservatives. This fact of Washington life means that a conservative president must be very careful to appoint "individuals who are committed to his views."[45] Eastland would extend this political penetration to crafting a litigation strategy for the Department of Justice. "When the government is a plaintiff in a case, and even more so when it has entered as a friend of the court, its lawyers have fewer institutional considerations to consider and can more freely pursue the President's interests." In toto, executive energy requires single-mindedness, because "[w]hatever the task—devising a legislative recommendation, drafting a State of the Union or veto message, enforcing a law, selecting a judge, negotiating a treaty, mapping a foreign policy—those who execute it must share the President's political premises. Personnel *is* policy."[46]

Eastland champions Reagan's strict screening of judicial appointees, because the Supreme Court "*does* jurisprudence, and the President can influence its jurisprudence through his Supreme Court choices," as did FDR, who was "perhaps the greatest example of a President who by design influenced the path of the law through judicial selection."[47] However, "Reagan did better on his terms at judicial selection than any President since FDR."[48] A failure to follow Reagan's appointment strategy is to fail the Constitution itself: "The oath obligates a President not only to execute the office faithfully but also to 'preserve, protect, and defend the Constitution.' The presidential office is essential to the constitutional order, and to the degree that a President effectively divests himself of the nominating and appointing powers vested in the executive as part of the overall design, he is in violation of the oath. At stake in judicial nominations and appointments is not only the political power of the President but also the very integrity of the constitutional order."[49]

Conclusion

Does presidential power derive from the prerogatives of office or from the incumbent? Given that Progressive and Liberal critics, who found the separated powers so deficient, logically turned to extraconstitutional methods (notably responsible partyism) to strengthen presidential leadership, one hypothesis is that conservatives would look toward Lockean prerogative as a natural remedy, since they would be very resistant to importing parliamentary forms to the American Republic. As was shown, the left-leaning scholars who feared Johnson, hated Nixon, and bemoaned Carter were intellectual outliers in the Progressive-Liberal tradition that typically exalted personalized power in the White House, though what was paradoxical was that the excesses of presidential war-making prerogative fueled the backlash against Vietnam.

Do these movement conservatives represent a departure from their forebears—Coolidge, Taft, and Corwin? Their fundamental grievance is that Congress encroached on presidential prerogative in foreign affairs, where historically the president's inherent powers have been most secure. On these terms, modern-day constitutionalists give the same principled arguments for Lockean prerogative that one would find in the writings of Hamilton, Taft, Coolidge, or Corwin. On the saliency of prerogative, therefore, Spitzer misspoke: there has been no flip-flop among the constitutionalists analogous to the way the 1960s Vietnam backlash caused liberals to seek redress from Lockean prerogative.

Does presidential influence depend upon the force of personality, rhetorical leadership, or partisanship? To say that the older generation of constitutionalists were antipolitical would be erroneous, since both Coolidge and Corwin were aware that the domestic role of legislative leadership required political skills, persuasive techniques, and party leadership. Yet it is not inaccurate to say that the movement conservatives have embraced Neustadtian orthodoxy to a degree unappreciated by the likes of Taft or Coolidge, even Corwin, though none of these early constitutionalists were adverse to presidential nudges of Congress. To engage the political opposition requires that conservative presidents wage war in the court of public opinion, not the court of law. Rhetorical leadership means a spirited defense of presidential prerogative, and priorities, against Congress. The Crovitz-Rabkin and Jones-Marini anthologies see the solution to weakened prerogative to be political, not legal. Terry Eastland and Irving Kristol are prominent advocates for Reagan's "going public" against Congress; support for that rhetorical counteroffensive is expressed by others, including Professors West and Best, and it is ultimately endorsed by coeditors Crovitz and Rabkin.

Does presidential leadership vary between domestic and foreign affairs?

From this perspective, Professor Spitzer may be right. Another question that guided our research was whether presidential leadership was influenced by domestic policy or foreign affairs. The left-right ideological divide is largely shaped by domestic policy, not foreign affairs, and this cleavage is primarily what Spitzer had in mind. However, Spitzer does not name the 1960s conservatives who bolstered Congress. If he was thinking of those anti-aggrandizement scholars, then his argument makes sense, since the fact that liberal congressional Democrats in the 1980s confronted a Republican in the White House upends the presumption by Kendall, de Grazia, and Patterson that Congress was the safe haven for conservatism. Of course the movement conservatives of today reject the kind of presidential passivity urged by Willmoore Kendall, Alfred de Grazia, and C. Perry Patterson. In sum, our argument is that the three anti-aggrandizement scholars are historical outliers in the constitutionalist tradition. A greater affinity exists between these movement conservatives and Taft-Coolidge-Corwin than between Kendall–de Grazia–Patterson and *either* the early-century constitutionalists or the late-century traditionalists. The ideological sympathies of all three groups of scholars are less important than how they assessed presidential leadership.

Does presidential leadership depend upon historical context, or is regime-building manifested through political, institutional, and constitutional developments? Here this question translates as, Does the prerogative-plus-politics model being advocated by the movement conservatives contradict Original Intent? Obviously this 1980s literature is time-bound, prompted by the executive-legislative tensions that surfaced under Reagan. However, these movement conservatives believe that it was the "imperial" Congress, not the president, who represents a repudiation of Original Intent. The Framers designed an energetic executive, to be independent of legislative cabals, whose base of authority flows directly from the Constitution. Indeed these apologists for Original Intent rally arguments that the Constitution mandates political leadership by the president. Even Tulis's argument (chapter 10) that the Framers feared demagoguery is sidetracked by an Eastland eager to rationalize energy in the executive.

Does the president actively or passively engage the legislative process and promote a policy agenda? This question is somewhat moot, since the traditionalist indictment argues that Congress has become an oligarchic tool in the hands of the Democratic Party, both unresponsive and irresponsible in policymaking. Congress is more attuned to special interests than to the public will, which explains why the movement conservatives collectively believe that a president can win by rallying public opinion. These new constitutionalists, like Taft and Coolidge before them, believe that the president is better positioned than Congress to defend the public good. Because a "going public" strategy involves mobilizing the public *against* Congress, rather than trying to bargain *with* Congress, clearly these scholars abandon any pretext that the executive-legislative relationship is a political partnership.

Does the organization of the executive branch service presidential leadership? Congress is imperial because it turned Original Intent upside-down with respect to administration. It unduly penetrates the bureaucracy and usurps executive functions, principally law enforcement via the use of independent counsels. The skepticism of Reagan was warranted, since federal bureaucrats are considered to be captive Democrats more willing to follow Congress than the chief executive. These critics add an ideological layer to the normal effects of organizational inertia, clienteleism, and congressional politics that have always allowed federal agencies to resist direction from the White House. Eastland saw hope in Reagan's ability to ideologically fine-tune the screening of administrative—and judicial—appointees. It seems less likely that Coolidge, given his criticism of Jefferson's meddling in judicial affairs, would subscribe to Eastland's robust defense of a full-court administrative presidency.

CHAPTER TEN

The Emerging Scholarly Consensus
A *New Realism, an Old Idealism*

It has been over forty years since Neustadt penned his Machiavellian study of presidential power, and though most of us still pay homage to his classic statement that presidential power is influence, many of the leading presidential scholars are abandoning the tenets of Neustadtian orthodoxy. The myth of the "heroic" presidency has given way to an emerging consensus that blends a new realism with an old idealism. The new realism is that the president is no master of Congress but rather one, albeit important, political actor in the legislative process. The old idealism is a renewed appreciation for the Framers' keen sense of why the separation of powers was essential both for liberty and for good government. Arguably the most holistic statement of this emerging consensus was the 1985 award-winning book by Theodore J. Lowi, but no one scholar can produce a working consensus.[1] Lowi got an assist from many presidency scholars, who represent a variety of traditions and approaches: some normative, others historicist, many empiricist and behavioral. We identify four interrelated themes that characterize this emerging consensus: (1) the expectations gap and the dangers of plebiscitary leadership, (2) divided government and policymaking, (3) the ennobled Congress, and (4) presidential constraints.

The Expectations Gap

Most fundamental to this scholarly consensus, as we see it, is the belief that an expectations gap exists between presidential power and presidential performance. Waterman and his associates claim that this thesis "has been a mainstay of the presidency literature for more than thirty years."[2] White House commentators long suspected that the official responsibilities were more than a match for one man, going back to Laski and, two decades later, to Herman Finer (see chapter 6), but that truism was no rallying cry to raise normative objections against heroic leadership. One example will suffice. Two decades ago Thomas E. Cronin diagnosed this "paradox" of the presidency, that we "ask our presidents to raise hopes, to educate, to inspire" but that "too much inspiration will invariably lead to dashed hopes, disillusion-ment, and cynicism." He explained that "few presidents in recent times have been able to keep their promises and fulfill their intentions"—but that pretty much ended his commentary.[3] Some commentators urged reforms to lighten the presidential load, but, like Cronin, no previous author suggested that the expectations gap held dire implications for the regime. Today, to pose this issue raises serious questions about presidential governing.

It was Lowi who dramatized the dangers to republicanism from the mismatch between presidential promises and performance. Some aca-demics embraced Neustadt, Lowi says, for "the selfish reason" of justifying JFK, but many also "sincerely accepted the redefinition of democratic theory with the presidency at its core."[4] By redefinition, Lowi means aban-doning representation as the basis for governmental legitimacy in favor of a "new social contract" based on service delivery. "They [the people] have invested fully in it [the presidency], they have witnessed the vesting of the 'capacity to govern' in the office, they have approved, and they now look for delivery on all the promises as their measure of democracy and legitimacy." Beware, however, for this new public philosophy has a serious downside. "There are built-in barriers to presidents' delivering on their promises, and the unlikely occasion of one doing so would only engender another round of new policies, with new responsibilities and new demands for help." Worse yet are the effects of this new public philosophy on the incumbent who faces the prospect of failure. "The desperate search is no longer for the good life but for the most effective presentation of appearances. This is a pathology because it escalates the rhetoric at home, ratcheting expecta-tions upward notch by notch, and fuels adventurism abroad, in a world where the cost of failure can be annihilation."[5] To correct this situation, Lowi argues, we need to begin "building down" the presidency, beginning with self-awareness by the president himself.

The problem of presidential plebiscites that Lowi identifies is given historical perspective by Jeffrey Tulis, who explains why the "rhetorical presidency" is at odds with Original Intent. Tulis distinguishes three eras in American history: the "old" way of the Founding; the "middle" way, person-ified by Theodore J. Roosevelt; and the "new" way of Woodrow Wilson. Of utmost concern to the Framers was majority tyranny from below and dema-goguery from above, and those concerns led our early presidents to address their policy agenda in written form to Congress. The proscription of dema-gogic leadership was never breached until President Andrew Johnson aimed his policy speeches at the populace, for which he nearly paid the ultimate political price of impeachment. Roosevelt's moderation was put asunder by Wilson. "By justifying Roosevelt's practice with a new theory that would make popular rhetoric routine, Wilson would transform the bully pulpit and Roosevelt's America."[6] Thus, Tulis sees Wilson as the first "modern" president, and surely the country is the worse because of it. Because Wilson regarded separated powers "the central defect" of our regime, impeding "true deliberation in the legislature" and "energy in the executive,"[7] his solution was the president as a " 'leader-interpreter' " who receives "his authority independently through a mandate from the people."[8]

The downside of rhetorical leadership was illustrated not only by Wilson's ill-fated popular campaign for the League of Nations but also, more recently, by the 1960s War on Poverty. President Johnson's rhetorical tactic "not only produced a hastily packaged program, his clear victory ensured that he and not Congress would be blamed if the program failed. And fail it did." At base, says Tulis, such leadership "is more deleterious than beneficial to American politics because the rhetorical presidency is not just the use of popular leadership, but rather the routine appeal to public opinion."[9]

Others cite the expectations gap as a drag on presidential credibility. In their study of legislative voting, Jon R. Bond and Richard Fleisher argue that one result of rising public expectations is "often the perception of a failed presidency," whereas Charles O. Jones claims that "[t]he American presidency carries a burden of lofty expectations that are simply not warranted by the political or constitutional basis of the office."[10] Those concerns are given added weight by Samuel Kernell as well as by Paul Brace and Barbara Hinckley. Kernell coined the phrase "going public" to describe "new strategies of presidential leadership" that promote the presidency "and his [the president's] policies in Washington by appealing to the American public for support." His analysis is validated by data showing that presidents travel more, give more speeches, have more public appearances, and secure more television time than they did in earlier years.[11] Kernell is troubled that going public has displaced bargaining as the essential tool of the popular presidents. But a "more damaging" consequence is that "public discussion tends to harden negotiating positions as both sides posture," both to rally supporters and to impress the opposition. Thus: "Even when a stalemate is avoided, the adopted policy may not enjoy the same firm foundation of support had it been enacted by a negotiated consensus."[12]

Paul Brace and Barbara Hinckley published an empirical analysis of public opinion and presidential popularity.[13] Modeling presidential popularity has become a fetish among quantitative analysts (usually devoid of any normative concerns), but Brace and Hinckley give serious thought to values. "At best, there is an uneasy balance between popularity and the tasks Americans expect a president to do," and "[a]t worst, the popular basis of government has slipped somehow, and democracy has been turned on its head," since presidents "govern in the name of the public, using poll reports and other devices as substitutes for more basic opinions and beliefs."[14] The fact is that elections no longer bestow legitimacy, because an "electoral mandate is continually updated and reviewed by public-opinion polls" as a "monthly referendum" on presidential performance.[15] This brings Brace and Hinckley back to the expectations gap: "We thus find an idealized portrait of the office that contrasts sharply with real-world events. This contrast supplies both power and limits to individuals in office: power insofar as they inherit the unrealistic expectations, limits when these expectations cannot be fulfilled."[16] For one thing, those unrealistic expectations largely explain why presidential popularity invariably falls during the term.

Is there escape from the dire implications of Brace and Hinckley? If the root of this governing problem is unrealistic public expectations, then one palliative is to achieve "a new realism" in our expectations regarding popular support. Presidents should "govern in a plural society by the same kind of margin that elected them" and not seek extraordinarily high approval ratings. And hopefully "increased consciousness on the part of the presidents, the news media, and the public" would help foster this new realism.[17] If this seems a bit myopic, a more sure-footed resolution of this governing dilemma is offered by Jeffrey E. Cohen, whose study builds upon Brace and Hinckley's by looking specifically at public opinion and legislative leadership.[18]

Cohen too begins with the contradiction that presidents should lead *and* follow public opinion, but the solution that Cohen unveils does not require the president to be the slave of opinion polls. After studying this relationship during the problem identification and position-taking (agenda-setting), policy formulation, and policy legitimation (or adoption) stages of the policy process, Cohen's bottom line is that presidents cater to public opinion early in the policymaking process but not later: "Presidents will be symbolically responsive to the public when doing so does not constrain substantive choices about policies; however, responsiveness to the public declines as decisions become more substantive."[19]

In drawing his normative conclusions, Cohen believes the presidency "is now arguably the most democratic of the three branches of government" yet "the least policy responsive." This "logic of responsiveness"—the gap between symbol and substance—"may be one cause of the high degree of public cynicism toward government during the past three decades." Says Cohen: "One implication may be the alienation and cynicism of the public from the political process because its expectations are not met in reality."[20]

Divided Government

For most of the early twentieth century, the norm of "unified" party government deeply influenced major party theorists such as V. O. Key, Pendleton Herring, and E. E. Schattschneider and led to a love affair between political science and the British-type responsible party doctrine. However since 1968 the normal state of affairs has been "divided government," most typically a Democratic Congress facing a Republican president. This new reality spawned a cottage industry among congressional researchers seeking to understand its causes and consequences. Various political variables were studied, but no behavioralist would suggest that divided government was a "rational" response by the electorate—that is, until Morris Fiorina dared a "purposeful" explanation that voters acted strategically to balance a conservative Republican executive against a liberal Democratic legislature to assure a moderate policy outcome. Fiorina thus answered the normative indictment against our separated regime by the constitutional activists, led by James L. Sundquist (see chapter 8). So emotionally charged was this debate, wrote Fiorina, that "divided government has the potential to become the new organizing principle of American politics research in the 1990s."[21] Since Fiorina justified divided government on democratic grounds, more germane for our purposes is how this debate was joined by David R. Mayhew and Charles O. Jones.

Although Mayhew is a congressional scholar, his *Divided We Govern* was honored as a singular contribution to presidency studies.[22] In it, he challenged those critics who attribute political deadlock and policy stalemate to divided government. "The political party, according to one of political science's best-known axioms about the American system," is (to quote James Sundquist) "the indispensable instrument that [brings] cohesion and unity, and hence effectiveness, to the government as a whole by linking the executive and legislative branches in a bond of common interest." This conventional wisdom, Mayhew demonstrates, is "wrong, or at least mostly or probably wrong," based on his analysis during 1947–90 of 31 high-profile congressional investigations and 267 pieces of major legislation. To the question of whether more oversight and lawmaking activity occurs during periods of unified or divided government, the results indicated "very little difference." Especially telling was his finding that "notable American laws tend to pass by broad majorities, regardless of conditions of party control," meaning they generally pass with two-thirds majorities and bipartisan support. Beyond the benefits of consensus-building, Mayhew attacks orthodoxy by arguing that unified party rule can lead to incoherent legislative enactments. Like Tulis, Mayhew showed that this dysfunction with LBJ's Great Society was "a 'politics of haste' in which 'solutions were often devised and rushed into law before the problems were understood.'"[23]

Since Mayhew was preoccupied with debunking the party theorists, it was left to Charles O. Jones to focus specifically on the presidential role.[24] Jones grounded his analysis in an issue as old as presidency studies—which branch had the more decisive role in shaping major legislation. Although Mayhew barely touched on this question, what he said puts him and Jones on the same page. The Fair Deal, the New Frontier, the Great Society, and Reaganomics may sound more impressive than the domestic agendas of Eisenhower, Nixon, Ford, Carter, and Bush, but Mayhew reminds us that Truman "largely failed," Kennedy "did little better," and Johnson "of course succeeded," but "so did Reagan," whereupon he favorably quotes Charles Jones. Says Jones: "Very few Presidents can claim legislative triumphs that are truly turning points in domestic policy."[25] The first lines of Jones's 1994 volume set the tone: "The President is not the presidency. The presidency is not the government. Ours is not a presidential system." Jones deliberately begins "with these starkly negative themes as partial correctives to the more popular interpretations of the United States government as presidency-centered,"[26] but his rebuttal is grounded in 28 legislative enactments (from Mayhew's data)—16 under divided and 12 under unified party control. For each, Jones details, step by step, the lawmaking process and finds that instances of "presidential preponderance" ($N = 6$) and "congressional preponderance" ($N = 7$) were fewer than cases of "joint presidential-congressional influence" ($N = 15$), indicating "that presidency-centered analysis of lawmaking is misleading if it conveys the impression of presidential dominance, either as an empirical fact or as a normative conclusion growing out of the principles upon which the system is built." A more accurate rendering of these cases shows that "when it comes to making laws in Washington, it is never done solely in the White House, it is sometimes done largely on Capitol Hill, and it is normally done with a substantial amount of cross-institutional and cross-partisan interaction through elaborate sequences featuring varying degrees of iteration." Jones comes away "quite in awe" of the American regime and believing that, though it is not perfect, ours is "the most intricate lawmaking system in the world. It will not be made better through simplification. Preponderance of one branch over the other should be a cause for concern, not celebration."[27]

The Ennobled Congress

That Congress should be valued is implicit in the Mayhew and Jones volumes. To denigrate the presidency-centered model is to elevate the political significance of Congress. As the most powerful legislature on earth, Congress is a uniquely American innovation in representative government. Some years ago Michael Mezey observed that congressional and presidential scholars hold very different views of the executive versus legislative roles.[28] The presidency scholars in the heroic school assumed that the White House could make demands on Congress, yet congressional scholars always knew that representatives and senators were subjected to many political forces, not only the White House. That bit of wisdom has been resurrected in the latest wave of empirical analysis by George Edwards, Jon Bond and Richard Fleisher, Mark Peterson, and Steven Shull.

At the Margins updated an earlier work by Edwards, with similar conclusions that all three presidential resources (party, popularity, and skills) operate "at the margins" of legislative leadership.[29] Party, says Edwards, "is unlikely to provide the basis for the direction of major change," and even worse, "[p]ublic support is not a dependable resource for the president, and it is not one that he can easily create when he needs it to influence Congress."[30] Based on his subjective evaluations of legislative skills, Edwards presumes that LBJ was superior to JFK, who, in turn, had better-honed skills than Carter. Among Republicans, anecdotal evidence suggests to him that Nixon was less effective than Ford, Eisenhower, and Reagan. Despite the methodological limits, Edwards tried but "failed to reveal systematic evidence of their [skills'] impact on presidential support." "It seems reasonable to assert that legislative skills are not at the core of presidential leadership of Congress . . . [since] [t]heir utility is at the margins, in exploiting rather than creating opportunities for change."[31] Edwards's grand conclusion is that since presidents "must largely play with the hands" dealt them by voters' electoral decisions and citizens' evaluations of their performance, "[t]hey are rarely in a position to augment substantially their resources. They operate at the margins as facilitators rather than as directors of change."[32] Even "presidents who appeared to dominate Congress were actually facilitators" (here Edwards cites FDR, LBJ, and Reagan). A facilitator is "a leader who constantly depends on his environment for creating favorable strategic positions from which he can exercise leadership at the margins to turn opportunities into accomplishments." All this seems very fragile, but Edwards is not troubled that presidents "are confined to the role of facilitator," because the "American system is such that they can be little else. Although there is a certain appeal to explaining major change in terms of personalities, the political system is too complicated, power too decentralized, and interests too diverse for one person, no matter how extraordinary, to dominate."[33]

Edwards's formulation of the president as "facilitator" of the legislative process has gained wide currency among his peers, including Bond and Fleisher.[34] Whereas Edwards limited his analytical search to the presidency, Jon R. Bond and Richard Fleisher incorporated presidential variables (skill and popularity) within a "Congress-centered" model of legislative voting behavior. Like Edwards, they ask under what conditions presidents succeed on floor votes in Congress. Although the "prevailing perspective" is to emphasize presidential variables (skill and popularity) "as the key to understanding presidential-congressional relations," they believe that "none of the[se] linkage agents are exceptionally strong." Again, the hidden hand of electoral forces is at work. Bond and Fleisher's central thesis "is that congressional support for the president is mainly a function of members' [of Congress] partisan and ideological predispositions operating within constraints imposed by the institutional structure of Congress. Between elections, the basic parameters of presidential-congressional relations set by these political and institutional forces in Congress are relatively fixed. Although presidential variables . . . may influence success at the margins, there is little that the president can do to move members of Congress very far from their basic political predispositions."[35]

After empirically verifying that the effect of party affiliation on congressional voting is "relatively weak," Bond and Fleisher proceed to assess other variables. Support from the rank and file is facilitated when party and committee leaders are in agreement, for example, but presidential popularity is not an influential force. Here the findings "are consistent and clear: the effects of the president's public approval on success in Congress are limited," because "the president does not consistently win more votes nor does he consistently receive higher levels of support from the party factions when he is popular than when he is unpopular." In judging legislative skills, the authors are forced to conclude that "the evidence . . . provides little support for the theory that the president's perceived leadership skills are associated with success on roll call votes in Congress. Presidents reputed as highly skilled do not win consistently more often than should be expected given the effects of the partisan balance in Congress, the president's popularity, and the cycle of decreasing influence over the course of his term."[36]

At base, although "presidency-centered explanations have dominated much of the literature," analyses "of presidential success on roll call votes . . . tend to support the Congress-centered thesis rather than the one emphasizing presidential variables." Bond and Fleisher chide Neustadt, who correctly disparaged the ability of parties to fuse the separated powers but who oversold the impact of presidential leadership or popularity. "In fact, the forces that Neustadt stressed as the antidote for weak parties are even less successful in linking the president and Congress than are weak parties."[37] Nor are Bond and Fleisher about to jump aboard the Sundquist bandwagon to reinvent the constitutional order. Instead they "recognize . . . that what some have called policy stalemate results from the difficulty of working out compromises among diverse interests in a highly pluralistic society. Giving increased power to the president to formulate solutions to complex problems does not guarantee that his solutions would be wise or benevolent, or would necessarily even work. The price of increasing presidential power and maximizing accountability would be the weakening of representation of diverse interests in government decision making."[38]

Mark Peterson also directly confronts the "presidency-centered perspective," which he calls "the most pervasive interpretation of . . . executive-legislative relations," in favor of a "tandem-institutions perspective" that offers "a more realistic prescriptive and descriptive appraisal of the symbiotic relationship" between the president and Congress. Whereas the previous studies looked at presidential influence on roll calls, Peterson looks at a four-stage continuum of conflict between the branches: "consensus and passive inaction"; then "compromise"; followed by "dominance," either by the president or the opposition; and finally "strategic inaction" (the highest degree of institutional conflict). Peterson, like Edwards or Bond and Fleisher, argues that the political hand a legislative leader plays is largely dealt to him by three types of contextual variables. The "pure" context is the institutional arrangement within Congress; the "malleable" context includes Congress's partisan makeup and general economic conditions;

and the "policy" context (agenda-setting) affords the only opportunity for a president to influence the legislative process. Whether the president recommends a small or a large program or an old or a new policy initiative may make a difference, but not that much of a difference. According to Peterson's summary, "[k]nowing something about the condition of major political institutions, the political position of the president and the opposition, the state of the economy, and the nature of the president's programs, we can say quite a bit about why Congress responded to the president by affirmation or condemnation, or by something in between."[39]

For many years Steven Shull has analyzed the policy process from a similar vantage point.[40] In a recent work, Shull and Thomas Shaw explain that "scholarship has moved away from viewing the president as the dominant actor in the relationship, toward . . . congressional influence, and ultimately toward emphasizing more equal power sharing between the two institutions."[41] Thus Shull and Shaw adopt a "multiple perspective approach" that studies presidential-congressional interactions on agenda-setting, legislative support, veto propensity, and budgetary agreement. Using a 1949–95 data base, they assess the impacts of the "executive environment" (e.g., public support), the "legislative environment" (e.g., the party margin), and the "exogenous environment" (e.g., the size of the government) and find differing effects depending upon the type of interaction. Their "most important contribution" is that the "multiple perspectives approach goes well beyond the tandem institutions by emphasizing the importance of not only the two institutional environments but also the exogenous environment. Our results show that the complexity of presidential-congressional relations is fully revealed only by incorporating all three environments in the analysis."[42]

Presidential Constraints

To sample this literature, we proceed from micro- to macro-level constraints.[43] One constraint inherent in the incumbent is personality. Neustadt wrote his classic to rebut Edward Corwin's legalistic view of executive power, but one especially prophetic insight from Corwin was that truly gifted presidents were few and far between and, for that reason, institutional arrangements were needed to support the presidency. That advice was rejected wholesale by the behavioralist Neustadt, who countered that presidents should be professional politicians with keen political antennae for maximizing their power options. The White House was no place for amateurs (meaning Eisenhower, whom Corwin admired), and presumably we would have no difficulty recruiting talented individuals for the highest office.

It took a scholar with the prestige of Fred Greenstein to challenge the Neustadtian stereotypes about Dwight D. Eisenhower and to single-handedly inaugurate a revisionist scholarship that has come to pervade presidency studies.[44] Ideology played no small part in how Eisenhower was portrayed, since "most writers on the presidency viewed him through the lens of his 1950s liberal critics as an aging hero who reigned more than he ruled and lacked the energy, motivation, and political know-how to have a significant impact on events." In short, to those commentators Eisenhower exemplified "how *not* to conduct the presidency."[45] Greenstein counters that the key to understanding Eisenhower was his unique style of "hidden-hand" leadership. He doubts that "many other presidents [would be] capable of adopting the full Eisenhower style," although one element—Ike's organizational sense (see below)—may be worthy of emulation. Regarding the expectations-gap thesis, moreover, Eisenhower did not raise public expectations. "Presidents who make judicious use of preventive politics may be more likely to sustain stable public support, mitigating the make-and-then-break pattern of most modern presidencies."[46]

Two years after Greenstein, a sympathetic critique of Neustadt was penned by Barbara Kellerman. Seeking to understand the "practice of leadership," using case studies from Kennedy through Reagan, Kellerman agrees with Neustadt that presidential power is political, not prerogative, but her focus was limited to understanding the "skill" of incumbents. Her game plan was "a detailed look at what they actually do," based on formulating presidential leadership as "the attempt to direct influential 'followers' to new ground."[47] Since leadership is conceptualized as a transactional (two-way) process between leader and followers, Kellerman inquires about the modes of influence used by the leader to solicit cooperation and, in turn, what motivates followers to accept his lead. Yes, personality matters, but too few have the requisite personality, because "the president who is motivated and equipped to be politically skilled will prove to be a more effective leader in the American political culture than the one to whom politicking is irrelevant or even distasteful." Unlike the heroic school, Kellerman dissents from any JFK hero-worship by declaring that "the best politicians, and the most effective directive leaders, were Lyndon Johnson and Ronald Reagan. Both were other-directed in the[ir] behavior and inner-directed in their rather fierce determination to see a very particular policy become law."[48]

If Franklin D. Roosevelt was the ideal-type heroic president, most commentators now doubt that we will see his analog anytime soon. Edwards and Bond and Fleisher empirically verify that skills are not so reliable a presidential resource. James David Barber affirmed that maladjusted "active-negative" personalities do get elected to our highest office (see chapter 8), and more recently, a well-received psychological study of William Jefferson Clinton argues that despite considerable political gifts, he suffers from serious character flaws.[49]

Another constraint is time. It is accepted wisdom that any president's popularity will decline over the four-year term; this fact, coupled with the normal midterm congressional losses by the presidential party (except in 1934, 1998, and 2002), suggests that any legislative victories must come during the early months or the year following the president's election. But this political reality has become mythologized, with FDR's One Hundred Days being elevated into holy grail by advocates of the heroic presidency. Only recently has empirical research confirmed what common sense implies: the Great Depression transformed Roosevelt's into a "crisis" presidency unlike anything experienced before or since.[50]

Time is one of the "internal" constraints (along with information, expertise, and energy), as opposed to "external" constraints (congressional support, public approval, and electoral margin) on presidential leadership, according to Paul Light.[51] Best known is Light's hypothesis that the ebb and flow of these variables create two distinct cycles: "The *cycle of decreasing influence* appears as time, energy, and congressional support drop. The *cycle of increasing effectiveness* enters as information and expertise grow."[52] In other words, to the plain-speaking advice—move it or lose it—Light would argue that things are not so simple. In fact Light sees the 1980s presidency (dubbed a "No Win Presidency") as decidedly weaker than the 1960s presidency, mainly because newly elected presidents are ill equipped to define and promote a policy agenda when their political capital is greatest, whereas later in their term, when presidents more fully understand the governing process, it is too late to promote ambitious domestic initiatives.

Thus, counsels Light, the "structure of incentives" must be changed to reward presidents "for patience, not haste; for planning, not short-term success." What we need is a fundamental revision in "how we view the policy process." Unless "Congress, the public, the media, even political scientists are willing to wait for careful policy, the President must respond to our impatience."[53] Shades of the expectations gap, with Light's calls for reeducation to permit our presidents to act with rational deliberation, not forced dispatch, when defining a policy agenda.

A third midrange constraint is organizational. When the President's Committee on Administrative Management, chaired by Louis Brownlow, proclaimed that the president "needs help," its advice that six presidential assistants be installed in a new Executive Office of the President (EOP) commenced the institutionalized presidency. Even so, Peri Arnold argues that there was a "nearly century-long [beginning with Taft] project of large-scale, official, administrative reorganization as it portrayed, justified, and attempted to implement a new, managerial role for the American presidency." This represents a "sharp contrast" with the previous century, given that the managerial presidency "has little foundation or precedent in either 19th-century practice (after the first third of the century) or in the Constitution."[54] Nonetheless, says Arnold, "[t]he plain fact is that no modern president has fully managed the executive branch."[55]

That observation is confirmed by two recent analyses showing that executive hegemony does not extend to the federal bureaucracy. According to Hugh Heclo, "[e]ven under the most favorable circumstances (typically at the beginning of a new administration), a modern chief executive and his personal aides face severe constraints in trying to breathe new life into the executive branch."[56] The relationship between political appointees and high-level careerists in the federal government is political, not hierarchical: Heclo argues that "Washington's political executives have as few incentives to pull together as they have resources to stand alone as political leaders. Like the President, they must persuade rather than command others, but they lack the President's preeminent position to improve their bargaining power."[57] One reason political appointees are disadvantaged is that, being "strangers" to government, their impatience, short tenures, and inexperience "are at war with what they most need—a patient fashioning of relationships of trust and confidence" in order to shape the behavior of civil servants.[58] To assist presidential management, therefore, Heclo urges the formation of a corps of middle-management "Federal Executive Officers"; such a group would be similar to the Senior Executive Service (SES) created by the Civil Service Reform Act of 1978.

Yet one wonders if the SES had much impact, given Colin Campbell's critical analysis of administrative politics under Carter and Reagan. Campbell argues that presidents "rely much less upon collegial cabinet dynamics and the resources of the permanent bureaucracy than do [British] prime ministers," because presidential styles and agendas "shape their administrations' policies" more than is the case in ministerial government.[59] Executive leadership Campbell calls a "struggle" between presidents who want "to leave their mark on history" and "the existing structures, folkways, and agendas of the institutional presidency."[60] Campbell's interviews uncover three bureaucratic cultures in the United States (unlike the fairly homogeneous civil service of Britain): politicos who are recruited from political campaigns; amphibians who are politically connected but also have expertise; and professional careerists, who dominate every agency except the White House. Reagan's management team is more praiseworthy than others, says Campbell, since its "strong networking ethos" during the first term "mitigated the possible dysfunctions" from their ideology and macro-approach to policy; he is more critical of Carter's politicos, who "generally proved themselves woefully inept at political operations in a 'governor's mansion' far beyond Georgian scale."[61] Thus, to engage this multifaceted bureaucracy is no easy task, which is why Campbell generally recommends "broker politics" as "probably the best assurance that an administration will optimize its preferred style."[62]

Scholars also have come to recognize the additional dimension of EOP expansion and the perplexing problem of coordinating White House–cabinet relationships. The "swelling" of the White House minibureaucracy under Nixon was not such a departure in what has been styled the "presidential branch" of government.[63] Most pundits now take for granted that the EOP has become a managerial problem in its own right—not simply the means for controlling line departments and agencies. According to Greenstein, Eisenhower's ultimate legacy was his "keenness as an organizer of the advice he received," because "[r]igorous staff work and systematic institutional back-up for policy making is persistently lacking in modern presidencies, as is the teamwork that is an informal offshoot of this procedure."[64] Eisenhower was omitted from Shirley Warshaw's analysis of White House–cabinet relations, but in the years since, only Ronald Reagan was successful at creating true "power-sharing," which she argues is the only appropriate remedy to deep-seated structural conflicts between presidential staffers and departmental secretaries.[65] Although Nixon failed at his "plot" to administratively gain control of the permanent government, Richard Nathan explains how Reagan was more successful by his adroit use of the appointment powers. Nathan's early impressions in 1983 suggested that "Reagan among recent presidents appears to have the best handle on the need for an administrative strategy. He has so far avoided the pitfalls of Nixon's heavy-handedness, Johnson's grand design, and Carter's atomic-submarine approach to management."[66]

Nathan's view is not the final word on Reagan, though Robert Durant's may be. Durant studied policy shifts by the Bureau of Land Management in New Mexico, research also predicated on Reagan's being "the quintessential practitioner of the administrative presidency, wielding its tools with a comprehensiveness, vigor, and relentlessness unparalleled in his predecessors."[67] Durant's analysis of public land policies shows that "the Administration's accomplishments were distinctly more modest than the rhetoric of its friends or its foes might suggest." "[T]hese results were not only the product of political missteps by [Interior Secretary James] Watt and his successors, of market conditions beyond anyone's control, of judicial reversals of the Administration's deregulatory agenda, and of the type of policy reorientation sought administratively." Moreover, "an implementation paradox developed to plague the administrative presidency . . . the more Reagan's appointees successfully used this strategy to pursue regulatory relief, the more difficult it became for them to meet their resource production, states' rights, and economic development goals in New Mexico."[68]

Informed observers agree that Reagan's judicial legacy may well be the most enduring legacy of his administrative presidency. In recruiting Supreme Court nominees, Reagan's "was a criteria-driven selection framework to be sure, but the most important criteria were ideological. In short, the Reagan administration wanted to sponsor ardently conservative candidates for the high court."[69] No wild inferences are required to appreciate that a "criteria-driven" approach—the most prevalent method by modern presidents—was first employed by Eisenhower, whose appointees, says David Yalof, "may rank historically as among the finest group ever to be appointed by one president."[70]

Eisenhower also gets high marks from the most comprehensive study of the White House since Leonard White chronicled the administrative Founding.[71] Contrary to the Neustadtian stereotype, Charles Walcott and Karen Hult claim that Eisenhower was a seminal figure in organizing the White House, noting that "by the time Lyndon Johnson left office, much of what Eisenhower had introduced to the White House Office remained—and persists today." As to impact, they "repeatedly observed" that "the Eisenhower system was far more diverse and flexible than the caricatured 'military model' its detractors envisioned. Indeed, given his governance duties, [chief of staff Sherman] Adams could scarcely have afforded to be simply the rigid martinet he was sometimes portrayed as being."[72]

Early observations that Democrats usually pursued a spokes-of-the-wheel advisory system, whereas Republican presidents tended to be hierarchical, has given way to more nuanced portraits of White House staffing.[73] Walcott and Hult merge the previously dominant paradigms, based on structural attributes or (presidential) personality needs, into a more inclusive "problem-contingency" analysis borrowed from organizational theory. They proceed "from the premise that staff structures emerge primarily from strategic responses by presidents to environmental demands" and then "add an organizational dimension. Once organizational structures are in place, even in such volatile settings as the ones the White House faces, structures can exercise an independent effect on the subsequent recognition and definition of problems that impinge from the external environment." In sum, "as the White House becomes more organizationally complex, that complexity itself shapes perceptions of and responses to the environment, and often constrains presidential choices."[74] Their multifaceted managerial analysis is not easily summarized. Suffice it to say that Walcott and Hult identify no fewer than seven distinctive "governance structures" that were reflected in various EOP staffing units during the period from Hoover to Johnson. Most important, "[i]t is crucial to underscore at the outset that hierarchy is by no means the only structural form that has characterized the White House. Of course, the White House Office as a whole must be viewed as a hierarchy, with the president at its apex. Within that hierarchical skeleton, however, a diverse array of subordinate structures has emerged."[75]

At the macro-level, the constraints on presidential leadership include the force of history and globalization. Both Schlesingers—senior and junior—have argued that "cycles" of American history alternate between periods of liberalism and conservatism, and the New Deal obviously signifies the consolidation of positive government.[76] Their crude formulations have been theoretically refined in more current scholarship,[77] with the most ambitious historicist interpretation being advanced by Steven Skowronek.[78] Since history repeats itself, Skowronek draws a line with those scholars who exaggerate the significance of the contemporary presidency, notably Richard Neustadt. Neustadt's "distinction between modern and premodern contexts for the exercise of power—introduced a sense of coherence" into presidency studies, but, argues Skowronek, "[t]he notion of a prior age when presidents did not *have* to be leaders . . . is nothing more than a conceit of modern times." What impressed Skowronek was that presidents "widely celebrated for their mastery of American politics" (Jefferson, Jackson, Lincoln, Roosevelt, and Reagan) were immediately preceded by others "judged politically incompetent" (Adams, John Quincy Adams, Buchanan, Hoover, and Carter).[79] To bring rationality to this discontinuity, Skowronek differentiates between political time, any moment in history when the political system shows an ideological bias, and secular (or chronological) time.

Skowronek's analytical questions are whether an incumbent *accommodates* or *opposes* the prevailing regime and whether that regime is politically *robust* or *vulnerable*. But there is a further complication because of the passing of secular time, which bears on "the progressive development of the institutional resources and governing responsibilities of the executive office," which is to say "the repertoire of powers the presidents of a particular period have at their disposal to realize their preferences in action." In other words, secular time poses obstacles to fundamental reforms, because the "repertoire of [presidential] powers" may not be adequate to the institutional "thickening" that allows "other actors to mount more formidable resistance to their [president's] will."[80]

Although Skowronek is impressed by the Reagan Revolution, he says our "[f]aith in the transformative capacities of the presidency seemed to be giving rise to ever greater expectations and ever more profound frustrations," absent any serious effort to understand "those capacities in a systematic way." Even Reagan could not fully impact the political regime at an optimal moment in political time, when the presidency was launching an ideological assault on a "vulnerable" (liberal) regime. Looking ahead, Skowronek's dialectic indicates that the "waning of political time" will offer fewer opportunities for "fashioning legitimacy anew." Therefore, he encourages "pragmatism" and "deliberation," because "[t]he experimentation that goes along with the pragmatic stance will have to become more collective, for no president will be able to tramp roughshod over the authority and independence of everybody else."[81] It is not too extravagant to suggest that Clinton and both Bushes were trapped in political time.

One reason for the institutional "thickening" of which Skowronek speaks is the decline of political party, the subject of Sidney Milkis's study. At the electoral level, the evidence seems clear: growing ranks of independents, weakened loyalty of partisans, greater split-ticket voting, and the rise of insurgent third-party candidates. Yet there is also an organizational side to the atrophy of parties, and on this score, if parties are in decline, then

Milkis places the blame on Franklin D. Roosevelt (and today's liberal Democrats). Milkis describes our party system as being in "transformation" and hints that the New Deal was the realignment to end realignments, because FDR conceived of welfarism in "rights" terms. His reforms were dedicated to liberating the president from the constraints of partisan politics, but in so doing, they also weakened the president's institutional base of support. Thus, presidents now subjected to the programmatic demands of the post–New Deal era "have been encouraged to rely on plebiscitary politics and unilateral executive action to circumvent the regular procedures of constitutional government, as well as formal partisan channels."[82]

Milkis's insight was that "the New Deal did not simply replace constitutional government with an administrative state; rather, the programmatic rights of the New Deal constituted the beginning of an administrative constitution, which was shielded from the uncertainties of public opinion, political parties, and elections." Nor was this New Deal legacy repudiated by the Reagan Revolution, which Milkis says "did not really challenge the aggrandizement of administrative power" but rather attempted "to extend the benefits of the national polity to those who wished to make new [conservative] uses of, rather than limit, the state." Of course the coming of the administrative state will affect the quality of democratic life, which troubles Milkis for many reasons, one being that weakened parties and executive hegemony will exalt "the *personal* responsibility of the president, thus making *collective* partisan appeals less meaningful in the eyes of the voters."[83]

We close with British political scientist Richard Rose, who directly raises the question of governing capacity. Rose delineates three epochs in U.S. history, beginning with the traditional presidents, who "had little to do"; then there are the moderns, who "had a lot to do at home and abroad," and today's "postmodern" presidents, who "may have too much expected" of them. The difference today is that presidents "can no longer dominate the international system," since "[i]nterdependence characterizes an international system in which no nation is the hegemonic power. The President is the leader of a very influential nation, but other nations are influential too." The megaconstraint arising from globalization is fairly obvious: "A postmodern President must start from the assumption: *To govern is to cooperate.* A President has always needed to cooperate with Congress in order to succeed in a constitutional system that separates powers. What is novel is that a postmodern President must cooperate with foreign governments to achieve major economic and national security goals. Cooperation requires a mutuality of interests between nations."[84]

Of course the problem is magnified because U.S. presidents are not especially trained in diplomacy. Rose underscores that *"[w]hat it takes to become President has nothing to do with what it takes to be President"* and, even more troubling, *"[w]hat it takes to become President actually makes it more difficult to be a successful postmodern President."*[85] To have any chance of succeeding, postmodern presidents face three imperatives: going public, going Washington, and going international. Any president "would like to take charge," but that is easier said than done, because postmodern presidents cannot calibrate foreign opinion or, for that matter, the views of the American people or official Washington, nor can presidents control events that happen worldwide. Worst yet, actions taken to appease one audience, such as domestic constituencies, may anger international elites. Given all the costs and benefits involved, is there any solution to what Rose calls "the responsibility gap" between these global challenges and the limitations of the Oval Office? Minimally, Rose hopes that postmodern presidents can avoid the pitfalls of illusion. "The biggest illusion is the belief that we can turn the clock back to the era when Franklin D. Roosevelt created the modern Presidency, and Dwight D. Eisenhower could rely on American wealth and military force to sustain a global *Pax Americana.*"[86]

Conclusion

Does presidential leadership depend upon historical context, or is regime-building manifested through political, institutional, and constitutional developments? This corpus of contemporary scholarship embodies four themes: the expectations gap, divided government, the ennobled Congress, and presidential constraints. Concerns about presidential plebiscites echo the Framers' fear of demagogic leadership, just as ennobling Congress reminds us that the Framers intended Congress to be the leading branch of popular government. Although expectations gaps and divided government are of recent vintage, reflecting new trends in political life, those themes along with the ennobled Congress and presidential constraints telegraph that mainstream scholars now explicitly repudiate the myopic teachings of the heroic-presidency advocates. Neustadt's paradigm has been challenged, because his idealized view was largely shaped by the model of Franklin D. Roosevelt. But Roosevelt is disconnected from "normal" politics, because his was a "crisis" presidency that followed the last realigning election.

Does presidential power derive from the prerogatives of office or from the incumbent? That presidential prerogative is not a salient issue in this emerging consensus deserves further comment (see the Conclusion). Here, although inherent authority is stronger than ever in foreign affairs, Richard Rose alleges that the decline of American hegemony in the postmodern era means that prerogative does not extend to global economics or politics. Just as bargaining is key to domestic policymaking, now presidents must negotiate one-on-one with other heads of state. No longer can the United States set terms. Bargaining offers no guarantees of success, but beyond that, this literature verifies the political frailty of leadership based on party and persuasion, whether with elites or the masses.

Does presidential influence depend upon the force of personality, rhetorical leadership, or partisanship? The 1960s fear of dysfunctional character has yielded to a more pragmatic view of personality as constraint. The president is a mortal with all the failings and potentialities—writ large—of any person, and there is no ready political recipe for recruiting the right person at the opportune time in history. Even a presidential tour de force must cope with the inexorable march of "political" time, his lonely status within a huge bureaucracy, and a party system assaulted by centrifugal forces. One significant theme in these currents of opinion is the demise of responsible partyism. Barely has a generation passed without some prominent thinker—Lord Bryce, Woodrow Wilson, Harold Laski, Herman Finer, James Sundquist, and now Richard Rose—praising parliamentary government as superior to our regime. Therefore, the next generation of presidency scholars may well proclaim the benefits of the separated powers.

Does the president actively or passively engage the legislative process and promote a policy agenda? The age-old adage that presidents propose and Congresses dispose may not be consistent with the Framers' intentions, but at least we contemporaries have come to terms with the fact that even though sometimes presidents do propose, and other times Congresses propose, at all times Congress must acquiesce. Interbranch agreement would seem virtually impossible given the prognoses of deadlock, gridlock, and stalemate that critics argue is a necessary by-product of divided government. Yet things appear to get done, and, curiously, it fell to those empiricists among us to confirm the rightful place of Congress in the legislative process.

Does presidential leadership vary between domestic and foreign affairs? It is readily apparent that the themes of divided government and the ennobled Congress are strongly grounded in domestic enactments. The expectations gap, a troubled Lowi fears, inexorably leads to presidential risk-taking and adventurism in foreign affairs, and the macroconstraint of globalism obviously implicates foreign affairs. Beyond our shores lies an interconnected, global political and economic system that has replaced the neat dichotomy between domestic and international with "intermestic" issues: trade, immigration, multinational corporatism, the global environment, and worldwide networks of capital flows. And we cannot forget that the 1960s critics of presidential imperialism (see chapter 8) worried that the tendency for national security "crisis" to centralize political power would have ominous implications if the president were an insecure personality type.

Does the organization of the executive branch service presidential leadership? "The New Institutionalism" is a recent wave in the varied subfields of comparative government, public administration, policy analysis, and international relations. Here it is reflected in some very innovative research on the administrative presidency. Perhaps because we have quantified to the nth degree a president's legislative support scores and approval ratings, scholars have turned to operational manifestations of presidential leadership. And the picture is not pretty, as any organizational theorist would have predicted. The heroic-presidency school overlooked administration, or perhaps assumed that the bureaucracy could be made to heel by a persuasive or charismatic leader. That falsity was learned by John Kennedy the hard way, after the Bay of Pigs fiasco, and relearned by a Reagan tarred with the Iran-Contra scandal. Administering the White House is now viewed as a challenge, or an obstacle, but managing the federal bureaucracy is much more daunting. For obvious reasons, president watchers usually focus on the upper administration—the EOP and the White House Staff, the cabinet, and the subcabinet—and leave to public administration scholars the task of digging deeply into the permanent government. When the analytical spotlight is focused on line agencies, as Durant did with the Bureau of Land Management, we cannot assume too much about the efficacy of an administrative strategy. In this light, Reagan was more successful in politicizing the upper and middle management of the executive branch and in recruiting federal judges than in subduing the machinery of big government.

Three Presidential Paradigms
Hamiltonianism, Jeffersonianism, Progressivism

Theodore J. Lowi identified an expectations gap and the political dangers accompanying presidential plebiscites. His insight in *The Personal President*, we argue, inaugurated the latest scholarly consensus on presidential leadership. Yet there is a second insight by Lowi that dates back to his pioneering 1964 work in public policy analysis.[1] He reversed the long-standing pluralist assumption that interest group politics influence public policy, saying instead that "policy affects politics." Whether the debate focuses on distributive, regulatory, or redistributive policies, says Lowi, will affect not only coalition-building among organized interests but also the relationship between Congress and the president. This new formulation of the means-ends relationship revolutionized the policy studies by urging researchers to classify policies according to their impact and then to look for salient variables in the policymaking process.

But virtually all the presidency literature that we reviewed has been concerned about the means—not the ends—of power, namely the levers by which presidents lead the separated system (see summary, Table 1, p. 230). That bias is the most compelling criticism of Neustadt's statecraft approach, but the same can be said about every other commentator, even those who are ideologically driven, such as Harold Laski, James Mac-Gregor Burns, and James Sundquist. Laski, Burns, and Sundquist tell us more about the optimal means of power than about the preferred ends of government. If the ends are not made explicit, how can we redirect our inquiries to the larger theoretical question of whether the means of presidential leadership are affected by policy objectives?

In *The Personal President*, Lowi applies his policy approach to presidential leadership by arguing that the policy regime affected the scope of presidential power. Following 1787 "was a period of 'state-building,' when the national government . . . did things and performed functions that were 'one time only,'" such as creating federal departments and a tax system, recognizing foreign governments, stabilizing the national debt, and "other matters that had to do with the establishment of legitimacy."[2] Afterward the

United States entered "the era of patronage politics," with the consequence that "the place of the presidency declined and with it the stature and accomplishments of presidents."[3] In other words, the nineteenth century saw Congress-centered government *because* it was an era of small government, just as positive government today requires a strong presidency. The end of the nineteenth century marked a turning point, but a political milestone came with the New Deal, when FDR abandoned the "patronage state" and pushed through Congress new programs that, although they "did not add significantly to the federal budget, . . . profoundly and permanently changed the nature of the national government." This Roosevelt Revolution inaugurated "an entirely new regime, which deserves to be called the Second Republic of the United States."[4] Even if the legislative leadership called for during the depths of the Great Depression is not required today, the management of those new domestic programs, as well as our global security and economic interests, necessitates a strong executive.

Assessing the presidential literature in light of Lowi's policy insight points to three distinctive presidential paradigms: Hamiltonian, Jeffersonian, and Progressive. In order to see how each of these paradigms conceptualizes the presidential office, let us revisit the six questions:

- Does presidential power derive from the prerogatives of office or from the incumbent?
- Does presidential influence depend upon the force of personality, rhetorical leadership, or partisanship?
- Does presidential leadership depend upon historical context, or is regime-building manifested through political, institutional, and constitutional developments?
- Does presidential leadership vary between domestic and foreign affairs?
- Does the president actively or passively engage the legislative process and promote a policy agenda?
- Does the organization of the executive branch service presidential leadership?

Hamiltonianism: A Strong President and Strong but Limited Government

The Framers crafted a strong president and a strong but limited government. Prerogative power looms large in Hamiltonianism because national security and the economic infrastructure (the Bank of the United States) were the foremost objectives of public policy. Hamilton's was the most distinctive voice of the Founders in articulating a rationale for an energetic executive. He argued for an executive capable of assuming decisive leadership in military and foreign affairs while obtaining a virtual equality with Congress in domestic policy. All students of the Founding believe the principles of the Constitution represent the enduring qualities of good government across time and circumstance. And some would argue that the Constitution empowered the "modern" president with all the resources necessary to govern this large republic. One is Jeffrey Tulis, who argues that the features of the modern presidency that Fred Greenstein and others attribute to Franklin D. Roosevelt originated with the Founding, specifically "Alexander Hamilton's theory of governance." Those features found "practical expression" with President Washington, who "with Hamilton's guidance—fashioned a legislative program, used the veto for policy purposes, and exercised all of the unilateral powers that are allegedly new today."[5]

The allegation that Madisonianism is Original Intent is laid to rest by Charles Thach, whose classic directly refutes the Progressive view. Indeed, most criticisms of Madisonianism should be redirected against Jeffersonianism. In the First Congress, which established the federal departments, as Thach points out, it was Madison's arguments favoring the presidential removal prerogative that carried the day. Madison's imprint on the crafting of Article 2, overstated by the Left and understated by the Right, has long been the straw man, or scapegoat, used by reformers of all stripes who have attacked the political frailty of our separated system. That the regime decayed into congressional government was Wilson's famous charge in 1885; during the 1950s–60s James MacGregor Burns alleged that the separated system yielded the deadlock of democracy; and later in the century, observers like Lloyd Cutler and James Sundquist attributed policy gridlock to a separated system overlaid with partisan rivalry.

The reality of the Founding was not an irrational fear of governing (majority rule, in modern parlance), because the separated system was designed to liberate the president from congressional interference and to empower the president with constitutional prerogative. For Hamiltonians, prerogative was the most decisive factor in their constitutionally grounded conception of the presidency. The Lockean prerogative armed the energetic executive in foreign affairs, and so enduring were the diplomatic precedents of Washington that he may be regard as the first "modern" chief diplomat.[6] This was later appreciated by Justice Story, a northern Jeffersonian, and feared by the Jeffersonian Henry Clay Lockwood; it served to reawaken Wilson in 1908 to the potentialities of executive energy.

Although Lockean prerogative was viewed at that time, as it is now, through the prism of national survival, the Founders' view of presidential prerogative powers in domestic policy is poorly understood. Hamilton argued that the veto power made the president equal to two-thirds of Congress, although the Framers recognized that Congress would be politically more popular than the president and thus would assert its popularity against him whenever the veto was cast. Nevertheless, the constant veto threat would force Congress to consider the president's views. The veto could be employed against bad domestic policy, the rationale given by Washington for one of his (two) vetoes, and Washington also used his veto threat to force Congress to alter a pending tariff bill. To be sure, the Federalists did not use the veto much, nor did they politicize its use—a development that awaited Jackson. But constitutionalists like William Howard Taft, Calvin Coolidge, and Edward Corwin all understood the veto in terms of legislative leadership. In other words, the commonly heard viewpoint that the Framers intended the veto as a defense only against unconstitutional encroachments by Congress should be attributed more to Jeffersonianism than to Hamiltonianism.

Nor was the veto the totality of Hamilton's legislative role, which so infuriated Madison and Jefferson, since his reporting to the House of Representatives on the nation's finances was the agency for Washington's policy agenda. His intimate involvement in agenda-setting, the presidential Recommending Clause, and Washington's decision to personally deliver the Annual Address to Congress are precedents that movement conservatives like Terry Eastland seize upon to justify more politically engaged Reagan-like presidents. Putting aside Tulis's objections to rhetorical leadership, Eastland and commentators like Irving Kristol urge more popular appeals from conservative presidents in the name of smaller government. Thus Eastland openly embraces Richard Neustadt as being entirely compatible with Hamiltonianism.

Hamilton had been Washington's chief of staff during the Revolutionary War, so both men understood the importance of organization. There was no administrative presidency during Washington's tenure, at least not as that concept is used today; Washington either worked one-on-one with his cabinet or simply did the administrative chores himself. In other words, there was little hierarchy to the federal government in 1789, no White

House minibureaucracy to manage, and no span-of-control problem for the chief executive. Washington operated through classic cabinet government, since his top aides debated all topics, though obviously Washington sided with his treasury secretary, more often than not, on matters of domestic and foreign policy. Thus, the literature dissents from David Nichols's interpretation that Washington set precedents for the administrative presidency.[7]

Since Madison played a minor role in authoring Article 2 and was not its defender in the *Federalist Papers*, those on the right who use Madisonianism as a rationalization to elevate Congress and to demonize presidential power must be judged intellectual outliers. Also required, therefore, is a clarification of the anti-aggrandizement position. It is not simply fear of presidential power or hostility to a robust domestic agenda. What distinguishes the anti-aggrandizement scholars—Patterson, Kendall, and de Grazia—is their wholesale denial of the Founding as the source of an invigorated (if not modern) presidency. The sine qua non of the Founding, to them, is the separation of powers, not Hamiltonianism to be sure. In contrast, read Corwin, Taft or Coolidge, or a contemporary conservative like Terry Eastland; they all look in some degree to the Constitution as the source for strong presidential leadership.

Jeffersonianism: A Weak President and Weak Government

Small government and weak presidents are precisely what the Jeffersonians had in mind—even the outlier Jackson used presidential power in the service of limiting government. When James MacGregor Burns applauded Jeffersonianism as the optimal model of presidential leadership, based on responsible parties, he surely understated that the Jeffersonians had no ambitious domestic or foreign policy agenda other than undoing the Hamiltonian legacy. On this score, there is more than a superficial harmony between Patterson, Kendall, and de Grazia, whom we consider true anti-aggrandizement scholars, and the extreme Jeffersonians of the mid-1800s, Buchanan biographer George Ticknor Curtis and the Southerner Frederick Grimke. Both Curtis and Grimke wanted to democratize the Founding by grounding presidential power in public opinion and political party. By those means, however, the body politic would act as a restraining influence on the president and not, as the Progressives later hoped, as a mobilizing force behind presidential leadership. They saw executive energy as regal, if not tyrannical, which is why Curtis and Grimke favored decentralization to the point of turning a blind eye to the dangers of secession. Both decried presidential prerogative—Grimke even in foreign affairs—thus locating themselves at the extreme of means-and-ends conservatism.

We argue that Willmoore Kendall should be grouped with C. Perry Patterson and Alfred de Grazia (but not Edward Corwin) as true anti-aggrandizement scholars. Faced with Burns's attack on Madisonianism as frustrating majority rule, Kendall was forced to the defensive side. Yet, for both men, ends justify means. Burns championed electoral mandates to legitimate presidential liberalism just as Kendall believed that Congress should be the lawgiver because it accurately reflected a conservative public opinion. Events have proved both of them wrong in attributing a right-wing bias to Congress and a left-wing tilt to the presidency. Like Kendall, Patterson and de Grazia were reacting to decades of liberal presidential rule during the New Deal and the Fair Deal. And de Grazia, like Kendall, made explicit what Patterson only implied, that conservative values will be politically dominant in the legislative branch. It is noteworthy that Patterson charged that Hamiltonianism—the theory of presidential power followed by Wilson and both Roosevelts—was at odds with Original Intent. De Grazia saw an Executive Force overpowering a Republican Force (lodged in Congress) and, similarly, argued that the Constitution of 1787 established a president, not the presidency, and surely no "all-seeing all-doing" executive.

Jefferson and his followers held steadfastly to the concept of a national government of limited scope, in which a relatively weak president derives his power not from prerogative but from popular support through national political parties. Congress should be supreme in domestic affairs. But what of Jackson, who ranks among the near-greats by virtue of his energetic uses of presidential power? Jackson was strong, but his presidential force was used to foster weak national power and to upend Hamiltonianism (except on the issue of nullification) through his opposition to the Bank, internal improvements, and tariff walls. And Jackson was surely the exception that proves the rule, because the nineteenth century was notable for its legacy of weak presidents confronting a dominant Congress (putting aside the Republican Lincoln and Jefferson himself). Although the Jeffersonian presidents before Abraham Lincoln had a few singular foreign policy successes when they used prerogative power, even their weak domestic agendas relied upon constant negotiation with, and deference to, their party leaders in Congress. After the Civil War, a new Republican majority emerged to continue the Jefferson tradition of decentralization, congressional dominance, and weak executives. In other words, Jeffersonianism remained the standard until the end of the nineteenth century.

The Jeffersonians disavowed the prerogative as monarchical and longed for an executive with only a ministerial role in war-making and a diplomatic role derivative from the Declaration Clause. As can be seen, the Jeffersonians built their political movement in opposition to Federalist policies at home and abroad. During his tenure in Washington's cabinet, Jefferson was the silent partner to Madison's criticism of Hamilton's open-ended view of implied powers, regarding the National Bank and Washington's Proclamation of Neutrality in the ongoing war between France and England.

James MacGregor Burns draws a distinction between Jefferson the "ideologist" and Jefferson the "politician," claiming that the latter was the real Jefferson, whose lessons are applicable to the mid–twentieth century. As evidence, Burns mentions Jefferson's purchase of the Louisiana Territory and, neglecting his use of presidential prerogative, focuses on Jefferson as the partisan leader of a congressional majority that funded his land acquisition. This dual personality smacks of political hypocrisy since, although Jefferson openly questioned the constitutionality of his action, that sentiment was a rhetorical device to assuage his followers. Privately Jefferson believed that he had the constitutional authority to consummate his deal with France. Also, when Jefferson justified engaging the Barbary Pirates in the Mediterranean Sea based only on statutory authority, even after war had been declared on the United States by the Pasha of Tripoli, the Federalists led by Hamilton, writing under the pseudonym Lucius Crassus, charged that Jefferson should rightfully employ his prerogative powers to defend American shipping from foreign attacks without going to Congress. Hamilton argued: "The first thing in [the President's message], which excites our surprise is the very extraordinary position, that though *Tripoli had declared war in form* against the United States, and had enforced it by actual hostility, yet that there was not power, for want of *the sanction of Congress*, to capture and detain her cruisers with their crews." He continues, saying the "plain meaning" of the Declaration Clause is "that it is the peculiar and exclusive province of Congress, *when the nation is at peace* to change that state into a state of war," but "when a foreign nation declares, or openly and avowedly makes war upon the United States, they are then by the very fact *already at war*; and any declaration on the part of Congress is nugatory; it is at least unnecessary."[8]

Since Burns was motivated in behalf of domestic policy, it was Jefferson's domestic philosophy—his embrace of democratic egalitarianism through party government—that caused Burns to favor Jeffersonianism over Hamiltonianism. As was already noted, however, Burns overstates the political case for Jefferson by, in effect, transporting his own twentieth-century liberalism to the early nineteenth century. Jeffersonians sought a weak national government of limited scope and headed by an executive without monarchical (read prerogative) tendencies, whereas Burns wants a strong president at the helm of a responsible majority party that stands ready to enact ambitious domestic programs (for Burns, apparently, the only limitation on what positive government can do is the Bill of Rights). Certainly Calvin Coolidge, long considered one of our passive chief executives, wrote in his autobiography that, despite Jefferson's faith in the people and opposition to bureaucracy, too many Americans invoke Jeffersonian democracy but do not follow his teachings. This internal contradiction suggests that Burns and other liberal advocates of the heroic president are more the intellectual heirs of Progressivism than of Jefferson.

Finally, by creating the first cabinet, Washington set a precedent that Jefferson followed. He certainly did not displace his formal advisers with a "kitchen" cabinet, as did Andrew Jackson. The Jeffersonians did not embrace a national administrative state—preferring that public policy be subnationalized to the states and localities rather than to empower the federal government. In staffing, Jefferson also had more in common with Washington than with Jackson, who proclaimed the virtues of the spoils system. All of these attributes are consistent with the Jeffersonian love of weak and limited government.

Progressivism: A Strong President and Unlimited Government

Which brings us to the Progressives, who championed strong presidents as essential for an administrative state of almost unlimited ends (certainly greater democracy, modernization, and regulation of capitalism, if not redistribution of wealth). Redistribution was added to the policy mix by the New Deal. The Progressives mark a radical turn, illustrating the necessity for presidential means to expand in tandem with the expansion of governmental ends. Deeply influenced by social reform movements in Europe and theorists of the administrative state, the Progressives embraced the new positive social sciences of economics, sociology, psychology, and politics. The social sciences represented a revolution in human thought, promising for the first time fully rational and practical policies capable of a rapid and far-reaching modernization of all aspects of American institutions and life. Progressives rejected the Hamiltonian Constitution, because its structures appeared to be antidemocratic devices designed to thwart the popular will, while protecting the rich and powerful. They also rejected Jeffersonianism, because its extreme liberalism destroyed the possibility of a truly national government. But a new Progressive majority could be created from both of these reactionary parties. The Progressive agenda would be deployed by newly elected Progressive presidents and governors to clean out the conservative, corrupt Augean stables of state legislatures and courts across the land. Reflecting the national will of a Progressive nation, the president should remove from office the reactionary elites and reform the legal structures (including the out-of-date constitutional principles such as separation of powers) that empower and protect them. The Progressive alternative to constitutional government was the administrative state. Applying popular pressure, presidents could secure or extort from Congress general mandates and funding for executive departments such as agriculture and labor that would direct and modernize American life under expansive presidential direction.

Progressives like Woodrow Wilson were relativists who embraced a "living Constitution" and argued that the 1787 document was, in reality, no longer relevant to the actual workings of American government. Changing times demanded constitutional changes enabling the present generation to achieve its ends. Since the Constitution was deemed an obstacle to modernity, all Progressives in varying degrees favored radical regime reconstruction. In this project, the Progressives and their Liberal progeny turned to the presidency as the medium for transforming the separated system into a finely honed political regime. The view that the Progressives had conceived of the "modern" presidency decades before FDR is gaining currency among historically oriented presidency scholars.

Jeffrey Tulis, for example, believes that every FDR-inspired presidential reform can be traced back to the Founding except one: "the rhetorical presidency *does* represent a true transformation of the presidency."[9] Critical to this transformation was Woodrow Wilson, who "settled modern practice for all presidents that were to follow him" and, more importantly, "legitimized these practices by justifying his behavior with an ambitious reinterpretation of the constitutional order."[10] Thus was born the plebiscitary presidency, which Tulis discredits as being directly at odds with the Framers' desire for deliberative government free from presidential demagoguery and the threat of populist coercion. Nearly a century passed following Wilson before a renewed concern about an expectations gap—between presidential promises and presidential performance—became embedded in mainstream presidency scholarship.

For Wilson and the Progressives, the president was the vital center of the political regime. But presidential prerogative was almost totally ignored by the Progressives. It was not viewed as being decisive in bringing about their ambitious programmatic objectives, which required presidential leadership of Congress. On this score, however, Theodore Roosevelt is a remarkable exception. His stewardship theory justified an expansive prerogative power in domestic affairs, and Roosevelt equated his intervention into labor-management strife with Lincoln's activism in defense of the Union. Such a sweeping interpretation of presidential prerogative deeply troubled William Howard Taft, but fellow constitutionalist Edward Corwin gave a more benign reading of that episode. Furthermore, Corwin basically identified Theodore Roosevelt with Wilson and FDR as inaugurating the presidential role of legislative leader.

Although prerogative was not a prominent theme in Progressive-Liberal scholarship, it was defended whenever Congress posed a threat to presidential leadership. During the 1950s, for example, advocates of the heroic presidency would rationalize "the need for presidential domination in foreign and military affairs. Eisenhower's deference to Congress in asking for resolutions authorizing American intervention in the Formosan Straits in 1955 and in the Middle East in 1957 was attacked as an abdication of responsibility and a dangerous precedent for the erosion of presidential authority in what should be a reserved domain for executive prerogative."[11] Of course, decades later the war prerogative forced liberal intellectuals, notably Arthur Schlesinger Jr., to rail against the imperial presidency. Neither World War II nor even the Korean War had troubled that generation of scholars, who so thoroughly subscribed to the heroic vision of FDR-style presidential leadership that they never contemplated a reconsideration of their assumption that, for presidents, might does make right. In our inventory of authors, only Harold Laski, though he favored the English parliamentary system for domestic matters, endorsed the American regime as superior to England's with respect to foreign policy. Pointing to the tragic consequences of a British prime minister who engaged in personal diplomacy with Hitler at Munich, without having to submit to parliamentary approval, Laski applauded the Senate's role in finalizing any treaty.

Progressives and their Liberal progeny saw legislative leadership as crucial, since Congress would need presidential prodding to enact new domestic programs. And the president should rightly prod, because his power was legitimated as superior to Congress's by virtue of his election by a national constituency and his possession of a popular mandate to govern. Whereas the Framers would have agreed that the president must safeguard the public well-being, for them presidential legitimacy flowed from the president's constitutional status, not his status as a charismatic leader of a popular following. One recurring reform proposal has been the advocacy of parliamentary government as the cure-all for our defective separation of powers. Woodrow Wilson, the Anglophile, much preferred the English model in 1885; British political scientist Harold Laski in 1940 lamented the presidential domestic weakness as opposed to the political muscle of his own prime minister; and in 1960 comparative politics specialist Herman Finer judged the American president to be the head of an inefficient regime as compared to European heads of state. It is surely ironic that what caused Wilson to abandon his earlier pessimism—and embrace of the English parliamentary system—were examples of decisive presidential leadership in foreign affairs, which as president he would transfer to the domestic arena. Despite Wilson's about-face, responsible partyism survived and was endorsed in 1950 by the Committee on Political Parties of the American Political Science Association and, during the 1970s, by such liberal thinkers as Charles Harden, Rexford Tugwell, James Sundquist, and, of course, James MacGregor Burns. Burns's thesis of four-party politics never gained widespread acceptance in political science, just as responsible party doctrine, which reached its high-water mark in 1950, has few disciples among today's presidency scholars.

Big government requires an administrative state; the administrative state is built upon bureaucracy; but no federal bureaucracy operating under conditions of separated powers in a nation of 50 states, 3,000-plus counties, and roughly 80,000 localities can operate on the hierarchical assumptions of organizational theory. However, this reality did not impinge upon the Progressive ideal of public administration. Although regulation of the national economy began under the Progressives, their view of Leviathan was more abstract than actual because many of their programmatic goals were not realized until the New Deal. Progressive thinkers, for example Wilson as political scientist, do more than hint that the administrative state exists to serve the president, with federal employees dutifully implementing the policies that the president campaigned on. Thus the president is both responsible for the bureaucracy and accountable to the electorate. No Progressive like Wilson, let alone a socialist like Harold Laski, entertained the notion that big government would become a managerial problem, an executive bureaucracy largely beyond presidential control.

In terms of its zeal for a strong and unlimited government, the Great Society was the last rhetorical invocation of the modernist Progressive agenda for American politics that began with Theodore Roosevelt's Square Deal, Woodrow Wilson's New Freedom, and continued with Franklin D. Roosevelt's New Deal, Harry Truman's Fair Deal, and John F. Kennedy's New Frontier. The successes of those Progressive-Liberal presidents still inspire the faith and ardor of liberals, just as Ronald Reagan inspires conservatives. Looking ahead, no doubt many will speculate that rallying the nation toward greater social perfection may well—again—require a "heroic" president armed with a renewed Progressive public philosophy, one that promises "to get the country moving again." But unless or until another FDR emerges, students of the presidency are turning away from the heroic assumptions of presidential leadership. The contemporary approach to presidential scholarship, we have argued, can best be described as "a new realism, an old idealism."

Wanted: A Theory of Presidential Power

The new realism and old idealism reflect four core themes: (1) expectations gap and plebiscites, (2) policymaking amid divided government, (3) the ennobled Congress as lawmaker, and (4) constraints on the president and the presidency. All are critical of the heroic-presidency approach—especially divided government and the ennobled Congress—but, as noted, the theme of presidential plebiscites reaches back to Woodrow Wilson, who legitimated rhetorical leadership as essential to grounding presidential leadership in public opinion, not the Constitution. Yet these themes, even when given empirical support, are normative and cannot define for us a comprehensive theory of presidential power. The primary concern of these contemporary authors is legislative-executive relations, and that leads them to appreciate the Framers for designing a system of deliberative politics to facilitate good government, not fast-acting government. This new outlook does not pertain to national security, nor is there any mention of prerogative power.

We conclude not with any full-blown theory of the presidency, although, with twenty-twenty hindsight, we feel that our six questions have defined the ingredients that any comprehensive theory must include. One sad consequence of Neustadt's embrace of behavioralism has been the nearly complete disregard of prerogative power in presidential scholarship. But any general theory must embrace presidential *prerogative*, institutionalized across time. A few scholars, for example Louis Fisher and David Adler, doubt that the war prerogative has any sanction in the Constitution,[12] but that dissenting opinion is refuted by the constitutionalists William Howard Taft and Edward Corwin and, more recently, Robert Scigliano and Richard Pious. For example, the 1973 War Powers Resolution, argues Scigliano, was a failed effort to erode the presidential war prerogative, because the Framers, to quote Montesquieu, wanted "a kind of constitution that has all the internal advantages of a republic, together with the external force of a monarchical, government."[13]

The most ambitious reading of prerogative is by Pious, who argues that prerogative is much more important than Neustadtian influence as a source of presidential power. Pious is entirely consistent with Hamiltonianism, insofar as prerogative is "the constitutional authority that the president asserts unilaterally through various rules of constitutional construction and interpretation, in order to resolve crises or important issues facing the nation."[14] To make his case, Pious employs historical cases. Successful "frontlash" efforts to establish prerogative power include Washington's assertion of diplomatic powers, Lincoln's Civil War actions, and Franklin Roosevelt's forging an Atlantic Alliance during World War II. All involve national security. Less effective are prerogative usages that provoke a "backlash," like Jackson's use of the veto and removal powers against the Bank, Tyler's frequent vetoes against the congressional Whigs, and Truman's seizure of the steel mills during the Korean War. For Jackson and Tyler, the veto was employed in a political brawl over domestic policy and, although Truman's use of wartime prerogative was repudiated, a common interpretation is that *Youngstown Sheet and Tube v. Sawyer* is the exception that proves the rule—normally the Supreme Court is deferential to the commander in chief.[15] The worst-case scenario, says Pious, is "overshoot and collapse"—a constitutional crisis following what is widely perceived to be an illegitimate assertion of presidential prerogative—as was illustrated by Andrew Johnson's unilateral actions to direct Reconstruction and Nixon's abuse of executive privilege during Watergate. These worst cases occur because "the president acts as if major national security issues were at stake in what is essentially a domestic political situation."[16]

But Neustadt's legacy will continue, because any theory of presidential power must include *political resources* at any moment in time. We cannot calibrate the relative proportions of prerogative and political power, and likely they would change depending upon context and presidential role.[17] It seems clear that prerogative power, for better or worse, clings more intimately to foreign policy and military affairs. In a classic essay, Aaron Wildavsky in 1966 argued that there were "two presidencies," one decidedly more successful in gaining congressional approval of the president's military and foreign requests than his domestic agenda. Steven Shull and others have tested—and basically validated—Wildavsky's thesis.[18] But there is a larger dimension to this insight, which, though underappreciated today, was immediately recognized by earlier generations of presidency observers. From the beginning, presidential power over national security policy was grounded in the president's inherent or prerogative powers, whereas his attempts to guide domestic policy have always been less effectively linked to his political resources.

The vital political resources are *rhetorical leadership* of public opinion; *party*, though not responsible parties; and the president's *personal skills*. If political resources pale alongside prerogative in national security policy, surely they may make the difference in the one area that remains a telling index of presidential effort and success: his ability to shape the policy process and bridge the separated powers. If Terry Eastland can urge his fellow constitutionalists to embrace Neustadt's leadership model, perhaps the time has come for behavioralists to look toward prerogative as legal grounding for their brand of presidential analysis.

Some empiricists have begun quantifying the use of presidential prerogative to explain the conditions under which those powers are used and to what effect. Thus, although we cannot say when the veto threat began to be regularly employed by presidents to shape the legislative process, one recent study recasts the presidential veto as a bargaining chip in executive-legislative relations rather than a means to simply kill legislation or dramatize a campaign issue.[19] And with respect to executive orders, Kenneth Mayer argues that "to see the importance of constitutional form to the presidency, studies of presidential power must include a broader understanding of the president's formal powers."[20]

More commonly behavioralists will discuss presidential approval in terms of Neustadt's concept of prestige, though they are less able to operationalize his concept of reputation (the president's standing with official Washington). Indeed, Barbara Kellerman may be alone in her effort to validate the core Neustadian concept of presidential "influence." Yet none of these methodological problems have deterred us from theorizing about the relevance of political resources to presidential leadership. So too, we urge, with respect to prerogative. Although, as Pious shows, there is a nebulous quality to assertions of prerogative, they can hardly be any more ephemeral than the art of politics, since prerogative is constitutionally mandated and has been so recognized by serious thinkers over the course of two centuries. Both prerogatives and politics belong in any holistic theory of presidential power.

There are good reasons why the New Deal is equated with big government, but consider whether—on these terms—Franklin D. Roosevelt *should* be called our first modern president. Although he "need[ed] help" and thus created the Executive Office of the President, in retrospect that advice from the Brownlow Committee was naive. In the 1930s the federal government was small in terms of budget, size, and reach, compared to even twenty years later, when Eisenhower showed real managerial acumen. Bureaucratization of government and institutionalization of the presidency have spawned daunting managerial problems for today's chief executive. The recent wave of organizational studies, though agreeing that an *administrative strategy* is required for presidents to have any prospect of controlling the bureaucracy, also hint that real top-down control cannot be achieved. Bureaucracy is more a constraint than a lever on presidential power.

Finally, we must factor into the equation *context*. The subtext of the emerging "new realism, old idealism" among contemporary presidency scholars bespeaks an implicit and belated admission that references to FDR as the standard for modernity make no intellectual or political sense. Lincoln was our greatest president, yet nobody applies Lincoln as the criterion for judging commanders in chief during the nineteenth or early twentieth centuries. Of FDR's greatness there is little doubt, yet his influence on modern presidential scholarship has been less benign. Harold Laski, at the end of the 1930s, offered a personal perspective on the American president that later scholars have forgotten. There is a qualitative difference between the "crisis" presidency of Franklin D. Roosevelt that called forth his greatness and the relatively "normal" times when the White House is graced by more average incumbents. The tremendous leverage that a deeply felt national emergency gave to FDR is not adequate for the exigencies of modern government during ordinary times.

This latest scholarly consensus questions the assumptions of the heroic presidential leadership. Yet was the generation of Burns and Neustadt wrong to believe that executive hegemony is essential in the modern era of big government? Even scholars like Lowi who now bemoan overreaching presidents do not necessarily reject the positive state. Herein lies the dilemma: whether the presidency can be downsized when the country has grown used to federal action to resolve pressing national problems (e.g., President Bush signing legislation to add thirty thousand more federal employees as airport baggage screeners).

The movement conservatives who follow in Reagan's wake, and who have embraced both Hamiltonian prerogative and Neustadtian persuasion, fancifully believe that strong presidents can be employed to defend small government. We have doubts that presidential energy, though it surely empowers the Oval Office, will bring about a reversal of modern trends toward a federal government of ends more unlimited than what the Framers had in mind. Is the new point of view, what we call "a new realism, an old idealism," simply the latest stage in the ongoing reevaluation of the presidency, or is it the final statement? The latter we doubt, though no cyclical interpretation is implied here. Only a prophet can forecast events (like another 9/11), but likely *none* of the three paradigms outlined in this book will be sufficient to explain the evolution of presidential power in the twenty-first century. We suspect, maybe fear, that the means of presidential power, given the expansive ends of contemporary government, will be greater than this, or any, generation of admirers of the Founding is willing to bear.

Table 1. Scholarly Views of Six Criteria for Presidential Leadership

Scholar	Prerogative or Incumbency	Personality, Party, or Rhetoric	Regime-Building
Alexander Hamilton	Open-ended prerogative is key, and few constitutional exceptions	Constitution empowers all presidents, no rhetoric or party needed	Founding era did not anticipate rise of democratic politics
Woodrow Wilson	In 1908 felt incumbency is important, as shown by TR and Cleveland	Links rhetoric with party for "mandate" based on popular election	A "living" Constitution must replace the 1787 version, which is anti-modern
Charles C. Thach Jr.	Vague wording of Article II offers strong prerogative potential	Personality can shape the office; party and rhetoric not relevant	Founding was a blueprint for future political development; rejects the Progressive criticism
Edward S. Corwin	Prerogative is primary, but incumbency plays a role	Lincoln, TR, FDR show personality matters, but personality "cult" is dangerous	Office becomes stronger due to precedents established by earlier presidents
Richard E. Neustadt	Incumbent must employ "influence" as prerogative is ineffectual	Personality is key to use of statecraft, but sees no role for party	Modernity is a fundamental departure from presidency in history
James MacGregor Burns	Incumbency only matters	Party government is key to presidential success	Ahistorical, as Jeffersonian model optimal at all times
Arthur M. Schlesinger Jr.	Concerned about prerogative power over war-making	Anti-democratic personality is dangerous	Historically grounded, and shifted from apologist to critic of strong presidents
Theodore J. Lowi	Incumbent personalizes the office	Presidential rhetoric breeds expectations gap	FDR's Second Republic began a new regime for the United States

Domestic and Foreign Policy	Legislative Leadership	Executive Branch
President is leading actor in foreign policy and war; also implied powers over domestic life	Veto is lever over Congress, coupled with ability to recommend legislation	President oversees his administrative subordinates; no patronage hiring in government
Congressional control of domestic policy (1885) but presidents make foreign policy (1908)	Presidential leadership of Congress is essential for innovation	Assumes that administrative state will serve the chief executive
Senate role in foreign affairs is limited; the president's is expansive	Separation of powers was designed to give president autonomy via the Congress	Department heads are subordinate to presidential appointive and removal power
Is more accepting of New Deal than other conservatives of his time	TR, Wilson, and FDR defined this role for the modern period	Is naive to believe that president has control over the entire government
Statecraft is ultimate goal, not to achieve any explicit policy agenda	No discussion whatsoever of legislative leadership of Congress	Original view of Eisenhower dominated by staff amended in updates
Presidents should pursue liberal policy agenda	Presidential election mandate legitimizes agenda-setting	Presidential control over government tied to span of control
Messianic foreign policy is underlying threat to constitutional government	Congress must reassert war authority, but War Powers Resolution is a failure	Large White House staff acts to isolate president from bureaucracy
President is responsible for service delivery (e.g. prosperity)	Public views president as embodying the regime, not Congress	Risk-adversity shifts policy initiative from bureaucracy to White House

Notes

The following works are cited parenthetically by abbreviated titles:

A   Theodore Roosevelt. *An Autobiography.* New York: Charles Scribner's Sons, 1925.

AC   James Bryce. *The American Commonwealth.* Vol. 1. 1888. New York: Macmillan, 1914.

AP   Clinton Rossiter. *The American Presidency.* 2d ed. New York: Harcourt, Brace & World, 1960. The first edition was published in 1956.

API   Harold J. Laski. *The American President, an Interpretation.* New York: Harper & Brothers, 1940.

CGAP   Woodrow Wilson. *Congressional Government: A Study in American Politics.* 1885. New York: Meridian Books, 1956.

CP   Charles C. Thach Jr. *The Creation of the Presidency, 1775–1789.* Baltimore: Johns Hopkins Press, 1969.

F   Alexander Hamilton, John Jay, and James Madison. *The Federalist.* 1799. Middletown, Conn.: Wesleyan University Press, 1961. Originally published in 1799.

IP   Arthur M. Schlesinger Jr. *The Imperial Presidency.* Boston: Houghton Mifflin, 1989.

NT   Frederick Grimke. *The Nature and Tendency of Free Institutions.* 1848. Cambridge, Mass.: Harvard University Press, 1968.

POP   Edward S. Corwin. *The President: Office and Powers.* 4th ed. New York: New York University Press, 1957.

PP   Richard E. Neustadt. *Presidential Power and the Modern Presidents: The Politics of Leadership from Roosevelt to Reagan.* New York: John Wiley, 1990.

RG   Henry Jones Ford. *The Rise and Growth of American Politics: A Sketch of Constitutional Development.* New York: Macmillan, 1898.

INTRODUCTION. Scope of Study

1. The first history of the presidency, now a classic but dated, was Wilfred E. Binkley, *The Powers of the President: Problems of American Democracy* (Garden

City, N.Y.: Doran, 1937). The best contemporary account is Sidney M. Milkis and Michael Nelson, *The American Presidency: Origins and Development, 1776–1990* (Washington, D.C.: CQ Press, 1990). The work by Forrest McDonald is called an intellectual history, but, although he does a superlative job in tracing the intellectual currents that influenced the American Founding, his chronicle of developments into the twentieth century is more history than intellectual history. See Forrest McDonald, *The American Presidency: An Intellectual History* (Lawrence: University Press of Kansas, 1994).

2. Richard M. Pious, *The American Presidency* (New York: Basic Books, 1979), 16.

3. David L. Paletz, "Perspectives on the Presidency," in "The Institutionalized Presidency," ed. Norman C. Thomas and Hans W. Baade, *Law and Contemporary Problems* 35 (summer 1970): 438–39.

4. Erwin C. Hargrove, *The President as Leader: Appealing to the Better Angels of our Nature* (Lawrence: University Press of Kansas, 1998), 27–28.

5. Although most contemporary commentators on the presidency regard Franklin D. Roosevelt as the first "modern" president, the scholar who formalized this thesis was Fred Greenstein, "Change and Continuity in the Modern Presidency," in *The New American Political System*, ed. Anthony King (Washington, D.C.: American Enterprise Institute, 1978), 45–85. Also see Fred Greenstein, "Introduction: Toward a Modern Presidency," in *Leadership in the Modern Presidency*, ed. Fred Greenstein (Cambridge, Mass.: Harvard University Press, 1988), 1–6.

6. David K. Nichols extends this argument too far, by arguing that Washington was *the* first modern president in every leadership domain: David K. Nichols, *The Myth of the Modern Presidency* (University Park: Pennsylvania State University Press, 1994). See our rejoinder: Thomas Engeman and Raymond Tatalovich, "George Washington: The First Modern President? A Reply to Nichols," in *George Washington and the Origins of the American Presidency*, ed. Mark J. Rozell, William D. Pederson, and Frank J. Williams (Westport, Conn.: Praeger, 2000), 37–76.

CHAPTER ONE. Constitutional Mythology

1. See James MacGregor Burns, *Roosevelt: The Lion and the Fox* (New York: Harcourt, Brace & World, 1956), and *John Kennedy: A Political Profile* (New York: Harcourt, Brace & World, 1960).

2. Willmoore Kendall, "The Two Majorities," *Midwest Journal of Political Science* 4 (November 1960): 317–45.

3. Ibid., 318–20.

4. Ibid., 325–26.

5. Ibid., 320–21.

6. See Scott E. Yenor, Travis S. Cook, and Raymond Tatalovich, "The Normative Study of the Presidency," in *Presidential Frontiers: Underexplored Issues in White House Politics*, ed. Ryan J. Barilleau (Westport, Conn.: Praeger, 1998), 3–21.

7. Kendall, "The Two Majorities," 321–22.

8. Robert A. Dahl published a series of lectures as *A Preface to Democratic Theory* (Chicago: University of Chicago Press, 1965). It was first published in 1956.

9. Kendall, "The Two Majorities," 329–30.

10. Ibid., 331.

11. Ibid., 336.

12. Ibid., 345.

13. James MacGregor Burns, *The Deadlock of Democracy: Four-Party Politics in America* (Englewood Cliffs, N.J.: Prentice-Hall, 1963), 6.

14. Ibid., 16–18.

15. Ibid., 21–22.

16. Ibid., 24–25.

17. Ibid., 36.

18. Ibid., 40–41.

19. Ibid., 41.

20. Ibid., 45–46.

21. *Dialogues in Americanism* (Chicago: Henry Regnery Co., 1964), 112–13, 115–17.

22. Ibid., 117–20.

23. Ibid., 121, 123.

24. Ibid., 127.

25. Ibid., 128–29.

26. Ibid., 131–32.

27. Ibid., 134.

28. Ibid., 134, 136.

29. Ibid., 143–44.

30. Ibid., 144–45.

31. One highly publicized assault on antimajoritarianism in the congressional process was authored by a Democratic senator from Pennsylvania, who had been a reform mayor of Philadelphia: Joseph S. Clark, *Congress: The Sapless Branch* (New York: Harper & Row, 1964).

CHAPTER TWO. Original Intent and the Presidency

1. Alexander Hamilton, John Jay, and James Madison, *The Federalist* (1799; Middletown, Conn.: Wesleyan University Press, 1961); this work is cited parenthetically in the text, with the abbreviation *F*.

2. Robert J. Spitzer, *The Presidential Veto: Touchstone of the American Presidency* (Albany: State University of New York Press, 1988), 18.

3. Ibid., 17–18.

4. Alexander Hamilton, *Pacificus Papers*, in *Selected Writings and Speeches of Alexander Hamilton*, ed. Morton J. Frisch (Washington, D.C.: American Enterprise Institute for Public Policy Research, 1985), 400.

5. David K. Nichols, *The Myth of the Modern Presidency* (University Park: Pennsylvania State University Press, 1994).

6. See Thomas S. Engeman and Raymond Tatalovich, "George Washington: The First Modern President? A Reply to Nichols," in *George Washington and the Origins of the American Presidency*, ed. Mark J. Rozell, William D. Pederson, and Frank J. Williams (Westport, Conn.: Praeger, 2000), 37–76.

7. Ibid., 63–67.

8. Thomas Jefferson, *The Kentucky Resolutions*, in *The Portable Thomas Jefferson*, ed. Merrill D. Peterson (New York: Penguin Books, 1975), 283–84.

9. Lynton Caldwell, *The Administrative Theories of Hamilton and Jefferson: Their Contribution to Thought on Public Administration* (Chicago: University of Chicago Press, 1944), 128.

10. Ibid., 129.

11. Thomas Jefferson to William Stephens Smith, November 13, 1787, quoted in Harry V. Jaffa, *A New Birth of Freedom: Abraham Lincoln and the Coming of Civil War* (Lanham, Md.: Rowman & Littlefield, 2000), 29.

12. Thomas Jefferson, *Notes on the State of Virginia*, in Peterson, *Portable Thomas Jefferson*, 217.

13. Jefferson, *First Inaugural Address*, in Peterson, *Portable Thomas Jefferson*, 292–93.

14. Ibid., 292.

15. Jefferson, *Kentucky Resolutions*, 281.

16. Gary J. Schmitt, "Thomas Jefferson and the Presidency," in *Inventing the American Presidency*, ed. Thomas E. Cronin (Lawrence: University Press of Kansas, 1989), 337–38. Schmitt argues that Jefferson exercised his "constitutional dissembling" in the Tripoli and *Chesapeake* affairs as well in the Louisiana Purchase. In each case Jefferson exercised legitimate presidential powers and then, to protect himself from party criticism, publicly denied that he had done so. As Schmitt observes, "Jefferson's decision to resort to prerogative is important to note; however, it is equally important that he made absolutely no attempt to give it the slightest constitutional justification" (340).

17. Presidents Jackson, Tyler, and Polk used the veto for policy reasons but often claimed that they did so for constitutional reasons. Jackson vetoed the second bank bill, citing constitutional reasons even though the first bank had passed muster before the Supreme Court and had been renewed by Congress. "At the same time, he [Jackson] also believed that he had the right to interpret the

Constitution, a right that he would exercise not only against the contrary opinions of Congress but against those of the Supreme Court as well. In his famous bank veto message (July 10, 1832), he cited constitutional grounds for his disapproval but also emphasized concerns of social and economic justice for the 'humble members of society' to support his action." Jackson used presidential prerogatives to guarantee social justice and oppose the new economic nationalism issuing now from Congress. Quoted in Richard A. Watson, *Presidential Vetoes and Public Policy* (Lawrence: University Press of Kansas, 1993), 15–16.

18. Congress threatened to impeach President Tyler for exercising this "unconstitutional prerogative." His opponents accused him of "the high crime and misdemeanor of withholding his assent to laws indispensable to the just operations of government, which involved no constitutional difficulty on his part." Watson, *Presidential Vetoes*, 16. During the nineteenth century, Congress introduced constitutional amendments twelve times to change the veto override to a simple majority (1833, 1835, 1836, 1838, twice in 1841, three times in 1842, 1849, 1850, and 1884). Senator Joseph Kent offered such an amendment in 1835, with the comment that

> the veto power unites executive and legislative powers, and such a combination in the hands of a president leads to despotism and oppression. He then observed that the veto was designed "only to prevent legislative encroachment upon the executive authority" and for bills raising constitutional authority. Kent also noted Jefferson's contrasting nonuse of the veto in his eight-year presidency and cited other sources to argue that the veto should be used sparingly and with caution, while Jackson had used it "till it has become an occurrence of everyday." (Spitzer, *Presidential Veto*, 38)

Jackson used the popular support for his vetoes to gain reelection in 1832. Sidney Milkis and Michael Nelson, *The American Presidency: Origins and Development, 1776–1990* (Washington, D.C.: CQ Press, 1990), 128.

19. Watson, *Presidential Vetoes*, 15.

20. Glenn A. Phelps, "George Washington: Precedent Setter," in Cronin, *Inventing the American Presidency*, 267. Rhetorically, President Washington followed the Jeffersonian view of the veto as an anticongressional and antidemocratic prerogative. Replying to Edmund Pendleton, Washington wrote: "You do me no more than justice when you suppose, that, from motives of respect to the legislature (and I might add from my interpretation of the Constitution), I gave my signature to many bills, with which my judgment is at variance." Watson, *Presidential Vetoes*, 14–15.

21. Alexis de Tocqueville, *Democracy in America*, trans. and ed. Harvey C. Mansfield and Delba Winthrop (Chicago: University of Chicago Press, 2000), 91, 96, 97, 110.

22. Joyce Appleby, "Economics: The Agrarian Republic," in *Thomas Jefferson*

and the Politics of Nature, ed. Thomas S. Engeman (Notre Dame, Ind.: University of Notre Dame Press, 2000), 143–63.

23. Milkus and Nelson, *American Presidency*, 102.

24. Ibid., 105.

25. Ibid., 103.

26. Ibid.

27. Wilfred E. Binkley, *The Powers of the President: Problems of American Democracy* (Garden City, N.Y.: Doubleday, Doran, 1937), 50.

28. Milkus and Nelson, *American Presidency*, 115 n. 46.

29. Binkley, *Powers of the President*, 64.

30. Ibid., 112.

31. Ibid., 113.

32. Milkus and Nelson, *American Presidency*, 113.

33. Ibid., 139–40.

CHAPTER THREE. Jeffersonianism Sustained

1. An excellent discussion of a contemporary view of Andrew Jackson is Sidney Milkis and Michael Nelson, *The American Presidency: Origins and Development, 1776–1990* (Washington, D.C.: CQ Press, 1990), 117–28.

2. Alexis de Tocqueville, *Democracy in America*, trans. and ed. Harvey C. Mansfield and Delba Winthrop (Chicago: University of Chicago Press, 2000), 377–78.

3. Ibid., 379.

4. Joseph Story, *Commentaries on the Constitution of the United States* (1833; New York: Da Capo Press, 1970), vol. 1, sec. 1411, 280–81.

5. Ibid., sec. 1412, p. 281.

6. Ibid., sec. 1427, p. 294; sec. 1457, p. 321.

7. Ibid., sec. 1504, p. 357.

8. Ibid., sec. 1523, p. 374.

9. Ibid., sec. 1555, p. 413.

10. Ibid., sec. 1560 n. 2, p. 417.

11. Ibid., vol. 2, sec. 879, p. 345.

12. Ibid., sec. 881, p. 347.

13. Ibid., sec. 882, pp. 348–49, emphasis added.

14. Ibid., sec. 883, p. 349.

15. Ibid., vol. 3, sec. 1566, p. 421.

16. Tocqueville, *Democracy in America*, 119, emphasis added.

17. Ibid., 169.

18. Ibid., 168.

19. Ibid., 123.

20. Ibid., 118.

21. Ibid., 119.

22. Ibid., 121

23. Frederick Grimke, *The Nature and Tendency of Free Institutions* (1848; Cambridge, Mass.: Harvard University Press, 1968); this work is cited parenthetically in the text, with the abbreviation *NT*.

24. Tocqueville, *Democracy in America*, 60.

25. George Ticknor Curtis, *Constitutional History of the United States from Their Declaration of Independence to the Close of the Civil War* (New York: Harper & Brothers, 1889), 2:302. For Abraham Lincoln, see 2:286.

26. Ibid., 2:315.

27. Roy P. Basler, ed., *The Collected Works of Abraham Lincoln*, 8 vols. (New Brunswick, N.J.: Rutgers University Press, 1952), 4:426.

28. Ibid., 2:249. For other declarations of Lincoln's attachment to Jefferson, see 1:487, 1:310, 1:502–3, 3:124, 3:220, 3:375–76, 4:112, 4:240, 5:48.

29. James Bryce, *The American Commonwealth*, vol. 1 (1888; New York: Macmillan, 1914); this work is cited parenthetically in the text, with the abbreviation *AC*.

30. "Lord Bryce . . . observed that 'the tendency everywhere in America to concentrate power and responsibility in one man is unmistakable.'" Quoted in Milkis and Nelson, *American Presidency*, 199.

31. Henry C. Lockwood, *The Abolition of the Presidency* (New York: R. Worthington, 1884), 84.

32. Ibid., 147.

33. Ibid., 204.

34. Ibid., 298.

35. Ibid., 299.

36. Ibid., 305.

37. Ibid., 302–3.

38. Ibid., 302–6.

39. Ibid., 303–5.

CHAPTER FOUR. Indictment of Constitutionalism

1. Woodrow Wilson, *Congressional Government: A Study in American Politics* (1885; New York: Meridian Books, 1956); this work is cited parenthetically in the text, with the abbreviation *CGAP*.

2. Woodrow Wilson, *Constitutional Government in the United States* (New York: Columbia University Press, 1908), 56, emphasis added.

3. Ibid., 57.

4. Ibid.

5. See Eldon Eisenach, *The Lost Promise of Progressivism* (Lawrence: University Press of Kansas, 1994).

6. Ibid., 54–55.

7. Wilson, *Constitutional Government*, 46.

8. Ibid., 54.

9. Ibid., 60.

10. Ibid., 59.

11. Ibid., 70–71.

12. Henry Jones Ford, *The Rise and Growth of American Politics: A Sketch of Constitutional Development* (New York: Macmillan, 1898); this work is cited parenthetically in the text, with the abbreviation *RG*.

13. Theodore Roosevelt, *An Autobiography* (New York: Charles Scribner's Sons, 1925); this work is cited parenthetically in the text, with the abbreviation A.

14. "Toward the end of his presidency, and more decidedly, during his years as the leader of the progressive movement after he left the White House, Roosevelt insisted that the government could not confine itself simply to mediating issues of wealth . . . he seemed to anticipate the welfare state that later was associated with the presidential initiatives of his cousin Franklin." Sidney M. Milkis and Michael Nelson, *The American Presidency: Origins and Development, 1776–1990* (Washington, D.C.: CQ Press, 1990), 199.

15. J. Allen Smith, *The Spirit of American Government*, ed. Cushing Strout (Cambridge, Mass.: Harvard University Press, 1965), xxx.

16. Ibid., xxxvi.

17. Ibid., 111–12.

18. Ibid., 135.

19. Ibid., 141.

20. Ibid., 386–87. "Democracy would raise government to the rank and dignity of science by making it appeal to the reason instead of the fear and superstition of the people. The governments of the past, basing their claims upon divine right, bear about the same relation to democracy that astrology and alchemy do to the modern sciences of astronomy and chemistry . . . More and more man is coming to look upon government as a purely human agency which he may freely modify and adapt to his purposes" (386).

21. Ibid., 402.

22. Charles Beard, *An Economic Interpretation of the Constitution of the United States* (1913; New York: Free Press, 1965), 32–38, 149–50.

23. Ibid., 38–40.

24. Ibid., 156–72, 190, 192, 195, 199, quotation on 202–3.

25. Charles Beard, *The Rise of American Civilization* (New York: Macmillan, 1930), "The Agricultural Era," 151–59, 738–63, quotation on 737.

26. Herbert Croly, *The Promise of American Life* (1909; Boston: Northeastern University Press, 1989), 37–44.

27. Thomas S. Engeman and Raymond Tatalovich, "George Washington: The First Modern President? A Reply to Nichols," in *George Washington and the*

Origins of the American Presidency, ed. Mark J. Rozell, William D, Pederson, and Frank J. Williams (Westport, Conn.: Praeger, 2000), 37–76.

CHAPTER FIVE. Critics of Progressivism

1. It is not uncommon for a presidency text to reference the unlike governing philosophies of Taft and Roosevelt. For example, see George C. Edwards III and Stephen J. Wayne, *Presidential Leadership: Politics and Policy Making*, 3d ed. (New York: St. Martin's Press, 1994), 7.

2. William Howard Taft, *The President and His Powers* (New York: Columbia University Press, 1916), 5–6.

3. Ibid., 11–12.

4. Ibid., 16, 27.

5. Ibid., 31.

6. Ibid., 40.

7. Ibid., 76.

8. Ibid., 94–95.

9. Ibid., 108, 110, 112–13, 115–16.

10. Ibid., 129.

11. Ibid., 138–39.

12. Ibid., 144, 147–48.

13. Ibid., 156–57.

14. Coolidge is classified as a "Madisonian" in James MacGregor Burns, *Presidential Government: The Crucible of Leadership* (Boston: Houghton Mifflin, 1973). He is a "Buchanan" type according to Sidney Hyman, "What Is the President's True Role?" *New York Times Magazine*, September 7, 1958. Erwin C. Hargrove calls Coolidge a "restraint" president in his *Presidential Leadership: Personality and Political System* (New York: Macmillan, 1966). And Coolidge was psychoanalyzed to be a passive-negative who responded unenthusiastically to the call of duty, says James David Barber, *The Presidential Character*, 3d ed. (Englewood Cliffs, N.J.: Prentice-Hall, 1985).

15. Calvin Coolidge, *The Autobiography of Calvin Coolidge* (New York: Cosmopolitan Book Corp., 1929), 197.

16. Ibid., 198–99.

17. Ibid., 214.

18. Ibid., 213.

19. Ibid., 212.

20. Ibid., 209.

21. Ibid., 223–24.

22. Ibid., 224–25.

23. Ibid., 228–30.

24. Ibid., 230–31.

25. Ibid., 231–32.

26. Ibid., 230–32.

27. Herbert J. Storing, introduction to *The Creation of the Presidency, 1775–1789*, by Charles C. Thach Jr. (Baltimore: Johns Hopkins University Press, 1969), vi; this work is hereafter cited parenthetically in the text and subsequent notes, with the abbreviation *CP*. Storing took note of "this 'excellent volume,' as Edward S. Corwin has justly called it" (v).

28. Woodrow Wilson, "The Study of Administration," *Political Science Quarterly* 2 (June 1887): 197–222.

29. Quoted in *CP*, 98–99.

30. Cited in *CP*, 115, 117.

31. *CP*, 159–60, Madison quote on 159.

CHAPTER SIX. Sowing the Seeds of Progressivism

1. Harold J. Laski, *The American President, an Interpretation* (New York: Harper & Brothers, 1940); this work is cited parenthetically in the text, with the abbreviation *API*.

2. "Toward a More Responsible Two-Party System," *American Political Science Review* 44 (September 1950): supplement.

3. Herman Finer, *The Presidency: Crisis and Regeneration* (Chicago: University of Chicago Press, 1960), 32.

4. Ibid., 20–21.

5. Ibid., 27–28.

6. Ibid., 303, 307, 309, 317.

7. Clinton Rossiter, *The American Presidency*, 2d ed. (New York: Harcourt, Brace & World, 1960); this work is cited parenthetically in the text and subsequent notes, with the abbreviation *AP*. The first edition was published in 1956.

8. In an earlier work he more fully developed the thesis that Lincoln effected a constitutional dictatorship during the Civil War. See Clinton Rossiter, *Constitutional Dictatorship: Crisis Government in the Modern Democracies* (New York: Harcourt, Brace & World, 1963). Originally published by Princeton University Press in 1948.

9. *AP*, 143–44, 152. His listing of eight "major" and six "creditable" presidents is found on pages 89–106.

10. Both polls were commissioned by the father of Arthur Schlesinger Jr., who is identified within the heroic tradition of presidential scholarship. See Arthur Schlesinger Sr., "The U.S. Presidents," *Life*, November 1, 1948, 65; "Our Presidents: A Rating by 75 Historians," *New York Times Magazine*, July 29, 1962, 12ff.

11. James MacGregor Burns, *Presidential Government: The Crucible of Leadership* (Boston: Houghton Mifflin, 1973). It was first published in 1965.

12. Ibid., xix.

13. Ibid., 7.

14. Ibid., 10–14. There are at least two errors of interpretation in Burns's rendition of the vital precedents from President Washington. First, regarding the Proclamation of Neutrality, Burns states that "because of American feelings about France and Britain this was a most controversial step, but the precedent stood" (13). Not so, because Edward Corwin documents that "[i]n 1794 Congress passed our first neutrality act, and ever since then the subject of neutrality has been conceded to lie within its jurisdiction." Edward S. Corwin, *The President: Office and Powers* (New York: New York University Press, 1957), 181. Second, on the matter of war-making, recent scholarship finds that the Framers authorized presidential prerogative only with respect to "defensive" actions, not offensive warfare, and that President Washington operated according to the Framers' intentions. See Louis Fisher, *Presidential War Power* (Lawrence: University Press of Kansas, 1995), 16–17. Says Fisher: "President Washington acted expressly on authority delegated to him by Congress. Legislation in 1792 provided that whenever the United States 'shall be invaded, or be in imminent danger of invasion from any foreign nation or Indian tribe,' the President may call forth the state militias to repel such invasions and to suppress insurrections" (16).

15. Burns, *Presidential Government*, 17.

16. Ibid., 16–18.

17. Ibid., 20–22.

18. Ibid., 29. Burns's claim that Hamilton held no vision about the kind of political economy he had engineered for the American republic would be disputed by Forrest McDonald, *Alexander Hamilton: A Biography* (New York: W. W. Norton, 1979), esp. chaps. 7, 8, and 9.

19. Richard E. Neustadt, *Presidential Power and the Modern Presidents* (New York: John Wiley, 1990); this work is cited parenthetically in the text and subsequent notes, with the abbreviation *PP*. The subtitle shows the scope of his coverage: "The Politics of Leadership from Roosevelt to Reagan." A previous revision of 1980 extended his original 1960 interpretation through Carter.

20. David L. Paletz, "Perspectives on the Presidency," in "The Institutionalized Presidency," ed. Norman C. Thomas and Hans W. Baade, *Law and Contemporary Problems* 35 (summer 1970): 429–44.

21. Peter W. Sperlich, "Bargaining and Overload: An Essay on *Presidential Power*," in *The Presidency*, ed. Aaron Wildavsky (Boston: Little, Brown, 1969), 168–69. See the major reviews of Neustadt by Don K. Price, *American Political Science Review* 54 (September 1960): 735–36; Harvey Walker, *Western Political Quarterly*, December 13, 1960, 1096–97; Edward H. Hobbs, *Journal of Politics* 23 (February 1961): 146–47; John H. Millett, *Midwest Journal of Political Science* 5 (February 1961): 89–90.

22. Paletz, "Perspectives on the Presidency," 439. One who explicitly compares Neustadt against Machiavelli is William T. Bluhm, *Theories of the Political*

System (Englewood Cliffs, N.J.: Prentice-Hall, 1965), 247–83. For Neustadt, as with Machiavelli, Bluhm argues that there is a disconnect between goals and values, as both thinkers reduced politics to a "purely technical affair" (269).

23. Paletz, "Perspectives on the Presidency," 439.

24. *PP*, 37; chapter 2 discusses "Three Cases of Command." The quotations are on 23–24.

25. Sperlich, "Bargaining and Overload," 186.

26. Ibid.

27. Actually, Neustadt identifies six developments worthy of note since the Eisenhower years: (1) perceptions of legitimacy and sentiments of loyalty; (2) changes of institutional detail, of which there are eight—(a) appointment schedules, (b) press relations, (c) cabinet contacts, (d) congressional relations, (e) bipartisan consultations, (f) war-making, (g) impoundments, and (h) renominations; (3) changes in the policy environment; (4) human qualities and "temperamental fitness"; (5) the failed power calculations by Johnson and Nixon, leading toward self-destructive policies; and (6) the "institutionalized presidency" (this growth of the White House staff is treated separately, though Neustadt says that it rightly can be viewed as a ninth change in "institutional detail" as noted above). *PP*, 183–229.

28. Burns, *Presidential Government*, 210.

29. Finer, *The Presidency: Crisis and Regeneration*, 121, 129, 159.

30. Burns, *Presidential Government*, 122–23. Referring to Corwin and Patterson, Burns said that "[t]hese two critiques could be discounted somewhat on the grounds that the authors were cool to the trend toward bigger national government with its vast regulatory and social welfare programs and hence to the office that had been so instrumental in the broadening of federal responsibility" (122). Burns's view of Corwin puts him at odds with William G. Andrews, who includes Corwin with Neustadt, Rossiter, Finer, and others—Louis W. Koenig, Wilfred Binkley, Walter Johnson, Francis H. Heller, and Rexford G. Tugwell—as illustrative of the 1960s presidency scholars who "tied themselves in knots explaining why the presidency was superior to Congress and should, therefore, wield commensurately greater power." William G. Andrews, "The Presidency, Congress, and Constitutional Theory," in *Perspectives on the Presidency*, ed. Aaron Wildavsky (Boston: Little, Brown, 1975), 24–45, quotation on 24. In chapter 7, Corwin was labeled an anti-aggrandizement scholar by David Paletz, indicating his fear of executive power, but we think both Burns and Paletz are wrong. We characterize Corwin as a constitutionalist who did not express ideologically conservative views, nor was he paranoid about the growth of presidential power. During the Vietnam era (see chapter 8), Arthur Schlesinger Jr. charged that Corwin was a "high prerogative" scholar who justified expansive presidential power in foreign affairs. On that, Schlesinger is more accurate than Burns or Paletz.

31. Burns, *Presidential Government*, 136, 154.

32. Ibid., 124. Besides Neustadt, Burns mentions Rossiter, Pendleton Herring, Wilfred E. Binkley, and Arthur N. Holcombe as having a "more confident" view of presidential power.

33. Finer, *The Presidency*, 256, 215.

34. Ibid., 251, 262.

CHAPTER SEVEN. Anti-Aggrandizement Scholars

1. David L. Paletz, "Perspectives on the Presidency," *Law and Contemporary Problems* 35 (summer 1970): 440.

2. C. Perry Patterson, *Presidential Government in the United States: The Unwritten Constitution* (Chapel Hill: University of North Carolina Press, 1947), v.

3. Ibid., v–vi.

4. Ibid., 6, 14.

5. Ibid., 38, 39.

6. Ibid., 49–50, 56, 65, 69.

7. Ibid., 77–80.

8. Ibid., 84, 94–95.

9. Ibid., 132–33, 142.

10. Ibid., 233, 237.

11. Ibid., 239–40.

12. Ibid., 251.

13. Ibid., 269, 268.

14. Alfred de Grazia, *Republic in Crisis: Congress against the Executive Force* (New York: Federal Legal Publications, 1965), foreword.

15. Ibid., 48–49, 66.

16. Ibid., 74–75, 77, 79.

17. Ibid., 104–5.

18. Ibid., 110–12.

19. Ibid., 164, 172.

20. Edward S. Corwin, *The President: Office and Powers*, 4th ed. (New York: New York University Press, 1957); this work is cited parenthetically in the text, with the abbreviation *POP*.

CHAPTER EIGHT. From Imperialism to Impotency

1. James Fallows, "The Passionless Presidency: The Trouble with Jimmy Carter's Administration," *Atlantic Monthly*, May 1979, 33–48.

2. Dorothy Buckton James, *The Contemporary Presidency* (New York: Pegasus, 1969), xii.

3. Philippa Strum, *Presidential Power and American Democracy* (Pacific Palisades, Calif.: Goodyear Publishing Co., 1972), 16, 20.

4. Ibid., 29.

5. Raoul Berger, *Executive Privilege: A Constitutional Myth* (Cambridge, Mass.: Harvard University Press, 1974). Mark J. Rozell, *Executive Privilege: The Dilemma of Secrecy and Democratic Accountability* (Baltimore: John Hopkins University Press, 1994).

6. George E. Reedy, *The Twilight of the Presidency* (New York: New American Library, 1970), 17–18.

7. Ibid., 22–33.

8. Ibid., 26.

9. Ibid., 29–30.

10. Ibid., 31.

11. Ibid., 40.

12. Ibid., 99.

13. Ibid., 160–61.

14. Ibid., 165.

15. James David Barber, *The Presidential Character: Predicting Performance in the White House*, 2d ed. (Englewood Cliffs, N.J.: Prentice-Hall, 1977). The first edition appeared in 1972.

16. Sidney Hyman, "What Is the President's True Role?" *New York Times Magazine*, September 7, 1958; James MacGregor Burns, *Presidential Government: The Crucible of Leadership* (Boston: Houghton Mifflin, 1973).

17. Erwin C. Hargrove, *Presidential Leadership: Personality and Political Style* (New York: Macmillan, 1966), 1.

18. Erwin C. Hargrove, "What Manner of Man?: The Crisis of the Contemporary Presidency," in *Choosing the President*, ed. James David Barber (Englewood Cliffs, N.J.: Prentice-Hall, 1974), 17.

19. Ibid., 19–21, 30–33.

20. Louis W. Koenig, *The Chief Executive*, 3d ed. (New York: Harcourt Brace Jovanovich, 1975), 336–39. Aaron Wildavsky and Sanford Weiner, "The Prophylactic Presidency," *Public Interest*, no. 52 (summer 1978): 9.

21. Barber, *The Presidential Character*, ix. The original preface was reprinted in this second edition.

22. Ibid., 4.

23. Ibid., 445–46.

24. Ibid., 6.

25. See James David Barber, *The Presidential Character* (Englewood Cliffs, N.J.: Prentice-Hall, 1993), and "Predicting Hope with Clinton at Helm," *Raleigh News*, January 17, 1993.

26. Barber, *The Presidential Character* (1977), 12.

27. Ibid., 13.

28. Ibid., 12–13.

29. Sigmund Freud and William C. Bullitt, *Thomas Woodrow Wilson, Twenty-*

Eighth President of the United States: A Psychological Study (Boston: Houghton Mifflin, 1967). Also see Alexander L. George and Juliet L. George, *Woodrow Wilson and Colonel House: A Personality Study* (New York: John Day), 1956).

30. In 1974 Erwin Hargrove, an analyst of presidential personality, indicated that Lincoln was "[p]robably not" an active-positive "in the strict definition of the typology." Erwin C. Hargrove, *The Power of the Modern Presidency* (New York: Alfred A. Knopf, 1974), 77. Another scholar who gave this question serious thought concluded that Lincoln came the closest to being an active-negative president. See Jeffrey Tulis, "On Presidential Character," in *The Presidency in the Constitutional Order*, ed. Joseph M. Bessette and Jeffrey Tulis (Baton Rouge: Louisiana State University Press, 1981), 283–313.

31. Arthur M. Schlesinger Jr., *The Imperial Presidency* (Boston: Houghton Mifflin, 1989); this work is cited parenthetically in the text and subsequent notes, with the abbreviation *IP*. This revised edition had a new epilogue by Schlesinger; the original was published in 1973. Also see Arthur M. Schlesinger Jr. and Alfred de Grazia, *Congress and the Presidency: Their Role in Modern Times* (Washington, D.C.: American Enterprise Institute for Public Policy Research, 1967). This debate between Schlesinger and de Grazia was held toward the end of 1966.

32. Schlesinger and de Grazia, *Congress and the President*, 2–3

33. Ibid., 5, 8.

34. Ibid., 13.

35. Ibid., 15–16.

36. Ibid., 27–28.

37. Ibid., 28.

38. Ibid., 105–6.

39. Ibid., 187–88.

40. One simple measure of Schlesinger's focused coverage of the Nixon administration is the number of pages referenced to Presidents Lyndon Johnson (87) and Ronald Reagan (41) as compared to the number devoted to Richard Nixon (463).

41. Schlesinger also disparaged the impact of the Congressional Budget and Impoundment Control Act of 1974 (see *IP*, 435–36).

42. Schlesinger omitted the Japanese relocation incident despite his inclusion of the following, as one of eight "standards that warrant presidential resort to emergency prerogative": "None of the presidential actions can be directed against the domestic political process and rights" (see *IP*, 459). In his own mind, apparently, Schlesinger absolves FDR from undue responsibility for that decision, since elsewhere in his account of World War II, he wrote: "The most shameful abuse of power within the United States during the Second World War—the removal of the Japanese Americans—was not a unilateral presidential act. It was quickly ratified by Congress and, regrettably, upheld by the Supreme Court in a series of cases" (*IP*, 116). Any impartial observer, of course, would draw

the distinction that the military forces that removed those Japanese-American citizens acted pursuant to FDR's executive order, not pursuant to legislation or any judicial decree!

43. Eventually those six essays in *Society* magazine were collected in revised form by Vincent Davis, ed., *The Post-Imperial Presidency* (New Brunswick, N.J.: Transaction Books, 1980). The Cronin quotation is found in Thomas E. Cronin, "An Imperiled Presidency?" in Davis, *The Post-Imperial Presidency*, 137. Cronin developed similar themes more fully in Thomas C. Cronin, *The State of the Presidency* (Boston: Little, Brown, 1975). Also see his 1980 edition.

44. Mark J. Rozell, *The Press & the Carter Presidency* (Boulder, Colo.: Westview Press, 1989), 2. Also see Mark J. Rozell, *The Press and the Ford Presidency* (Ann Arbor: University of Michigan Press, 1992).

45. Cecil V. Crabb Jr. and Kevin V. Mulcahy, "The Elitist Presidency: George Bush and the Management of Operation Desert Storm," in *The Presidency Reconsidered*, ed. Richard W. Waterman (Itasca, Ill.: Peacock Publishers, 1993), 276.

46. Thomas M. Franck, ed., *The Tethered Presidency: Congressional Restraints on Executive Power* (New York: New York University Press, 1981); Hugh Heclo and Lester M. Salamon, eds., *The Illusion of Presidential Government* (Boulder, Colo.: Westview Press, 1981).

47. Franck, *The Tethered Presidency*, x.

48. Theodore C. Sorensen, "Political Perspective: Who Speaks for the National Interest?" in Frank, *The Tethered Presidency*, 7.

49. Ibid., 14–15.

50. Dean Norman Redlich, "Concluding Observations: The Constitutional Dimension," in Franck, *The Tethered Presidency*, 284–85.

51. Ibid., 295.

52. Hugh Heclo, "Introduction: The Presidential Illusion," in Heclo and Salamon, *The Illusion of Presidential Government*, 1–2. Here he references Richard E. Neustadt, "Presidential Government," *International Encyclopedia of the Social Sciences* (London: Collier-Macmillan, 1968), 12:451.

53. Heclo, "Introduction," 7, 9.

54. Lester M. Salamon, "Conclusion: Beyond the Presidential Illusion— Toward a Constitutional Presidency," in Heclo and Salamon, *The Illusion of Presidential Government*, 287–88.

55. Ibid., 291–92.

56. Ibid., 292–93.

57. Ibid., 294.

58. Charles Jones, *The Trusteeship Presidency: Jimmy Carter and the United States Congress* (Baton Rouge: Louisiana State University Press, 1988), 6. Also see Erwin C. Hargrove, *Jimmy Carter as President: Leadership and the Politics of the Public Good* (Baton Rouge: Louisiana State University Press, 1988).

59. Jones, *The Trusteeship Presidency*, 153.

60. Ibid., 200.

61. Hargrove, *Jimmy Carter as President*, 188.

62. Ibid., 13.

63. Ibid., 33.

64. Ibid., 78.

65. Ibid., 107, 105.

66. Ibid., 111. See Robert A. Strong, *Working in the World: Jimmy Carter and the Making of American Foreign Policy* (Baton Rouge: Louisiana State University Press, 2000). Given his purpose "to challenge some of the initial accounts" that called Carter "weak, indecisive, inconsistent, and the victim of conflicts among his advisers," Strong argues the opposite: "That is a portrait that does not conform with the evidence now available . . . [which shows] an active, intelligent, and sincere individual in command of a complicated foreign policy agenda that often involved the conscious acceptance of substantial political risks" (274–75).

67. Hargrove, *Jimmy Carter as President*, 192.

68. Phillip G. Henderson, "Carter Revisionism: The Flight from Politics," *Political Science Reviewer* 24 (1995): 322–53, quotation on 333.

69. Charles M. Hardin, *Presidential Power & Accountability* (Chicago: University of Chicago Press, 1974), 1–2. A professor at the University of California at Davis, Hardin acknowledged support from colleagues at the Center for the Study of Democratic Institutions, notably Robert M. Hutchins and Rexford G. Tugwell.

70. Ibid., 7. His reform agenda is summarized in the introduction and chapter 10 of his book.

71. Ibid., 9.

72. Ibid., 10, 12.

73. Ibid., 13.

74. Ibid., 63.

75. Ibid., 17, 19–20.

76. James L. Sundquist, *Constitutional Reform and Effective Government* (Washington, D.C.: Brookings Institution, 1986), 9.

77. Douglas Dillon, address at Tufts University, May 30, 1982, reprinted in Donald L. Robinson, ed., *Reforming American Government: The Bicentennial Papers of the Committee on the Constitutional System* (Boulder, Colo.: Westview Press, 1985), 24–29.

78. Lloyd N. Cutler, "To Form a Government," *Foreign Affairs* 59 (fall 1980): 127, 132.

79. Sundquist, *Constitutional Reform*, 239.

80. Ibid., 5–7.

81. Ibid., 10, 11, 12.

82. Ibid., 251.

83. Rexford G. Tugwell, *The Emerging Constitution* (New York: Harper's

Magazine Press, 1974); Rexford G. Tugwell and Thomas E. Cronin, eds., *The Presidency Reappraised* (New York: Praeger, 1974). The latter is a collection of essays by various presidency scholars who attended conferences at the Center for the Study of Democratic Institutions. A much shorter version of Tugwell's argument was published in his *The Compromising of the Constitution* (Notre Dame, Ind.: University of Notre Dame Press, 1976).

84. Rexford G. Tugwell and Thomas E. Cronin, "The Presidency: Ventures in Reappraisal," in Tugwell and Cronin, *The Presidency Reappraised*, 3, 4–5.

85. Tugwell, "On Bringing Presidents to Heel," in Tugwell and Cronin, *The Presidency Reappraised*, 293.

86. Tugwell, *The Emerging Constitution*, 528, 534.

87. Ibid., 543–44.

88. Ibid., 559, 558.

89. Ibid., 560.

90. Ibid., 564–65.

91. Ibid., 161, 163, 165.

92. Ibid., 173.

93. Ibid., 186.

94. Ibid., 604, 608.

CHAPTER NINE. Return to Hamiltonianism

1. L. Gordon Crovitz and Jeremy A. Rabkin, eds., *The Fettered Presidency: Legal Constraints on the Executive Branch* (Washington, D.C.: American Enterprise Institute for Public Policy, 1989); Gordon S. Jones and John A. Marini, eds., *The Imperial Congress: Crisis in the Separation of Powers* (New York: Pharos Books, 1988); Terry Eastland, *Energy in the Executive: The Case for the Strong President* (New York: Free Press, 1992).

2. Robert J. Spitzer, *President & Congress: Executive Hegemony at the Crossroads of American Government* (New York: McGraw-Hill, 1993), 248–54. Spitzer calls their thesis the "imperial Congress/weak President" argument.

3. Ibid., 252.

4. Robert H. Bork, foreword to Crovitz and Rabkin, *The Fettered Presidency*, ix, xiii. In addition to Bork and coeditor Rabkin, eight of the other seventeen contributors have been somehow affiliated with the American Enterprise Institute, a conservative think tank.

5. Ibid., 1, 3, 5.

6. Ibid., 6–7.

7. Ibid., 7–8.

8. Ibid., 11.

9. Ibid., 12.

10. Gary J. Schmitt and Abram N. Shulsky, "The Theory and Practice of

Separation of Powers: The Case of Covert Action," in Crovitz and Rabkin, *The Fettered Presidency*, 60–61.

11. Caspar W. Weinberger, "Dangerous Constraints on the President's War Powers," in Crovitz and Rabkin, *The Fettered Presidency*, 96–97.

12. Judith A. Best, "Budgetary Breakdown and the Vitiation of the Veto," in Crovitz and Rabkin, *The Fettered Presidency*, 125.

13. Ibid., 129.

14. Louis Fisher, "Micromanagement by Congress: Reality and Mythology," in Crovitz and Rabkin, *The Fettered Presidency*, 141, 145.

15. G. Boyden Gray, "Special Interests, Regulation, and the Separation of Powers, in Crovitz and Rabkin, *The Fettered Presidency*, 211–13.

16. Michael J. Malbin, "Legalism versus Political Checks and Balances: Legislative-Executive Relations in the Wake of Iran-Contra," in Crovitz and Rabkin, *The Fettered Presidency*, 284, 288.

17. William French Smith, "Independent Counsel Provisions of the Ethics in Government Act," in Crovitz and Rabkin, *The Fettered Presidency*, 253–61.

18. Suzanne Garment, "Talking about the President: The Legacy of Watergate," in Crovitz and Rabkin, *The Fettered Presidency*, 304.

19. See "Commentary and Exchanges on Politics and Public Debate," in Crovitz and Rabkin, *The Fettered Presidency*, 315–17.

20. Newt Gingrich, foreword to Jones and Marini, *The Imperial Congress*, x.

21. Jones and Marini, *The Imperial Congress*, 1. The book was published under the auspices of the Heritage Foundation and the Claremont Institute, and of the fifteen contributors to this volume, the four whom we discuss (Kesler, West, Wettergreen, and Jeffrey), as well as the coeditors, were affiliated with one or both of those organizations.

22. Ibid., 2.

23. Ibid., 17–18.

24. Charles R. Kesler, "Separation of Powers and the Administrative State," in ibid., 21.

25. Douglas A. Jeffrey, "Executive Authority under the Separation of Powers," in Jones and Marini, *The Imperial Congress*, 53–54.

26. John Adams Wettergreen, "Bureaucratizing the American Govenment," in Jones and Marini, *The Imperial Congress*, 92, 95, 97.

27. Herman A. Mellor, "Congressional Micromanagement: National Defense," 107–29; and John Hiram Caldwell, "Congressional Micromanagement: Domestic Policy," 130–50, both in Jones and Marini, *The Imperial Congress*. Also see Margaret N. Davis, "The Congressional Budget Mess," 151–82; Mark Crain, "The House Dynasty: A Public Choice Analysis," 183–203; and Clifford Barnhart, "Using the Rules for Abuse," 204–21, all in Jones and Marini, *The Imperial Congress*.

28. Gordon Crovitz, "The Criminalization of Politics," in Jones and Marini, *The Imperial Congress*, 239.

29. Ibid., 243, 256.

30. Gordon S. Jones, "Overthrowing Oligarchy," in Jones and Marini, *The Imperial Congress*, 295–97.

31. Ibid., 297.

32. Ibid., 299.

33. Ibid., 308.

34. Thomas G. West, "Restoring the Separation of Powers," in Jones and Marini, *The Imperial Congress*, 309.

35. Ibid., 314, 316–17.

36. Ibid., 326.

37. Gabriel Prosser, "Comes the Revolution," in Jones and Marini, *The Imperial Congress*, 331, 352.

38. Eastland, *Energy in the Executive*, 2–3.

39. Ibid., 279–80.

40. Ibid., 13, 71, 92–93.

41. Ibid., 283.

42. Ibid., 120.

43. Ibid., 125.

44. Ibid., 295.

45. Ibid., 152.

46. Ibid., 166, 278.

47. Ibid., 236.

48. Ibid., 266.

49. Ibid., 267.

CHAPTER TEN. The Emerging Scholarly Consensus

1. Given the volume and variety of presidential studies during the past two decades, as compared to the first fifty years of the twentieth century, the boundaries for this contemporary literature are less obvious. One noteworthy criterion is that several books included have won the Neustadt Award, given yearly since 1985 by the Presidency Research Section of the American Political Science Association for the best book on the topic. Of the eighteen books so distinguished from 1985 to 2002, ten are included in this discussion, as follows: Lowi, *The Personal President* (awarded 1986); Campbell, *Managing the Presidency* (1987); Mayhew, *Divided We Govern* (awarded 1992); Brace and Hinckley, *Follow the Leader* (awarded 1993); Skowronek, *The Politics Presidents Make* (awarded 1994); Jones, *The Presidency in a Separated System* (awarded 1995); Walcott and Hult, *Governing the White House* (awarded 1996); Renshon, *High Hopes: The Clinton Presidency and the Politics of Ambition* (awarded in 1997); Cohen, *Presidential Responsiveness and Public Policy-Making* (awarded 1999); and Yalof, *Pursuit of Justices*

(awarded in 2000). An eleventh winner was discussed in chapter 8, namely Hargrove, *Jimmy Carter as President* (awarded 1989).

2. Richard W. Waterman, Robert Wright, and Gilbert St. Clair, *The Image-Is-Everything Presidency* (Boulder, Colo.: Westview Press, 1999), 4. They also cite a "classic article" by James Stimson, who attributed the downward spiral of presidential popularity to unrealistic expectations by less informed segments of the electorate who had rallied behind the electoral victor but later became disillusioned (8). See James A. Stimson, "Public Support for American Presidents: A Cyclical Model," *Public Opinion Quarterly* 40 (spring 1976): 1–21; James A. Stimson, "On Disillusionment with the Expectations/Disillusion Theory: A Rejoinder," *Public Opinion Quarterly* 40 (winter 1976–77): 541–43. A previous Waterman anthology was based explicitly on the expectations gap thesis: Richard W. Waterman, ed., *The Presidency Reconsidered* (Itasca, Ill.: F. E. Peacock, 1993).

3. Thomas E. Cronin, *The State of the Presidency*, 2d ed. (Boston: Little, Brown, 1980), 9–10. A recent volume detailing nine paradoxes argues that "[w]hen Americans realize that the presidency is incapable of dealing with everything well and that democratic politics, in general, is not suited to provide quick answers to every social and economic malaise, then we will be more responsible in the way we judge presidents." Thomas E. Cronin and Michael A. Genovese, *The Paradoxes of the American Presidency* (New York: Oxford University Press, 1998), 28.

4. Theodore J. Lowi, *The Personal President: Power Invested, Promise Unfulfilled* (Ithaca, N.Y.: Cornell University Press, 1985), 9.

5. Ibid., 20.

6. Jeffrey K. Tulis, *The Rhetorical Presidency* (Princeton, N.J.: Princeton University Press, 1987), 116.

7. Ibid., 119–20.

8. Ibid., 125, 128.

9. Ibid., 172, 181.

10. Jon R. Bond and Richard Fleisher, *The President in the Legislative Arena* (Chicago: University of Chicago Press, 1990), 220. Charles O. Jones, *The Presidency in a Separated System* (Washington, D.C.: Brookings Institution, 1994), 281.

11. Samuel Kernell, *Going Public: New Strategies of Presidential Leadership* (Washington, D.C.: CQ Press, 1986), 1.

12. Ibid., 218.

13. Paul Brace and Barbara Hinckley, *Follow the Leader: Opinion Polls and the Modern Presidency* (New York: Basic Books, 1992).

14. Ibid., 7.

15. Ibid., 18–19.

16. Ibid., 23.

17. Ibid., 176, 178.

18. Jeffrey E. Cohen, *Presidential Responsiveness and Public Policy-Making: The Public and the Policies That Presidents Choose* (Ann Arbor: University of Michigan Press, 1999).

19. Ibid., 27.

20. Ibid., 240, 242, 244.

21. Morris Fiorina, *Divided Government* (New York: Macmillan, 1992), 3. Also see Gary C. Jacobson, *The Electoral Origins of Divided Government* (Boulder, Colo.: Westview Press, 1990). Claiming that Fiorina assumes a too highly sophisticated voter, Jacobson counters that divided government results because voters have different reasons for voting for Republicans and Democrats. They want Democratic legislators who cater to their local interests but Republican executives who safeguard the national well-being (106).

22. David R. Mayhew, *Divided We Govern: Party Control, Lawmaking, and Investigations, 1946–1990* (New Haven, Conn.: Yale University Press, 1991).

23. Ibid., 1–2, 3, 100, 119, 181.

24. Jones, *The Presidency in a Separated System.*

25. Mayhew, *Divided We Govern,* 92. The Jones quote that Mayhew references is from Charles O. Jones, "Ronald Reagan and the U.S. Congress: Visible-Hand Politics," in *The Reagan Legacy: Promise and Performance,* ed. Charles O. Jones (Chatham, N.J.: Chatham House, 1988), 37.

26. Jones, *The Presidency in a Separated System,* 1.

27. Ibid., 209, 210–11, 273, 297.

28. Michael L Mezey, "The Legislature, the Executive, and Public Policy: The Future Quest for Congressional Power," *Congress & the Presidency* 13 (spring 1986): 1–20. This article won an award for being "the Best Paper Published in the First Ten Years of *Congress & the Presidency.*"

29. George C. Edwards III, *At the Margins: Presidential Leadership of Congress* (New Haven, Conn.: Yale University Press, 1989). Also see George C. Edwards III, *Presidential Influence in Congress* (San Francisco: W. H. Freeman, 1980), where he concluded: "Presidential legislative skills do not seem to affect support for presidential policies, despite what conventional wisdom leads us to expect" (202).

30. Edwards, *At the Margins,* 100, 143.

31. Ibid., 185.

32. Ibid., 221.

33. Ibid., 223–24.

34. This concept was referenced in the last sentence of a new study of land-mark enactments that ranked contemporary presidents according to legislative effectiveness: "Presidents can fulfill crucial roles in this process as they exercise their leadership skills and make their strategic choices, but—like Roosevelt—as facilitators rather than directors of policy change." William W. Lammers and

Michael A. Genovese, *The Presidency and Domestic Policy* (Washington, D.C.: CQ Press, 2000), 356–57.

35. Bond and Fleisher, *The President in the Legislative Arena*, 40–41.

36. Ibid., 120, 194, 218.

37. Ibid., 222–23.

38. Ibid., 238.

39. Mark A. Peterson, *Legislating Together: The White House and Capitol Hill from Eisenhower to Reagan* (Cambridge, Mass.: Harvard University Press, 1990), 41–42.

40. See Steven A. Shull, *Presidential-Congressional Relations: Policy and Time Approaches* (Ann Arbor: University of Michigan Press, 1997); Lance T. LeLoup and Steven A. Shull, *Congress and the President: The Policy Connection* (Belmont, Calif.: Wadsworth, 1993); Steven A. Shull, *Domestic Policy Formulation* (Westport, Conn.: Greenwood Press, 1983); Steven A. Shull, *Presidential Policy Making: An Analysis* (Brunswick, Ohio: King's Court Communications, 1979).

41. Steven A. Shull and Thomas C. Shaw, *Explaining Congressional-Presidential Relations: A Multiple Perspective Approach* (Albany: State University of New York Press, 1999), 2.

42. Ibid., 155.

43. During the 1960s this approach was heavily colored by the experience of John F. Kennedy, "whose rhetoric proclaimed vast responsibilities for his office"; that rhetoric in turn led "inevitably [to] an inclination for those who served in his administration to blame his frustrations, disappointments, and failures on the constraints surrounding the presidency and the President's lack of power to overcome them." David L. Paletz, "Perspectives on the Presidency," in "The Institutionalized Presidency," ed. Norman C. Thomas and Hans W. Baade, *Law and Contemporary Problems* 35 (summer 1970): 435. The Theodore C. Sorenson monograph was based on his Gino Speranza Lectures at Columbia University: *Decision-Making in the White House: The Olive Branch or the Arrows* (New York: Columbia University Press, 1963). The heart of Sorenson's defense was that "too often a President finds that events or the decisions of others have limited his freedom of maneuver—that, as he makes choices, that door closes behind him" (21). Later he lists these limitations on presidential decision-making: permissibility, available resources, available time, previous commitments, and available information (23).

44. Fred I. Greenstein, *The Hidden-Hand Presidency: Eisenhower as Leader* (New York: Basic Books, 1982). Examples of revisionism that cast doubt on Neustadt's interpretation include Phillip G. Henderson, *Managing the Presidency: The Eisenhower Legacy—From Kennedy to Reagan* (Boulder, Colo.: Westview Press, 1988); John W. Sloan, *Eisenhower and the Management of Prosperity* (Lawrence: University Press of Kansas, 1991); Meena Bose, *Shaping and Signaling*

Presidential Policy: The National Security Decision Making of Eisenhower and Kennedy (College Station: Texas A&M University Press, 1998).

45. Greenstein, *The Hidden-Hand Presidency*, 5–6.

46. Ibid., 233, 248.

47. Barbara Kellerman, *The Political Presidency: Practice of Leadership from Kennedy through Reagan* (New York: Oxford University Press, 1984), xi–xii.

48. Ibid., 53, 256.

49. Stanley A. Renshon, *High Hopes: The Clinton Presidency and the Politics of Ambition* (New York: Routledge, 1998). First published in cloth in 1996.

50. See John Frendreis, Raymond Tatalovich, and Jon Schaff, "Predicting Legislative Output in the First One-Hundred Days, 1897–1995," *Political Research Quarterly* 54 (December 2001): 853–70. Not only were most of FDR's enactments Depression-specific laws (many of which did not survive the 1930s), but statistical analysis verifies that presidential success is linked to structural variables, such as economic conditions and electoral outcomes. An earlier version of this paper won the Best Paper Award from the Presidency Research Group of the APSA in 1999.

51. Paul C. Light, *The President's Agenda: Domestic Policy Choice from Kennedy to Carter* (Baltimore: Johns Hopkins University Press, 1983). The hardback was published in 1982.

52. Ibid., 10.

53. Ibid., 233.

54. Peri E. Arnold, *Making the Managerial Presidency: Comprehensive Reorganization Planning, 1905–1980* (Princeton, N.J.: Princeton University Press, 1986), xi–xii. This book won the Brownlow Award from the National Academy of Public Administration in 1986.

55. Ibid., 361.

56. Hugh Heclo, *A Government of Strangers: Executive Politics in Washington* (Washington, D.C.: Brookings Institution, 1977), 10. This book won the Brownlow Award from the National Academy of Public Administration in 1978.

57. Ibid., 88.

58. Ibid., 170–71.

59. Colin Campbell, *Managing the Presidency: Carter, Reagan, and the Search for Executive Harmony* (Pittsburgh: University of Pittsburgh Press, 1986), 9–10.

60. Ibid., 259.

61. Ibid., 200, 255.

62. Ibid., 270.

63. Perhaps the first scholar to target Nixon's excessive use of staff was Thomas Cronin, "The Swelling of the Presidency: Can Anyone Reverse the Tide?" in *American Government: Readings and Cases*, ed. Peter Woll, 8th ed. (Boston: Little, Brown, 1984). Also see John Hart, *The Presidential Branch* (Chatham, N.J.: Chatham House Press, 1987).

64. Greenstein, *The Hidden-Hand Presidency*, 247.

65. Shirley Anne Warshaw, *Powersharing: White House–Cabinet Relations in The Modern Presidency* (Albany: State University of New York Press, 1996).

66. Richard P. Nathan, *The Administrative Presidency* (New York: John Wiley & Sons, 1983), 88; also Richard P. Nathan, *The Plot That Failed: Nixon and the Administrative Presidency* (New York: John Wiley & Sons, 1975). The administrative presidency is also endorsed by Terry M. Moe, "The Politicized Presidency," in *The New Direction in American Politics*, ed. John E. Chubb and Paul K. Peterson (Washington, D.C.: Brookings Institution, 1985), 235–72.

67. Robert F. Durant, *The Administrative Presidency Revisited: Public Lands, the BLM, and the Reagan Revolution* (Albany: State University of New York Press, 1992), xi. This book won the Gladys M. Kammerer Award for the best book on United States national policy, awarded by the American Political Science Association.

68. Ibid., 76.

69. David Alistair Yalof, *Pursuit of Justices: Presidential Politics and the Selection of Supreme Court Nominees* (Chicago: University of Chicago Press, 1999), 134.

70. Ibid., 68, 177.

71. Charles E. Walcott and Karen M. Hult, *Governing the White House: From Hoover through LBJ* (Lawrence: University Press of Kansas, 1995). See the four classic volumes by Leonard D. White: *The Federalists: A Study in Administrative History* (New York: Macmillan, 1948), *The Jeffersonians: A Study in Administrative History, 1801–1829* (New York: Macmillan, 1951), *The Jacksonians: A Study in Administrative History, 1829–1861* (New York: Macmillan, 1954), and *The Republican Era, 1869–1901: A Study in Administrative History* (New York: Macmillan, 1958).

72. Walcott and Hult, *Governing the White House*, 8, 245.

73. One of the few studies of White House organization (which Jimmy Carter purportedly read for his guidance) was Stephen Hess, *Organizing the Presidency* (Washington, D.C.: Brookings Institution, 1976).

74. Walcott and Hult, *Governing the White House*, 5.

75. Ibid., 14.

76. Arthur M. Schlesinger, "Tides of American Politics," *Yale Review* 29 (December 1939); Arthur M. Schlesinger Jr., *The Cycles of American History* (Boston: Houghton Mifflin, 1986).

77. Another more sophisticated model views presidential leadership relative to the three cycles of preparation, then achievement, and finally consolidation. See Erwin C. Hargrove and Michael Nelson, *Presidents, Politics, and Policy* (New York: Alfred A. Knopf, 1984), 66–83.

78. Stephen Skowronek, *The Politics Presidents Make: Leadership from John Adams to George Bush* (Cambridge, Mass.: Harvard University Press, 1993).

79. Ibid., 5, 8.

80. Ibid., 30, 31.

81. Ibid., vii, 444–45.

82. Sidney M. Milkis, *The President and the Parties: The Transformation of the American Party System since the New Deal* (New York: Oxford University Press, 1993), 10.

83. Ibid., 145, 262–63, 301.

84. Richard Rose, *The Postmodern President: The White House Meets the World* (Chatham, N.J.: Chatham House Press, 1988), 2–4.

85. Ibid., 6.

86. Ibid., 44, 73, 304.

CONCLUSION. Three Presidential Paradigms

1. Theodore J. Lowi, "American Business, Public Policy, Case Studies, and Political Theory," *World Politics* 16 (July 1964): 677–715.

2. Theodore J. Lowi, *The Personal President: Power Invested, Promise Unfulfilled* (Ithaca, N.Y.: Cornell University Press, 1985), 32.

3. Ibid., 34.

4. Ibid., 45, xi.

5. Jeffrey K. Tulis, *The Rhetorical Presidency* (Princeton, N.J.: Princeton University Press, 1987), 7–8. In criticizing the view that modernity begins with FDR, Tulis cites the following to support this interpretation: Fred I. Greenstein, "Change and Continuity in the Modern Presidency," in *The New American Political System*, ed. Anthony King (Washington, D.C.: American Enterprise Institute, 1977); Arthur Schlesinger Jr., *The Imperial Presidency* (Boston: Houghton Mifflin, 1973); Richard Neustadt, "The President at Mid-Century," *Law and Contemporary Problems* (autumn 1956): 610–11.

6. Thomas Engeman and Raymond Tatalovich, "George Washington: The First Modern President? Reply to Nichols," in *George Washington and the Origins of the American Presidency*, ed. Mark J. Rozell, William D. Pederson, and Frank J. Williams (Westport, Conn.: Praeger, 2000), 37–76. Like Tulis, David K. Nichols argues that the Framers created an executive with all the power of a modern-day president. See David K. Nichols, *The Myth of the Modern Presidency* (University Park: Pennsylvania State University Press, 1994).

7. Nichols, *The Myth of the Modern Presidency*, 6–7.

8. John C. Hamilton, ed., *The Works of Alexander Hamilton* (1851), 7:745–47.

9. Tulis, *The Rhetorical Presidency*, 7.

10. Ibid., 118.

11. William G. Andrews, "The President, Congress, and Constitutional Theory," in *Perspectives on the Presidency*, ed. Aaron Wildavsky (Boston: Little, Brown, 1975), 27.

12. Louis Fisher, *Presidential War Power* (Lawrence: University Press of Kansas, 1995); David Gray Adler, "The Constitution and Presidential Warmaking: The Enduring Debate," *Political Science Quarterly* 103 (1988).

13. Robert Scigliano, "The War Powers Resolution and the War Powers," in *The Presidency in the Constitutional Order*, ed. Joseph M. Bessette and Jeffrey Tulis (Baton Rouge: Louisiana State University Press, 1981), 149.

14. Richard M. Pious, *The American Presidency* (New York: Basic Books, 1979), 16. An edition that gives many sources for Pious's understanding of prerogative power is Christopher H. Pyle and Richard M. Pious, eds., *The President, Congress, and the Constitution* (New York: Free Press, 1984).

15. One who criticizes the Supreme Court for its rigidity in the Steel Seizure case is Glendon A. Schubert Jr., *The Presidency in the Courts* (Minneapolis: University of Minnesota Press, 1957), 284.

16. Pious, *The American Presidency*, 50.

17. For more than twenty years, the senior author has argued that, whatever the exact proportions of political and prerogative power, each co-varies depending upon the role involved in presidential leadership. See Raymond Tatalovich and Byron W. Daynes, "Towards a Paradigm to Explain Presidential Power," *Presidential Studies Quarterly* (fall 1979): 428–41; reprinted in *The American Presidency: Historical and Contemporary Perspectives*, ed. Harry A. Bailey Jr. and Jay M. Shafritz (Chicago: Dorsey Press, 1988).

18. Aaron Wildavsky, "The Two Presidencies," *Trans-Action* (December 1966): 7–14. Steven Shull, ed., *The Two Presidencies* (Chicago: Nelson-Hall, 1991).

19. Charles M. Cameron, *Veto Bargaining: Presidents and the Politics of Negative Power* (New York: Cambridge University Press, 2000).

20. Kenneth R. Mayer, *With the Stroke of a Pen: Executive Orders and Presidential Power* (Princeton, N.J.: Princeton University Press, 2001), 223.

Index

Adams, John, 36, 37, 71, 115, 153, 209
Adams, John Quincy, 38, 39, 59, 66, 209
Adler, David G., 226
American Political Science Association, Committee on Political Parties, 111, 224
Anti-aggrandizement thesis, 9, 12, 131, 132, 142, 143, 191, 218, 219
Arnold, Peri E., 205; on executive branch organization, 205

Barber, James David, 10, 122, 147, 151, 152–54, 160, 169, 175, 204; *The Presidential Character*, 152; on presidential personality, 151, 152–54
Beard, Charles, 9, 69, 82, 83, 84, 85, 108; on class politics, 83–84; on domestic policy, 84; *An Economic Interpretation of the Constitution of the United States*, 82, 83
Berger, Raoul, 148
Best, Judith A., 181, 190
Binkley, Wilfred E., 38
Bond, Jon R., 195, 199, 200, 201, 204. *See also* Bond, Jon R., and Richard Fleisher
Bond, Jon R., and Richard Fleisher: on expectations gap thesis, 195; on legislative leadership, 200–201
Bork, Robert H., 179
Brace, Paul, 195–96. *See also* Brace, Paul, and Barbara Hinckley
Brace, Paul, and Barbara Hinckley: on expectations gap thesis, 196; on presidential popularity, 195–96
Brownlow, Louis, 128, 130, 146, 205, 228
Bryce, James (Lord), 8–9, 39, 44, 57–61, 65, 108, 212; *The American Common-wealth*, 9, 44, 57; on domestic policy leadership, 57, 58; on foreign policy leadership, 58; on legislative leadership, 57–58; on prerogative power, 58; on presidential personality, 59–60; on presidential rankings, 59–60; on rhetorical leadership, 58–59
Buchanan, James, 40, 44, 55, 56, 59, 67, 77, 92, 154, 209, 218
Burns, James MacGregor, 8, 9, 12, 14–18, 18–21, 22–24, 107, 113, 116–18, 126, 127, 128, 129, 137, 170, 171, 177, 214, 216, 218, 219, 220, 221, 224, 228, 230–31; Burns-Kendall debate, 18–21; on domestic policy, 23, 117–18, 128; on executive branch organization, 22–23, 129; on foreign policy, 117; four-party thesis, 14, 224; on Hamiltonian model, 15, 18, 116, 118, 127, 128; on Jeffersonian model, 15–18, 116, 118, 127, 128; on legislative leadership, 22, 117, 128; on Madisonian model, 14, 15–18, 116, 118, 128; on majority rule, 17; on party leadership, 16, 17, 22; on prerogative power, 22, 117, 126–27; *Presidential Government*, 127; on presidential personality, 16, 116; on regime-building, 23, 117, 127–28
Bush, George Herbert Walker, 23, 153, 186, 187, 188, 198, 209
Bush, George W., 1, 2, 3, 5, 6, 7, 23, 209, 229

Calhoun, John C., 35, 38, 45, 59
Campbell, Colin 205–6; on executive branch organization, 205–6
Carter, James Earl, 10, 122–23, 147, 153, 159, 160, 161, 164–67, 170, 171, 175, 176, 177, 178, 181, 190, 198, 199, 205, 207, 209